INSIDE THE SMT:
Teamwork in Secondary School Management

Mike Wallace works at the National Development Centre for Educational Management and Policy at the University of Bristol. He has acted as a consultant and researcher for LEAs, the DES and the School Management Task Force. Recently he has carried out research on the management of multiple innovations at school level and on planning for change in multiracial primary schools. He is currently researching into the role of the mass media in the education policy process. Previously he was a teacher in primary and middle schools and his doctoral research was based on action research into his own practice as a deputy headteacher.

Valerie Hall is a lecturer at the National Development Centre for Educational Management and Policy at the University of Bristol. She has taught in schools, and in further, higher and adult education in Britain and the United States. She was a member of the research teams looking at the selection of secondary heads (POST Project) and the changing role of the secondary head. She has written distance learning materials for schools on management development and materials on managing collaboration. She currently coordinates the EdD programme at the School of Education and is conducting research on women headteachers.

INSIDE THE SMT:
Teamwork in Secondary School Management

Mike Wallace
and
Valerie Hall
National Development Centre for
Educational Management and Policy,
School of Education, University of Bristol.

P·C·P
Paul Chapman
Publishing Ltd

Copyright © 1994 Mike Wallace and Valerie Hall

Paul Chapman Publishing Ltd
144 Liverpool Road
London
N1 1LA

British Library Cataloguing in Publication Data

Wallace, Mike
Inside the SMT: Teamwork in Secondary
School Management
I. Title II. Hall, Valerie
373.12

ISBN 1-85396-208-2

Typeset by Dorwyn Ltd, Rowlands Castle, Hants
Printed and bound by
Athenaeum Press, Newcastle-upon-Tyne, UK

A B C D E F G H 9 8 7 6 5 4

ACKNOWLEDGEMENTS

Our research was funded by a grant from the Economic and Social Research Council (reference number R000232699), for whose support we are most grateful.

Staff in the two LEAs where we worked were very helpful to us in identifying the study schools. We are indebted to the heads, their SMT colleagues, other staff and chairs of governors in the six study schools who were willing to find time for interviews during such a hectic period of reform. A special vote of thanks goes to all SMT members in two of these schools who put themselves on the line by enabling us to observe and interview them extensively during the second phase of the project. We wish to pay tribute to their readiness to expose their arduous and often emotionally demanding professional lives to our scrutiny so that others' learning may be informed by their experience.

We have been ably supported by our present and past colleagues at the National Development Centre for Educational Management and Policy: David Oldroyd and Ray Bolam conducted three of the initial case studies, providing many insights on which we were able to build; while Agnes McMahon and Eric Hoyle have always been ready to share and advise. June Collins, Angela Allen, Norma Meechem and Joan Moore of the support staff facilitated the research throughout with their usual efficiency and good humour. Mike Wallace acknowledges the generosity and – as the wordprocessor increasingly took over his life – stoicism of Liz Lindsay in helping to make this book happen.

Mike Wallace
Valerie Hall

CONTENTS

1

Outside Looking In

The good things in life don't always come easy. We will develop the argument that a team approach to managing secondary schools is a 'high gain, high strain' strategy for senior staff to adopt. The pay off – if it works – is synergy, where the team achieves more than the aggregate of what its members could do as individuals. In this sense an effective team consists of more than the sum of its parts:

> Synergy can be summed up as 2 plus 2 equals 5. In other words, when two or more talented people come together they can often produce an energy and creativity that is beyond the simple combination of them both.
> (Spencer and Pruss, 1992, p. 12)

If unified commitment to working towards shared goals can be achieved and sustained, it offers senior staff the prize of mutual empowerment. The ability of headteachers to carry out their responsibility for managing the school is enhanced through the support of senior colleagues. Team members other than heads have the opportunity to contribute to school-wide policy, enabling them to have a significant impact on management concerns beyond the sphere of their individual responsibility.

Yet there lurks a booby prize for heads. Their legally enshrined power to operate unilaterally and to direct colleagues is constrained by allegiance to beliefs and values about teamwork: all members have the right to participate in policy debates and the obligation to work towards consensus on important decisions. Where synergy is achieved, the potential for stripping heads of their power remains latent. Embarking on a team approach to management carries the risk that the team will prove to be less than the sum of its parts. Unless all members – heads included – commit themselves fully to teamwork and carry out their own responsibility competently, the team may be less effective than a more individualistic approach relying on a hierarchical chain of command. Suppose that one or more members do not pull their weight within the team, perhaps by refusing to accept the value of consensus building, or underperforming in connection with their individual responsibility. In such cases 2 plus 2 equals 3: heads are either inhibited from employing their power as individuals, or use it and alienate their colleagues by contravening the beliefs and values on which teamwork is built.

The strain of securing the gain offered by a team approach is not just a technical matter and cannot be wished away with a few rules and procedures. A central theme of this book is that there is a contradiction between two sets of beliefs and values held by senior secondary school staff with consequences for the way they use resources to achieve their ends within a team approach. There is a long tradition where the distribution of posts among professional staff in secondary schools has been viewed as a *management hierarchy*. Staff in the higher echelons are entitled to supervise and direct the work of colleagues lower down the pecking order for whom they are responsible. Headteachers are set apart since they alone are ultimately responsible for the working of the school, with a unique ability to affect the career prospects of other staff through their part in the staff selection process.

The last few decades have also witnessed the emergence of more egalitarian beliefs and values about management which are widely held among secondary school staff. The interdependent nature of the enterprise is emphasised: all staff (whatever their position in the hierarchy) are part of management since managerial tasks can only be carried out with and through other people. In other words, managers ultimately depend upon those they manage. It has become commonplace for senior staff to opt for team approaches to management, whose hallmark is interdependence amongst members. Each is perceived to have an *equal contribution* to make to debate, whatever his or her position in the management hierarchy. Heads are leaders of their teams who set the parameters for teamwork. They are also team members, whose opinion is on a par with that of colleagues.

Teams of senior staff are known as senior or school management teams (SMTs). We will show how the culture of the SMTs in our study reflected beliefs and values connected with a management hierarchy and those linked with equal contribution as team members to the work of the SMT. Team members interacted without conflict while there was congruence in the beliefs and values underpinning their actions. Unity in working towards consensus on a decision reflected a belief in the right of each member to contribute equally to the debate and in the obligation to make a commitment to implementing the agreed decision. Yet heads decided unilaterally whether to adopt a team approach, an action accepted by other staff as their prerogative as the person at the top of the management hierarchy. Potential for conflict arose if team members differed over whether they were acting in accordance with a management hierarchy or as team members with an equal right to contribute to the SMT's work. Heads who used their power within the management hierarchy to make a unilateral decision could be unpopular with other SMT members where the latter believed that it should have been a team decision to which all members had contributed. All team members were equal, but heads were more equal than their colleagues in the SMT.

This theme highlights the importance of developing a perspective for understanding how SMTs work through interaction among their members. Such a perspective must address both the beliefs and values which underpin individual and group actions and the differential abilities of SMT members to use power according to particular beliefs and values. A cultural perspective offers concepts for grasping how beliefs and values are shared; a political perspective offers concepts for exploring how people make differential use of resources in forming and developing a team and in carrying out team tasks. Combining cultural and political perspectives into a dual perspective offers a more comprehensive understanding of the way beliefs and values are linked with the use of resources by different individuals and groups within SMTs. It also enables us to grasp how team members contribute to shaping, sustaining and changing the beliefs and values connected with teamwork which underpin the work of SMTs.

Our purposes in this book are fourfold. First, we report on the outcomes of a study of SMTs at work. Second, we develop a cultural and political perspective for grappling with the complexities of SMTs (which may have wider application in the study of organisations). Third, we point to gender issues related to SMT membership and working practices. Finally, we make a tentative assessment of approaches to teamwork which appear to be effective in enabling senior staff to cope with an expanding range of management tasks.

In this chapter we clear the ground by defining key concepts connected with team approaches to management; examine the evolution of the national policy context favouring a management hierarchy while rendering the management of secondary schools increasingly complex, so putting pressure on senior staff to coordinate their work; discuss how SMTs emerged within this context; consider what is known about effective and ineffective teamwork in secondary schools and organisations outside education; describe how we attempted to get the inside story on SMTs through our research focus and methods; and introduce the rest of the book.

WHAT IS A TEAM?

Our research focuses upon the attempt of SMT members to work together within their conception of teamwork. We have followed Larson and LaFasto (1989) in adopting a broad definition of a *team*:

> A team has two or more people; it has a specific performance objective or recognisable goal to be attained; and coordination of activity among the members of the team is required for the attainment of the team goal or objective.
>
> (p. 19)

This definition begs the questions of who determines the team's goal and how far it is clearly specified. We have noted how the role of SMTs in our study was largely prescribed by the heads, but how far their conception was realised in practice depended on the contribution of other team members.

Individuals within any group, however temporary or informal, may *collaborate* in so far as they combine their resources to achieve agreed goals over a period of time (Hall and Wallace, 1993). Collaboration may be defined as 'joint work for joint purposes', the foundation of synergy. Joint work within teams does not imply that team members are clones or that working together is harmonious. Collaboration within an SMT may include shared commitment to reaching a decision that all members agree must be made. However, individuals may disagree profoundly about the content of the decision; collaboration implies that they are committed to working towards a mutually acceptable compromise.

Individual team members' motivation to collaborate may vary from voluntary commitment to compulsion by others. In SMTs, some members may ultimately be compelled to collaborate since they are expected to behave according to agreed groundrules as a condition of membership which, in itself, may be purely voluntary for heads alone. *Teamwork* refers to collaboration within a group which is formally constituted and endures over time. A team is an identifiable entity, and may be viewed as one end of a continuum from an established team, through an informal group, to an aggregate of individuals who come together temporarily.

While headteachers are the formal *leaders* of SMTs, they use their resources to develop this team role by sharing it to a greater or lesser degree with other team members. *Leadership* may be defined, following Louis and Miles (1990), as actions which set the course for maintaining the *status quo* and change within an organisation or a team within it. These actions include making strategic plans; stimulating and inspiring others to act and creating conditions favourable to action; and monitoring progress. Leadership actions entail attending to various tasks and the needs of people concerned (Halpin, 1966).

MANAGEMENT HIERARCHY AND MANAGERIAL COMPLEXITY

By the time senior staff come to occupy their present post, they will probably have been teachers for at least a decade. Most will continue to serve in a senior post for the rest of their career. They tend to have experience of management responsibilities, salary levels and working practices of the past, whose legacy is a set of assumptions which may affect their current perceptions. Beliefs and values about a management hierarchy are likely to reflect experience of the distribution of posts connected to nationally negotiated salary differentials; those connected with teamwork may reflect experience of participation in management, of team-building training, and of an increasing range of managerial tasks (following mainly from central government policies) which necessitate coordination between senior staff.

In this country a hierarchical distinction has long been drawn between headteachers and other professional staff, exemplified by the autocratic style of (almost exclusively male) heads of the past within what Baron (1975) termed the 'headmaster tradition'. This distinction has become less clear since the 1950s as the greater complexity of secondary school management has made heads more dependent upon senior colleagues. A single deputy headteacher post also existed in grammar and secondary modern schools over many years (Burnham, 1968). By contrast with headship this role lacked definition beyond deputising for heads and acting as their administrative assistant (Lawley, 1988).

A central government policy (widely adopted at the local level) with enormous impact on secondary school management was 'comprehensivisation', beginning in the 1950s and continuing over two decades. The system of grammar schools for more able pupils and secondary modern schools for the less able was largely replaced with comprehensive schools encompassing the full range of ability. Amalgamation of schools to create many comprehensives meant that the new institutions were much larger and split sites were not uncommon. By the 1970s the largest comprehensives had over 2,000 pupils. Falling rolls in the next decade led to smaller staffs and site closures, facing heads with the unwelcome task of managing contraction (Briault and Smith, 1980).

Morgan, Hall and Mackay (1983) argued that five influences reducing the feasibility of heads remaining the sole senior manager were:

> changes in pupil numbers and ability range; changing expectations of parents and their children; the development of new power bases such as teacher unions and curriculum pressure groups within the school; external demands for accountability; and an interest in the relationship between running costs and school performance. These changes have combined to make secondary headship much more concerned with the running of the school as a complex organization and with the political management of the array of professional and public interest groups wanting a say in school policy . . . Heads in the 1980s cannot promote their policies without contest, or impose their own values or ethos without debate, bargaining and compromise. Other social changes such as staff assertion, union groupings, subject lobbies, and the interests of ancillary staff, must also be taken into account. They are influences which combine to modify a head's traditional role from that of determining policy to that of leading the policy forming process.
>
> (pp. 11–12)

An additional influence favouring shared management, related to union power and pressure groups within the school, was teachers' mounting concern to participate more fully in decision making. Hoyle (1986) suggested that this pressure was linked to the wider political climate of the 1960s which highlighted individuals' right to have their say in the running of social affairs; the need for coordination among teachers resulting from curriculum changes; the increasing complexity of schools; and the provision of in-service training courses emphasising participation.

A second policy originating long before comprehensive schools, and extended by comprehensivisation, was a piecemeal transition from separate schools for girls and boys to co-educational institutions. This policy led to a gender-related hierarchy among senior staff whose legacy may remain in gender-linked responsibilities for a minority of deputies. According to Burnham (1968) men gained the headship of the vast majority of mixed grammar and secondary modern schools formed by amalgamation of girls' and boys' schools:

> The post of senior mistress became established, in many cases to accommodate the obsolete headmistress, and some authorities stated that where the head was a man, the senior assistant must be a woman, and vice versa. Her function was to watch over the girl pupils . . . This dilemma of having a senior mistress as deputy head was increasingly circumvented by the appointment of a senior master as well as a senior mistress; a ruse to avoid the necessity of men having to serve under a woman.
>
> (p. 176)

Towards the end of the 1980s Litawski (1993) analysed job descriptions relating to 378 advertisements for deputy headships of co-educational comprehensive schools. Almost a quarter described stereotypical responsibilities, in all instances naming the previous incumbent as a woman. Tasks required of female deputies emphasised aspects of a traditional woman's role – 'people orientated and pastoral but, more revealingly, low-level operational tasks'. An extreme case was the job of 'checking the skirting boards, toilets and curtains'. Litawski interviewed thirteen female deputies and found that over half were responsible for tasks which were primarily pastoral and of lower status than their male deputy colleagues. A gender-linked element of hierarchy may therefore be alive and well among a minority of senior staff with the same job title and salary level. On the other hand, McBurney and Hough (1989) showed that the creation of SMTs in secondary schools has contributed to fewer women being confined to stereotyped roles compared with a decade ago.

National salary negotiations leading to differential pay and conditions of service have reflected the increasing managerial load of senior staff. The agreement of employers and unions on the 1956 Burnham Committee established the role of deputy head for all schools over a minimum size. A system of graded posts for teachers was introduced, replaced in 1971 by a wider range of five salary scales (consolidated into four in 1974). An additional post of 'senior teacher' was added in 1972 for the largest schools, carrying a salary above that of the highest scale. Teaching posts above the basic scale were often allocated to reward good class teaching but by the 1980s such posts were increasingly linked to management responsibility (Wallace, 1986). Senior teacher posts were variably allocated in practice: some for management responsibility, others to acknowledge good teaching and management work or the loyal service of heads of department (Straker, 1984).

The 1971 agreement also acknowledged the size of comprehensive schools by enabling a senior master or mistress post carrying a deputy head's salary to be created in middle- to large-sized schools. This post was additional to the deputy headship, and in large schools a second deputy could be appointed, allowing the possibility that senior managers might include the head, two deputies and a senior mistress or master. The gender-related senior mistress or master post was replaced by the designation of deputy head in 1987, so freeing it of any gender connection, although we have seen how stereotypical beliefs and values about responsibilities linger on in a minority of schools.

Central government imposed a new salary structure in this year, while spelling out conditions of service for the first time (DES, 1987). The system of scales and senior teachers was replaced by a basic teaching scale with five grades of 'incentive allowance'. In addition to management responsibility, incentive allowances could still be given for reasons such as outstanding ability as a class teacher.

Conditions of service also implied hierarchical status. Senior teachers could be given the highest (E) grade incentive allowance but their conditions of service were identical to those of other teachers. The conditions for deputies were a hybrid between those of teachers and heads. Conditions for heads stipulated that, subject to legislation and articles of government for the school, 'the headteacher shall be responsible for the internal organisation, management and control of the school'. However, heads could not be autocrats: they must consult various interested parties.

A further element of hierarchy between deputies (where schools are large enough to have two or more) may relate to arrangements for deputising for the headteacher. It is common for one deputy to be nominated to take charge of the school in the head's absence. The label 'senior deputy' may be used to reflect this deputy's elevated status. Alternatively a ranking of first, second and even third deputy may indicate differential status, whether based on length of service or level of responsibility.

In recent years, changes imposed by central government in the process of salary negotiation and in the financing of schools have given heads and governors more room to manoeuvre in distributing senior staff posts. The recommendation of the Teachers' Review Body in 1992 that statutorily required numbers of deputy heads for schools of given sizes should be abolished was followed by what a *Times Educational Supplement* (1992) article described as

> a savage little outbreak of redundancy among deputy headteachers. In most cases, schools with their backs to the wall financially are seizing upon the biggest possible saving on staff costs for the smallest short-term impact on the curriculum.
>
> (p. 23)

The question arose whether reducing the number of deputies would increase the hierarchical separation of heads from other staff. In principle, it was also possible to increase the number of deputies. Since our fieldwork finished, more changes in the salary structure are afoot, teaching staff other than deputies and heads being placed along a single scale according to criteria which include management responsibility.

MULTIPLE CHANGES – MULTIPLE MANAGEMENT TASKS

Over the years, local education authorities (LEAs) have undertaken many initiatives for schools which reflect changing local circumstances and the political imperatives of local councils. Notable examples were the promotion of equal opportunities for pupils and staff and the development of multicultural and antiracist education. LEAs also responded to central government creation of funding arrangements to help meet the educational needs of the increasing proportion of pupils from minority ethnic groups. Managing the work of specialist staff funded through the 'Section 11' legislation became a new task for senior staff in schools receiving this support. Overhaul of the allocation system added the new managerial task of working within a system of time limited 'projects' (Bagley, 1992), exacerbated by recent government cutbacks affecting Section 11 (Yaseen, 1993).

The launching of new central and local government policies with implications for the complexity of secondary school management has gathered pace since the early 1980s. Most policies have added management tasks to the existing load. Demands for greater external accountability following the 'great debate about education' of the late 1970s led to initiatives such as school self-review and to closer links with governors. The Technical and Vocational Education Initiative (TVEI) required coordination within and between schools and colleges to manage the local initiatives. A novel management task was the preparation of competitive bids for funding.

The associated arrangements for in-service training, backed from 1987 by a new central government approach to allocating in-service training funds, required a systematic approach to identifying staff development needs and priorities and to implementing and evaluating programmes to meet high priority needs (Wallace and Hall, 1989; Oldroyd and Hall, 1991). Coordinators were commonly appointed at middle or senior level within the management hierarchy for TVEI and for staff development.

The mid-1980s saw an increase in central government commitment to developing school staff with management responsibility, especially heads and deputies. Pressure was placed on the providers of government-sponsored management training to use approaches and techniques employed within industry. Team-building activities were an increasingly prominent feature of such programmes. As news of training in teamwork spread within the education sphere, team building became a feature of many management development courses for school managers, often modelled through syndicates or action-learning sets (Wallace, 1991a). Participants on these courses were encouraged to adopt a team approach to their managerial work in school, reinforcing the tendency towards sharing managerial work as a result of the new tasks.

A long period of industrial action over teachers' pay during the mid-1980s gave senior managers a novel context for their work: intermittent disruptive action necessitating ongoing negotiation with staff unions. The central government approach to resolving the dispute was, in 1987, to impose a new salary structure and conditions of service (as discussed above), including the requirement that each teacher may be directed to work for 1,265 hours per year. Deputies and heads were exempted from this stipulation, further differentiating them as the most senior staff in the management hierarchy. A new annual management task was to work out individual teaching loads and compulsory attendance at meetings and in-service training within the framework of the 1,265 hours of 'directed time'. The government package included provision of five 'training days' each year, whose organisation fell to staff development coordinators. They were also generally responsible for managing, at school level, the extensive in-service training of teachers which accompanied the launch of the General Certificate of Secondary Education (GCSE) examination system in 1988.

This year saw the passing of the Education Reform Act (ERA) which, with provisions in the 1986 Education Act, set in train massive changes in secondary school management. The privatising of school inspections under the 1992 Education Act added yet another task at school level. Central government reform policies leading to new management tasks for all secondary schools include:

- a national curriculum, divided into ten subjects and phased in year by year;
- formal assessment of the national curriculum, whose raw results are to be published as 'league tables', together with information about the rate of truancy among pupils;
- tighter regulation of religious education and a daily collective act of worship;
- increased representation of parents and local community representatives on governing bodies;
- responsibility for financial management and the appointment and dismissal of staff falling to headteachers and the governing body under the local management of school initiative (LMS), entailing greater liaison between the professional staff and governors;
- biennial appraisal of all teaching staff;
- more open enrolment of pupils to promote competition between schools within the same phase, resulting in a new emphasis on marketing the school to prospective parents and to liaison between secondary schools and their feeder primary schools;
- the possibility of individual schools opting out of LEA control and becoming 'grant maintained', funded directly by central government;
- the duty imposed upon LEAs of developing local schemes within reforms such as LMS and supporting schools with their implementation. School staff must work within these schemes;
- the inspection of schools every four years according to published critera, putting pressure on staff to ensure their work conforms to them.

The multiplicity of management tasks implicit in the reforms of the past decade puts heavy pressure on headteachers to delegate. The complexity of these tasks lies not only in the new jobs to be done once changes are made, but also managing the implementation of each change and orchestrating the implementation of all concurrent and often interrelated changes alongside the rest of the school's work (Wallace, 1992; Wallace and McMahon, 1993). Delegating a task such as administering the LMS budget entails the implementation tasks of securing resources such as the services of a bursar and use of a computer. Implications must be taken into account of allocating resources to LMS for those needed for other changes and the maintenance of existing practice elsewhere in the school. Delegation does not remove the need for coordination.

Heads remain externally accountable for performance of the tasks they delegate. A counter-pressure upon them is to retain a high level of control over the work of the staff to whom they delegate management tasks through some form of monitoring. These conflicting pressures were reflected in the work of the SMTs we studied.

ENTER THE SMT

The creation of SMTs has never been a central government policy; the label emerged during the early 1970s as new management structures developed in secondary schools after comprehensivisation where a larger number of senior staff were being appointed. Richardson (1973) studied the first years of expansion after one comprehensive was created from a grammar school, tracing the establishment of a new 'top management' structure. The headteacher believed in consulting staff about changes as the school began to cater for the full pupil-ability range. Initially, weekly meetings of the top management group consisted of a 'triumvirate' of the head, deputy and senior mistress. Membership was broadened by the inclusion of three middle managers – heads of lower, middle and upper school – in a 'standing committee'.

Richardson noted how this committee contained three hierarchical levels of management responsibility, yet senior staff including the head resisted the notion of hierarchical relationships inside it and between the committee and other consultative groups. The head tacitly accepted a hierarchical ordering of responsibilities while, publicly, expressing his wish to sustain more egalitarian relationships with staff. Teachers held notions of 'the hierarchy' as a separate entity, some encompassing just the head and deputy while others also included the senior mistress and the three section heads.

Perceptions of a management hierarchy persisted: the senior mistress described how many staff wanted her to remain the stereotypical 'school mum', primarily concerned with girls' welfare, when she had shed most of this work and was now responsible for other tasks including timetabling. The view of hierarchy among some staff outside the top management group seems to have included gender-related assumptions about who should perform particular management tasks.

A few years later, an account of secondary schools (DES, 1977) judged by Her Majesty's Inspectors (HMI) to be effective indicated that heads had begun to open up management: 'Emphasis is laid on consultation, teamwork and participation, but, without exception, the most important single factor in the success of these schools is the quality of leadership of the head'. The SMT label probably came into use in large secondary schools with at least two deputies.

Maw (1977), in discussing the allocation of management responsibilities among senior staff, referred to the need to define them within a plan for a 'comprehensive and mutually supportive team', commenting that stereotypical gender-related responsibilities should be avoided.

The term SMT had become widespread by the mid-1980s. Research on new secondary heads by Weindling and Earley (1987) revealed that all 47 schools in the sample had an SMT, as did the 24 schools studied by Torrington and Weightman (1989). However this research and the observational study of four heads by Hall, Mackay and Morgan (1986) showed that the composition of SMTs and their working practices varied widely according to heads' preferences.

Hall and her colleagues reported four SMT meetings each week in one school whose SMT consisted of the head, first and second deputies, second master and director of studies; another head never held a meeting with all three senior staff. The membership of the SMTs in the study by Torrington and Weightman also varied between head and deputies (seven SMTs); head, deputies and senior teachers (fourteen SMTs); and 'idiosyncratic' arrangements (three SMTs), in one case including two 'elder statesmen' on Scale 4. The frequency, timing, process and content of SMT meetings and the relationship between SMTs and the rest of staff was equally variable, interpreted by the researchers as reflecting the culture of each school.

These studies indicate that the SMT label had become widely employed in conceiving a group of senior staff as a single entity and that heads had a key influence on who was in the SMT and what it did. This influence was not exclusive: Weindling and Earley documented how new heads were dominated by recent 'institutional history'. They inherited the SMT of the previous incumbent and had to take existing practices into account. Although most of the new heads were committed to a team approach to management, it could prove difficult to secure a full contribution from other SMT members.

Hall and her co-workers showed how heads had considerable scope to express often idiosyncratic beliefs and values in their management style; the research evidence on SMTs suggests that equivalent room to manoeuvre exists for heads to promote a team approach, but it is tempered by the actions of other SMT members. New heads in the study by Weindling and Earley took the lead in team development, taking opportunities to appoint senior staff who shared their views; negotiating delegation of individual tasks and the procedure for SMT meetings; and attempting to develop a structure for communication which would avoid divorcing the SMT from other staff.

According to Murgatroyd (1986), such an aspiration was not always achieved. He documented a school where the head was seen by many staff outside the SMT to have 'retreated to management by memo', with the support of a management 'clique'. There was lack of communication with other staff about the SMT agenda, which included little emphasis on staffing and staff concerns. Conversely, middle managers in a substantial study by Earley and Fletcher-Campbell (1989) commented favourably on heads who were readily accessible and 'the degree to which the SMT were working together and had a positive policy as regards the middle managers'.

Evetts (1992) examined secondary heads' powers to shape the management structure. Despite constraints posed by existing staffing (often including individuals on protected salaries as a legacy of falling rolls) and the national salary scales, heads found considerable room to manoeuvre to create a management structure according to their belief in a management hierarchy or more collegial structure of professional staff. As the newly appointed head of the school where he had been deputy, Taylor (1992) reorganised the SMT. It was extended to include 'staff whose contributions were expected to be of considerable value'; staff who wished to develop their ability as managers; and staff whose responsibilities were 'crucial to the success of the school'. Team membership was to reflect more closely the gender balance among the school staff. He excluded from the SMT staffing issues which 'proved too sensitive to discuss in this forum', discussing them with the deputies alone.

Recent research confirms how the burgeoning of management tasks associated with central government reforms resulted in an increasing proportion of school-wide management responsibilities being allocated within SMTs (Earley and Baker, 1989). This survey indicated that a major cause of low staff morale was the number and speed of the reforms, coupled with the lack of resources needed for implementation. Conversely a factor contributing to high morale among senior staff, despite these difficult circumstances, was 'the enthusiasm and commitment of senior staff, and the advantages of working as a team'. The response of eight heads studied by Gillborn (1989) to new demands connected with reforms included looking to SMT colleagues for support in coping with their new management responsibilities and the associated stresses. A large scale survey of deputy heads carried out by the Secondary Heads Association (SHA) (1992) showed how deputies were undertaking an increasingly strategic management responsibility, especially in consequence of new tasks linked with LMS. The most senior staff other than deputies (E or D allowance holders) were now shouldering more routine administrative tasks, such as arranging cover for staff absences, which used to be the province of deputies. According to respondents, where SMTs worked well they formed a powerful means of handling the new managerial burden.

EFFECTIVE AND INEFFECTIVE TEAMWORK

SMTs have arrived, at least in name, and look set to stay for the foreseeable future. Yet it is not easy to make a team approach work. Two-fifths of the new heads in the research by Weindling and Earley reported problems with the rest of the SMT. Heads commented on 'personality clashes' and difficulties with senior staff who were defensive and interpreted their tasks narrowly, near the end of their career and 'burned out', promoted beyond their ability and unable to cope, or disappointed internal candidates for the headship. On the other hand a few deputies complained of domination of the SMT by the head.

A follow-up investigation of the same heads (Earley, Baker and Weindling, 1990) five years later indicated that problems could endure. Almost half perceived that they and their senior staff colleagues worked well as a team. This study highlighted how a hierarchy among members of the SMT other than the head could cause internal tension: a few schools had a two-tier system where policy-making meetings included solely the head and deputies while other meetings, where policies were ratified, extended to the most senior teachers. Two-thirds of respondents to the SHA survey of deputies perceived that they were members of an effective SMT. Reasons given for ineffectiveness included 'carrying' a colleague who was not contributing fully, lack of delegation by the head and lack of clarity about individual responsibilities.

A recipe for success was distilled from the positive survey responses:

> Take collaboration, complementary skills and temperaments, add common values, flexibility and far sightedness. Stir well with a good head who provides clear roles and regular meetings and here we have a management team that feels ready for the future.
>
> (SHA, 1992, p. 9)

The assertion that SMTs can work effectively is backed by informed professional opinion. The report of the Committee of Enquiry into London's secondary schools (ILEA, 1984) argued that improving SMT performance was an important route to overall effectiveness. HMI in England (DES, 1988) and Scotland (SED, 1988) pointed to the contribution of teamwork among senior staff, led by heads, to effective schooling. A study of staff perceptions of effectively managed schools (Bolam *et al.*, 1993) found that SMTs were seen to function effectively in self-reportedly effective secondary schools, confirming that the team leadership role of the head remained crucial to teamwork and that deputies were being given greater control over day-to-day management. In a few schools, a negative consequence of the almost exclusive emphasis by senior staff on management tasks in the wake of central government reforms was to distance the SMT from other staff and pupils. Creating an in-group runs the risk of creating a disaffected out-group.

Evidence of the effectiveness of sharing school management tasks is not confined to Britain. In their large scale study of effective secondary schools in the United States, Wilson and Corcoran (1988) concluded that:

> leadership in secondary schools tends to be dispersed. Seldom do all of the desired qualities or all of the required energy reside in one person. In most of the schools there are a number of people who can and do take leadership roles at different times . . . However, the principal is always a key actor, developing and supporting these other school leaders, and orchestrating their efforts into a harmonious whole that moves the school closer to its goals. At the heart of this harmony is the ability of formal leaders in these schools to recognize the strengths of a diverse set of people and to encourage those people to make maximum use of their skills. Good leaders develop other leaders.
>
> (pp. 81–2)

As in British schools, how far staff could contribute to management depended upon the degree to which principals (headteachers) used their power to empower others.

What do we know about effective teamwork among senior managers in schools? A consistent message of research and informed opinion in Britain is that SMTs can make a difference to school effectiveness. Yet little detail is known about how they operate. These studies are based primarily on question-naires and interviews, with scant observation of the inner world of the SMT.

Practical handbooks for senior staff (e.g. Trethowan, 1985; Nicholson, 1989; Davies *et al.*, 1990; Bell, 1992), often drawing on concepts and tech-niques developed in organisational settings other than education, are strong on exhortation and practical tips for effective teamwork, and also warn against various pitfalls. As long as the tips are followed faithfully, such handbooks imply that effective teamwork will ensue. There is little acknowledgement of tension between the perception of a management hierarchy and the view that members have an equal contribution to make to team decisions, or of con-sequences of this tension for SMT effectiveness.

TEAMWORK OUTSIDE THE EDUCATION SPHERE

Ideas from research and industrial management training have influenced man-agement training for senior secondary school staff. Later chapters will describe how some of these ideas were employed in the SMTs we studied, whether in selection of team members or a team development effort. Many team-building guides (e.g. Woodcock, 1979; Spencer and Pruss, 1992) are based upon the authors' experience as trainers and consultants. The research underpinning exhortatory popular books (e.g. Peters, 1988; Kanter, 1990) and some training materials tends to have a strongly practical orientation, with a greater em-phasis on *processes* connected with a team approach to management than work on secondary schools. It offers insights into group interaction and con-siderable support for some of the factors already identified.

Yet several features of the research conducted outside education suggest we should be cautious in adopting the prescriptions or training techniques that draw upon it. First, the almost exclusive concern is for team effectiveness as defined within a framework of competitive business (as opposed to profes-sional service) values. Woodcock and Francis (1989) developed a values-clarification questionnaire whose starting point was their judgement about values associated with commercial success. Alongside teamwork, which offers synergy, they promote other values including competitiveness – 'the only sure-fire recipe for survival' – and elitism – 'successful organizations understand the vital importance of getting the best candidates into management jobs, and continually developing their competence'. Generally, teams are assumed to be good for achieving the goal of profitability in a competitive environment; the research and training enterprise is dedicated to finding how to develop 'win-ning teams' for this purpose.

Second, methodological limitations of research are often glossed over. A common approach is to identify companies, or teams within them, that are deemed by some measurement as effective, then to ask those concerned to divulge the secret of their success (e.g. Peters and Waterman, 1982). Larson and LaFasto (1989) took such a sample of teams, interviewed leaders and other members, and compiled a list of 'distinguishing features of high performance teams' based on analysis of the responses. These features were the foundation for a team self-review questionnaire which was tested with another sample of teams. The findings were – inevitably – limited to factors of which respondents were aware, and were not cross-checked through observation.

The influential work of Belbin (1981) was based on extensive experiments with participants attending courses at Henley Management Centre. Depending on their scores on personality tests, individuals were placed in small teams participating in a competitive simulation game which modelled company financial transactions. The amount of money each team accrued provided the outcome criterion for judging its effectiveness. The complementary team roles that Belbin identified and the associated questionnaire for assessing individual preferences have been widely used to create work teams whose members are expected to contribute to the creation of synergy by adopting complementary roles. However, the research findings were derived from artificially created teams, often of strangers from different companies, in an off-the-job setting, playing a simulation game where mistakes did not matter. The research did not extend to observation of real work teams tackling real management tasks in their real setting.

Third, it is uncertain how far findings from one organisational setting are transferable to another. Much research within companies refers to temporary project teams (e.g. Peters and Waterman, 1982) created to develop new products, whereas SMTs constitute a permanent entity for managing the organisation as a whole. While factors may be universally applicable to teams at a high level of generality, contextual factors may dramatically modify their expression. Cultural and political factors are acknowledged in the work on teams in commerce and industry; yet beliefs and values and the resources available to achieve various ends in SMTs are likely to reflect the social and political context of schooling in Britain. Secondary schools are public service institutions staffed by professionals and accountable to the local community – business values promoted by central government reforms notwithstanding!

MIXED MESSAGES

Let us therefore proceed with caution, bearing in mind the limitations of this work, and examine the overlap between studies of management teams inside and outside education. The central message from both sectors is consistent with our claim that team approaches can be a powerful way of working for managerial purposes, but effective teamwork is difficult to bring off. There is support for the idea that teams can be an effective way of offering a coordinated response to change (e.g. Chaudrey-Lawton *et al.*, 1992), and Critchley and Casey (1984) have argued that teams are needed in conditions of shared uncertainty for solving problems to which there is no simple solution. Considerable overlap exists between the ingredients of effective teams that have been identified. Some compare well with the SHA recipe for SMTs. The recipe for team success put forward by Larson and LaFasto (1989) includes:

- clearly understood and shared team goals;
- competent team members – with individual skills and the ability to work with others;
- unified commitment – loyalty to and identification with the team, fostered through a balance between respecting individual differences and requiring unity;
- a collaborative climate – marked by honesty, openness, consistent behaviour, and mutual respect;
- a shared expectation that high standards are to be achieved;
- principled leadership – establishing a vision, initiating change and unleashing the talents of members.

To which we may add ingredients from Chaudrey-Lawton and her colleagues (1992):

- openness to feedback and advice from outsiders;
- retaining flexible ways of working;
- sharing leadership according to the task;
- strong internal communication;
- continuous effort to improve performance, linked to internal monitoring;
- the ability of members to cooperate, rather than compete against each other.

The recipe for team disaster may be read off in part as lack of the ingredients for success, such as ambiguous goals, incompetent team members, individuals more committed to realising personal interests than team goals, failure to confront where individuals differ, isolation from the rest of the organisation or complacency. Most ingredients for success and failure relate to team and wider organisational cultures and to the use of power. Unified commitment indicates a culture shared throughout a team, leading to the synergistic use of resources; putting personal career interests first suggests a high value placed on individual advancement and resources directed towards this end.

Two factors identified elsewhere echo our assertion that there is a contradiction between the existence of a management hierarchy and the assumption that team members contribute to teamwork as equals. First, Kanter (1983) refers to 'the seductiveness of the hierarchy' where a project team consists of individuals with different organisational status. Deference patterns may re-emerge even where groundrules for team operation imply that the contributions of all members are equally important. There is collusion between members who together recreate the management hierarchy within the team.

Second, even where team members do create an oasis of equality within a hierarchical organisation, Chaudrey-Lawton and her colleagues reveal how difficulties may arise with relationships between team members and others. Action according to a belief in the 'flat structure' of a non-hierarchical team may lead to conflict with assumptions held by outsiders about the hierarchy elsewhere in the organisation. Despite the differences in organisational context between schools and companies, in so far as both settings exhibit a management hierarchy, it seems likely to constrain teamwork that transgresses hierarchical boundaries.

ON THE TRACK OF THE 'INSIDE STORY'

Our intention was to build on existing knowledge of SMTs which was strong on accounts of diverse structures but weak on the process of teamwork through a study which featured extensive observation. The project was funded by the Economic and Social Research Council for two years from January 1991. Its purpose was to address the question:

> Within the context of educational reform, how do SMTs operate in secondary schools where senior staff perceive themselves to be committed to teamwork as their core strategy for managing the school, and to what effect?

We decided to seek SMTs whose members were all positive towards the idea of teamwork. We felt that more would be learned than by investigating a randomly selected group of schools; the existing research had demonstrated how teamwork was inhibited in perhaps a third or more of SMTs.

Our hunch that LEA actions in promoting teamwork, supporting SMTs or selecting staff might affect teamwork at school level was reflected in the decision to work in two LEAs. Both were counties: Westshire, with extensive urban areas and rural dormitory villages; and Eastshire, with small towns separated by rural tracts. Senior LEA staff were asked to suggest schools whose SMTs met our criterion of unified commitment to a team approach.

We also sought an equal number of schools with female and with male heads, wishing to avoid the pitfall of gender blindness. Since the national proportion of women headteachers is only about 19% (DES, 1992), had we not specified schools with heads of either gender, it is likely that we would have studied SMTs led predominantly by men. North American research on school principals, where the under-representation of women is similar (Fullan, 1991), indicates that there are differences between the management styles of women and men as a group, although individuals vary widely. Women tend to behave more in the ways associated with other research findings on effective leadership (Smith and Andrews, 1989). A gender-blind study would run the risk that portraying the actions of male heads might be interpreted as encompassing the actions of (invisible) female heads.

The project design consisted of two phases. First, focused, interpretive case studies (Merriam, 1988) were carried out in three schools in each LEA. For each site, a semistructured interview was conducted with all SMT members, the chair or deputy chair of governors, and a sample of six other teaching staff which included main scale teachers and staff with middle management responsibility. One SMT meeting was observed and relevant documents were collected.

Second, longitudinal case studies were carried out over the 1991/92 academic year in two of these schools. Criteria for selecting second phase schools from the original six were to ensure that there was one from each LEA; one had a female head and the other a male head; and one SMT was developing its approach to teamwork while the other was an established team. The main method was non-participant observation of formal meetings: some 47 SMT meetings; nineteen middle management meetings involving SMT members; four governors' meetings; seven middle management meetings not attended by SMT members; and, in one school, a residential team review meeting. Each SMT member was shadowed for at least half a day and interviewed two or three times. A small sample of other staff was interviewed and documents relating to meetings were gathered.

Staff in all the schools were very supportive of the research, giving us unrestricted access to SMT and other formal meetings. No one refused to be interviewed. We were very rarely asked not to be present, as when a head was meeting a teacher to discuss a personal matter.

Our interpretation of the findings was checked out at a feedback session for the staff interviewed during each initial case study and a session for the SMTs in the second phase after fieldwork was complete. The staff most centrally involved in the projects were invited to comment on the draft of this book.

We integrated data analysis with data collection, so repeatedly refocusing our enquiry according to the interim findings. Our methods were informed by the approach to qualitative data analysis developed by Miles and Huberman (1984), who argue that analysis should start prior to and continue throughout data collection. A literature review led to an initial conceptual framework from which research questions were derived. Interview schedules for the initial case studies related to our research questions.

A site summary was prepared for each school and themes and hypotheses identified were investigated in the second phase. The aim in the autumn term 1991 was to develop an overview of how the two SMTs operated; in the spring term 1992 the theme of structured team development was explored in one school while the process of SMT restructuring was tracked in the other; and in the summer term 1992 the focus switched to links between the SMTs and other staff.

Extensive notes were taken during each observation and interview, and all interviews were taped. A summary tape was then prepared by referring back to the notes, schedule and field tape. Our interpretations and quotations to substantiate them were included. Summaries were transcribed and collated. Matrices were used to display data from the six initial case studies as part of the cross-site analysis. Some data analysis in the second phase, such as determining the pattern of interaction and typical content of SMT meetings, was carried out in this way. The data set for both schools was also scanned for the expression of various themes. Tabulated display of data was less suited to this purpose, as it risked losing the contextual richness and complexity of particular incidents.

TELLING IT LIKE IT ISN'T?

Our research had several limitations. It was a sociological study, and so did not address psychological factors except where they were expressed in interaction.

The small number of SMTs studied and our qualitative methods mean that our findings cannot be taken as representative of schools across the country. Nevertheless, they are likely to have implications for other schools. Any team has to be constituted, developed and its working practices negotiated. According to the research and informed professional opinion discussed earlier our SMTs reflected many features of teams elsewhere and the problems besetting them, not least those following from central government reforms. Our findings also suggest that, within certain parameters, there is room for variation in membership and interpretation of teamwork within SMTs according to the beliefs and values of members (particularly the heads), so it is unlikely that any of our SMTs will be 'typical' in every respect.

Secondary schools are large organisations and SMT members represent a small minority of school staff and others, such as governors, concerned with management issues. Our primary concern with what went on inside the SMT meant we could observe only a few meetings with other groups and sample the views of a few outsiders about the relationship between the SMT and those who interacted with it.

Our frequent presence in the schools during the second phase may have caused a 'halo effect', especially as we were party to many confidences and witnessed incidents which those involved found emotionally demanding. When asked towards the end of the fieldwork about the impact of our presence, SMT members were unanimous that it had made little difference to their practice.

We followed the causal chain of SMT effectiveness only part way, looking no further in the first phase than judgements of other staff and governors. In the second phase we sought evidence of the direct outcomes of the process of teamwork as a basis for considering the effectiveness of different approaches, recognising that there might be many intervening variables which could affect whether effective teamwork had any link with pupil learning. Yet despite the methodological limitations, we think our findings raise important practical and theoretical issues.

TOPICS COVERED IN THE REMAINING CHAPTERS

The book falls into two parts: first, an overview of our research and the range of approaches to teamwork revealed through the initial case studies; second, a detailed analysis of two SMTs. Chapter 2 develops a cultural and political perspective and discusses how gender issues articulate with such a framework. The next two chapters examine similarities and differences between the six schools studied in the first phase of our fieldwork. Chapter 3 puts the SMTs in context and looks at membership, the role of the team in managing the school, and structures for carrying it out. We move on in Chapter 4 to consider the selection of team members, ways of developing the capacity for teamwork, and the processes of carrying out team tasks.

In the second part we take forward the analysis by focusing more closely on two of these SMTs. Chapter 5 puts forward a framework for understanding complementary patterns of behaviour in teams and explores how the heads and other SMT members made their individual contribution to teamwork. Chapter 6 describes how SMT members operated in team meetings and examines the content of the agenda they sought to address, followed in Chapter 7 by an account of the links between the SMTs and other groups through which the SMTs worked in fulfilling their team role. We consider the consequences for those inside and outside the SMTs of identifying a group as the team with major responsibility for managing the schools as a whole.

In different ways, members of both SMTs made structured attempts to review and modify their team structure or process of operation. These efforts revealed some of the strains that may arise in adopting a team approach to school management and documents how SMT members attempted to get round them. Chapter 8 describes how one SMT went about team development, while Chapter 9 examines the process of restructuring in the other SMT. Finally, Chapter 10 reviews what has been learned about SMTs, considers issues connected with the effectiveness of approaches to teamwork and discusses the implications of our findings for researchers, practical issues for senior school staff and governors, and policy issues for LEA and national policy makers.

2

Towards a Cultural and Political Perspective

In this chapter a case is made for adopting a dual cultural and political perspective as a basis for interpreting how SMTs work. We begin by considering the nature of perspectives as metaphors providing a lens for guiding understanding, then look critically at two studies of school management where either a cultural or a political perspective was used. Concepts within a proposed dual perspective are defined and illustrated through examples drawn from our research. Finally, we consider how far this perspective encompasses gender-related differences over the use of power linked to cultural assumptions about women and men.

COMBINING METAPHORS: MIXED OR MULTIPLE?

Morgan (1986) suggests that any theoretical perspective on organisations constitutes a metaphor which directs attention to some features of phenomena under investigation, while ignoring other aspects. It is probably beyond human capacity to develop a single metaphor that provides an all-embracing explanation of social life. In recent years, an increasingly common approach to understanding organisations has been to mix metaphors by employing more than one perspective (Cuthbert, 1984; Bush, 1986; Bolman and Deal, 1991). Each perspective offers insights into different aspects of organisations. Drawing upon Cuthbert's work, Bush identifies five perspectives which, he suggests:

> represent conceptually distinct approaches to the management of educational institutions. However, it is rare for a single model to capture the reality of management in any particular school or college. Rather aspects of several perspectives are present in different proportions of each institution.
> (Bush, 1986, p. 131)

He argues that the ability of any perspective to offer insights depends upon factors such as the size of the organisation. A political perspective is claimed to be valid in comprehending large institutions such as secondary schools and colleges because subgroups of staff tend to compete for resources. This perspective is seen as less appropriate to small primary schools where policy is likely to be decided by all staff within the leadership of the head.

Bush's position appears to rest on two assumptions: that each perspective addresses a limited but distinctive proportion of organisational phenomena, and that the relevant phenomena may or may not be significantly in evidence within a given institution. As we will discuss below, the attempt by British researchers (Nias, Southworth and Yeomans, 1989) to analyse interaction between staff in primary schools from a cultural perspective and by another researcher (Ball, 1987) to use a political perspective in secondary schools are limited because the phenomena they explored in both types of institution could also be interpreted from the alternative perspective. We question Bush's assumptions about the exclusivity of each perspective and the presence or absence of the phenomena addressed by one or other perspective in particular types of institution.

A 'mixed metaphor' approach resting on different assumptions is offered by Bolman and Deal (1991), who identify four perspectives or 'frames' for interpreting organisations. Their concern is to broaden the range of ways in which managers interpret their experience as a platform for action. They suggest that managers should examine this experience from more perspectives than the single frame that many managers habitually use:

> The ability to reframe experience enriches and broadens a leader's repertoire and serves as a powerful antidote to self-entrapment. Expanded choice enables managers to generate creative responses to the broad range of problems that they encounter . . . it can be enormously liberating for managers to realize that there is *always* more than one way to respond to any organizational problem or dilemma. Managers are imprisoned only to the degree that their palette of ideas is impoverished.
>
> (Bolman and Deal, 1991, p. 4, original emphasis)

These writers assume, in contrast to Bush, that the same organisational phenomena may be interpreted from more than one perspective. Managers are exhorted to switch from one frame to another as each contains both a set of concepts offering a focus for interpretation and an image of how organisations should be managed. While they advise that (for simplicity) managers go back and forth between one frame and another, they acknowledge that an increasing range of organisational research and theory (for example Cohen and March, 1974; Perrow, 1986) employs concepts reflecting two or more perspectives in the same analysis. Bolman and Deal suggest that 'multiple frame' approaches represent a way of circumventing limitations imposed by single perspective work.

A key issue in developing a conceptual framework encompassing two or more metaphors lies in whether we assume that two into one won't go: a dual perspective must then be handled as a mixed metaphor – interpretation of phenomena first from one perspective, then from another. We wish to test the opposite assumption: that two into one will go where phenomena may be addressed through a multiple metaphor – applying concepts from two or more perspectives to a phenomenon simultaneously.

There seems nothing sacred about the grouping of particular concepts to form a perspective. The writers cited above opt for different sets of concepts in identifying the perspectives they use. Morgan identifies no less than eight perspectives and argues that there is no limit to the number of possible metaphors. Different typologies of perspectives combine some concepts that others keep separate. The political perspective adopted by Bush, and Bolman and Deal, is divided by Morgan into the 'organization as political system' and the 'organization as instrument of domination'. It seems plausible to draw on the concepts of more than one perspective in developing multiple metaphors, rather than using one metaphor at a time as in the mixed metaphor approach.

Giddens (1976, 1984) brings together concepts from several metaphors described by Morgan in developing his structuration theory. Our much less ambitious endeavour is, with reference to the conception of agency developed by Giddens, to combine two widely employed perspectives within a dual metaphor – a cultural and political frame for analysing interaction in SMTs. The essence of our *dual metaphor* is that we employ cultural and political perspectives together in developing a framework for interpreting interaction within organisations.

LIMITATIONS OF SINGLE PERSPECTIVES

We hope to avoid some limitations of single metaphor perspectives: while Deal and Kennedy (1982) interpret interaction solely in terms of the extent to which the values of an organisational culture are shared, Mangham (1979) views interaction primarily in terms of the interplay of power as individuals and groups seek to achieve different goals. Are these perspectives incompatible or may they be combined?

Like these writers, some organisational theorists and researchers into school management have adopted either a cultural perspective (e.g. Sergiovanni and Corbally, 1984; Deal, 1985; Nias, Southworth and Yeomans, 1989; Nias, Southworth and Campbell, 1992) or a political perspective (e.g. Ball, 1987; Radnor, 1990; Blase, 1991). Both approaches offer valuable insights but, in focusing the research, each may be constrained by its emphasis on one set of concepts to the detriment of the other. This point may be illustrated by examining how exponents of the two perspectives interpret the way headteachers interact with other staff.

The analysis of primary school staff relationships carried out by Nias and her colleagues employs the notion of organisational culture to explain the pattern of interaction that they observed between staff. They portray how staff develop and sustain a shared set of beliefs and values about 'the way we do things here'. Concepts employed in their analysis are listed in Table 2.1.

Table 2.1 Key concepts employed within different perspectives

Cultural (Nias et al., 1989)	Political (Ball, 1987)	Cultural and political
Culture of collaboration	Power	Culture of teamwork
Beliefs	Control	Beliefs
Values	Goal diversity	Values
Understanding	Ideology	Norms
Attitudes	Conflict	Role
Meanings	Interests	Status
Norms		Rituals
Symbols		Consensus
Rituals		Power
Ceremonies		Resources
Negotiation		Hierarchy
Consensus		Interests
		Dialectic of control
		Authority
		Influence
		Conflict
		Contradiction
		Coalitions

Conflicts between staff are interpreted as being addressed or avoided according to shared values about, say, the appropriateness of working towards compromise solutions. For Nias and her co-workers, conflicts give rise to the expression of underlying value consensus about how conflicts should be avoided or resolved: conflict on the surface masks consensus at a more implicit level.

Nevertheless, even in schools with a strong staff 'culture of collaboration', they accept that:

> . . . normative *control* was so pervasive that it is easy to lose sight of the fact that it too was the product of a *power differential*. Each school had a head with a strong 'mission' and well developed *political skills* who had been in post for at least ten years and to whom had accrued during that time a considerable amount of personal *authority*.
>
> (Nias, Southworth and Yeomans 1989, p. 15, emphasis added)

The concepts we have highlighted are pushed into the background in the analysis, yet help us grasp how headteachers were in a uniquely strong position to persuade other staff to adopt their managerial values and so obtain value consensus through negotiation.

Conversely, Ball (1987) analyses interaction amongst staff in secondary schools in terms of conflict:

> I take schools, in common with virtually all other organizations, to be *arenas of struggle*; to be riven with actual or potential conflict between members; to be poorly coordinated; to be ideologically diverse.
>
> (Ball, 1987, p. 19, original emphasis)

While Ball accepts that, overtly, much interaction is marked by apparent acceptance of a normative consensus amongst staff, he argues that implicit conflict lurks below:

interaction is centred upon the *routine*, mundane and, for the most part, uncontroversial running of the institution . . . routine organizational life is set within the *'negotiated order'* . . . a patterned construct of contrasts, *understandings, agreements and 'rules'* which provides the basis of con-certed action . . . In this way conflicts may remain normally implicit and subterranean, only occasionally bursting into full view.

(Ball, 1987, p. 20, emphasis added)

Key concepts employed in his analysis are listed in Table 2.1. Headteachers are interpreted as using various overt and covert strategies based upon their unique access to power to realise their interest in retaining control over other staff in the management of schools. SMTs are viewed as a means of supporting this interest, members other than heads being orientated towards them. Other staff, it is claimed, perceive the SMT as constituting 'the hierarchy': a group set apart from teachers who tend to exclude them from important aspects of decision making. The ability of the group to control the rest of the staff is reinforced by the 'norm of cabinet responsibility' whereby SMT members refrain from criticising SMT decisions in public.

The cultural concepts we have highlighted in the quotation above are under-played in his analysis but relate closely to that of Nias and her colleagues. In both analyses, concepts relating to the perspective that was *not* adopted are brought repeatedly into the account. The 'norm' of cabinet responsibility mentioned by Ball is essentially a cultural idea; the 'personal authority' of the head which fea-tures prominently in the analysis by Nias and her colleagues is a political notion. In order to explain the phenomena being studied, both analyses have actually used concepts from an alternative perspective in a subsidiary position within the domi-nant one. The way concepts from a second perspective creep in implies that the concepts of one perspective alone may not be up to capturing the range of pheno-mena encountered in the research to which this perspective was applied.

The limitations of a single perspective are not confined to studies in Britain. A recent cultural analysis of the role of principals in Canadian schools suggests that principals play a key part in promoting a collaborative professional cul-ture amongst their staff which is supportive of efforts to improve their schools (Leithwood and Jantzi, 1990). While this work reveals that certain principals share power with others, it is not clear how principals use power to develop a shared approach to leadership.

A contrasting example is a micropolitical analysis of leadership in an el-ementary school in the United States. Greenfield (1991) shows how the princi-pal was motivated by a moral commitment to doing what was best for the pupils, and how she used her commitment as a currency in persuading teachers to change their practice by cultivating a similar commitment in them. This analysis moves away from an emphasis on conflict towards the political strat-egies through which one person influences others to share certain beliefs and values. Yet this approach underplays how the principal's power derives partly from the existing staff culture which accepts such actions by the principal as legitimate. Cultural concepts offer a means of exploring the more collaborative use of power which Greenfield describes.

It is a truism that as social reality is infinitely complex any attempt at interpretation is guilty of simplification. A strength of any perspective is also a weakness: by directing attention to some aspects of social phenomena, it directs attention away from others. The conceptual framework derived from a perspective may lead to interpretive bias where it is assumed that the central concepts account for more of the phenomena than may be the case. As Ball (1987) acknowledges,

> having set an agenda for the study of micropolitics and institutional conflict in schools, I do not want to fall into the same trap as the social system theorists, of seeing conflict everywhere, where they saw consensus.
>
> (Ball, 1987, p. 19)

Yet despite recognising the possibility of consensus among staff in schools based upon shared values, Ball focuses very largely upon conflict.

Hargreaves (1991) argues that research on teachers may be biased where a cultural perspective has been adopted:

> the existence of shared culture is presumed no matter how complex and differentiated the organization being studied. The possibility that some highly complex organizations may have no shared culture of any substance is not acknowledged.
>
> Second, the theoretical and methodological emphasis on what is shared in the organization may exaggerate the consensus-based aspects of human relationships, according them an importance in research studies that outweighs their significance in practice. In some organizations, the differences and disagreements among participants are more significant than what they happen to share.
>
> (Hargreaves, 1991, p. 50)

The cultural perspective appears prone to directing attention away from conflict and over-emphasising consensus; the opposite can happen with the political perspective. In his definition of micropolitics, Blase (1991) includes 'both cooperative and conflictive actions and processes' but his review of research suggests that conflict has been the focus of most work in this area.

A complicating factor with significant methodological implications is the phenomenon that individuals may or may not behave according to their values, since in most situations they have some choice over whether to act (Giddens, 1976). What passes for consensus on the surface may, as Ball contends, belie some form of hidden conflict. Gronn (1986) distinguishes several types of conflict along a continuum between action and inaction. In addition to conflict which is overt (and so readily observable), it may be covert where individuals refrain from dissenting activity; or latent where expression of dissent is interpreted as arising from personal problems. Inaction may follow from a perception of the greater power of others; it may even be due to lack of awareness of conflicting interests where individuals' perceptions are shaped in such a way that they accept their situations without question. Our own research effort was limited in how far we could identify various forms of inaction. We may have got inside the SMT but we certainly did not get inside the minds of SMT members!

However, it was occasionally possible after the 'non-event' to explore instances with individuals where they had withheld from taking action, although they had the power to do so, by adopting a deliberate strategy of non-intervention. Such a strategy could amount to a long-term pattern of behaviour.

A DUAL PERSPECTIVE: PROBLEMS AND POTENTIAL

Given these constraints, is interaction best conceived, in common with Nias and her co-workers, as the rather cosy expression of shared values where conflict is bounded by underlying consensus on its resolution? Or is it, as Ball asserts, an often silent struggle between conflicting interests where apparent consensus masks suppressed conflict? We guess that interaction may be an expression of both the shared values of a culture and the differential use of power to realise particular interests. The position of authority, which we noted in the previous chapter is accorded to secondary headteachers, gives them greater power than their colleagues to shape the SMT culture relating to team-work. Combining the cultural and political perspectives into a more comprehensive framework may offer greater potential for explaining how and by whom the SMT teamwork culture is developed, maintained or threatened, than either a cultural or a political perspective alone.

An obvious drawback is the danger of conceptual indigestion, since concepts associated with both culture and power are employed in the same analysis. It is easy for the interpretation to be as complex as the phenomenon it is designed to render comprehensible.

Our starting point is the assumption that individuals make different use of resources to achieve desired goals through interaction according to their beliefs and values, which they share to a greater or lesser extent with others, and of which they have only partial awareness. Values may be sustained or changed through interaction. This conception, where both culture and power are seen as integral components of interaction, follows Giddens's (1976) view: individuals communicate meaning within the context of normative sanctions and relationships of power. All three elements are intrinsic to interaction and are empirically inseparable although they may be distinguished analytically.

In order to tease out the main elements of this perspective, we will define the main concepts to be employed. Since the range of possible concepts is doubled in bringing together two perspectives, we have restricted our selection to those which gave most purchase in our research so as to aid conceptual digestion. We recognise that in so doing we lose distinctions between related concepts within either a cultural or a political orientation – a second drawback of a dual perspective.

CONCEPTS DRAWN PRIMARILY FROM A CULTURAL PERSPECTIVE

Meanings and norms may be subsumed within the notion of *culture*: a set of shared or complementary symbols, beliefs and values expressed in interaction.

SMTs in our research developed a *'culture of teamwork'*: shared beliefs and values about working together to manage the school. Beliefs and values include those relating to *norms*, or rules of behaviour. A norm common to the SMTs we studied was that decisions must be reached by achieving a working consensus, entailing the acknowledgement of any dissenting views. Where the meanings and norms held by one individual are shared with others, they belong to a common culture.

Some shared meanings take the form of *myths*: stories and rumours related to the organisation which are passed on between individuals and whose authenticity may be based upon impressionistic or hard evidence. Certain myths were connected with the institutional history: some members of each SMT had worked in the school for much of their professional lives. They had a rich store of anecdotes about people and events from years gone by, which were often a basis for interpreting the present. Rumours amongst staff in the different schools varied widely, including the perception that certain SMT members had more influence on decision making than their colleagues. This myth was based upon the impressions of individuals who were not party to the decision-making process as they did not attend SMT meetings, but who were made aware of decision outcomes.

Meanings which may or may not be shared by all parties to the interaction include those relating to the *role* of an individual or group. When individuals occupy a social position their actions are determined by what others expect of anyone in that position in terms of their responsibilities and individuals' idiosyncratic preferences. We will discuss the group *role of the SMT* in managing the school, amounting to the aggregate of beliefs and values about each team's purpose among SMT members and others interacting with it. We will also consider team roles occupied by individuals within the SMT.

People may occupy many roles, giving rise to the possibility of *role conflict* where beliefs and values do not coincide. A few SMT members who were incentive-allowance holders had, in addition to their school-wide brief within the SMT, middle management responsibility for a faculty. They experienced some conflict between their beliefs and values as SMT members, where they were expected to serve the interests of the whole school, and those as middle managers where they were concerned to do the best for their own faculty.

A third area of shared meaning with significant implications for SMTs is *status*. This term refers to the relative position of a person on a socially defined scale or hierarchy of social worth. Common to all our research schools was a perception that the different grades of incentive allowance held by many teachers, generally awarded for increasing levels of management responsibility, represented a mark of their relative status. The management hierarchy extended further through deputies to heads.

Membership of an SMT, while distinguishing an individual's status from those who were not members, did not remove the status boundaries arising from different levels of remuneration, conditions of service and management responsibility. On one team, the two senior teachers were paid almost as much as the deputies. Yet their scope of responsibility and status within the SMT were considerably less. The difference in status created by salary scales was most evident when a member of the non-teaching staff was in the SMT, since she or he was paid on a lower salary than main-scale teachers, and tended to be accorded lower status. The considerably higher salary and different conditions of service of the head in all our SMTs ensured that they enjoyed higher status within the management hierarchy than their SMT colleagues, however much they valued equality as a component of a team approach to school management.

Symbolic elements of culture are those where patterns of action represent something else, typically a shared value. Such patterns include *rituals* – regularised and often habitual sequences of action (such as the seating arrangements for SMT meetings which demonstrated the value placed on everyone being able to contribute) – and, within this category, *ceremonies* which imply some form of celebration. Members of one SMT occasionally went out for a meal together. Hoyle (1986) suggests that much interaction amongst staff in schools is symbolic in that actions may have both an explicit managerial purpose and a part in signifying a shared value.

A study of the symbolic leadership behaviour of an elementary school principal in the United States by Reitzug and Reeves (1992) showed how his actions were designed to stimulate teachers into reflecting on their values about teaching methods. Although he indicated his own preferences when asked, he did not direct staff, insisting only that they be reflective and be able to justify what they did. He made a video of what he regarded as an exemplary lesson given by one of the teachers, which he made available to all staff. The video was a symbol of the principal's belief in a particular teaching style, used to influence staff without this intention being made explicit. Headteachers in our research variably attempted to demonstrate values about being fair in their dealings with colleagues through the way they chaired SMT meetings. Checking regularly that each team member had been given the opportunity to state a view demonstrated the heads' commitment to shared leadership of the school through the SMT.

CONCEPTS DRAWN PRIMARILY FROM A POLITICAL PERSPECTIVE

Power refers to the capability of individuals to intervene in events so as to alter their course, and is defined by Giddens (1984) as a 'transformative capacity': the use of resources to secure desired outcomes. These *resources* vary widely, including sanctions, rewards, reference to norms of behaviour, attitudes and skills linked to individual personalities, and various kinds of knowledge. Individual personalities are expressed in interaction through preferences in the use of power according to particular beliefs and values. Within SMTs, aspects of individuals' personality are expressed through these preferences in a pattern of behaviour which may be summarised as their personal style as managers and teamworkers.

Sanctions within SMTs included the potential of heads to take disciplinary action while other SMT members could potentially withdraw their commitment to the SMT and act to undermine its work, say by leaking confidential information. A reward for some members of SMTs other than heads, which motivated them to seek membership, was the status of being in the SMT. In one SMT when a member tried to push for a majority decision, a colleague referred to the long-established norm of continuing debate until a working consensus of all members was achieved on the decision at hand.

Very diverse forms of knowledge may be used to alter the course of events in myriad ways. Contextual knowledge may be employed by individuals to judge when to give or withhold information. All SMT members used their knowledge of the school to contribute to SMT debates. Each member had expertise related to her or his individual management responsibility, and the more experienced members were frequently expert in colleagues' areas of work as a legacy of their past responsibilities. Some members of SMTs kept in touch with the views of other staff and relayed their opinions to the team.

We found instances where heads withheld information from the SMT that they had been given in confidence by other staff concerning personal problems. Where heads were concerned about the performance of another SMT member, they generally addressed the issue with this person without divulging it to the full SMT. As we mentioned earlier, individuals had more or less extensive knowledge of the institutional history which influenced their current perceptions. Longer-serving SMT members referred, on occasion, to past experiences with a particular management strategy to support their argument in a current debate.

Power may be manifested in interaction yet, as we saw in the discussion of action and inaction, may also remain latent, since resources may still exist when they are not in use. Within interaction power may be regarded as a relationship, since action intended to secure particular outcomes involves the responses of others or their potential to act. The goals of each SMT member could only be met through the actions of colleagues inside (and often outside) the SMT. In two SMTs, where one deputy wished to change her or his delegated responsibilities, the necessary agreement of other SMT members to change theirs could not be secured.

For Giddens, power may or may not imply conflict. His conception contrasts with the 'zero-sum' formulation of Weber (1947) and Dahl (1957), the latter defining power as 'the ability to get someone to do something that he or she would not otherwise do'. Giddens' view of power allows for each protagonist within a conflict to use his or her transformative capacity in attempting to achieve interests that contradict those of others. It also suggests that, where there is consensus, individuals may have great capacity for working together to bring about change or to maintain the *status quo* both within and outside the SMT. Unanimous agreement among members in all SMTs on certain decisions led to a concerted effort to implement them. Within Giddens' conception, therefore, power does not disappear where individuals interact in attaining the same goal without resistance from inside or outside the group. Zero-sum conceptions of power, adopted by many conflict theorists, tend to define power out of existence where someone has the ability to get others to do something that they also want to do. Power exists in a zero-sum conception only where there is potential conflict, as opposed to potential synergy, and so fails to account for the ways in which people may use resources to achieve a shared goal.

Two types of power may be distinguished (Bacharach and Lawler, 1980). *Authority* implies the use of resources to achieve desired ends in a way which is perceived by an individual as legitimated by beliefs and values associated with formal status. It includes the right to apply sanctions if necessary to secure compliance of others. Headteachers have extensive authority as managers which is enshrined in their conditions of service. Bacharach and Lawler regard authority as an all-or-nothing affair: people either have overall or delegated authority. In the area of schooling, it is difficult to see how any individual has complete authority. Even the authority of the Secretary of State for education is delegated by the Prime Minister and his or her authority is, in turn, delegated by the electorate. Nevertheless, heads are legally empowered to delegate aspects of their authority for day-to-day management of the school to other staff.

The authority delegated to heads is itself part of a network of legally backed authority held by others inside and outside the school, including governing bodies, which have representatives of teachers, parents, local government and the community; LEA staff in the case of local authority maintained schools; and the central government Department for Education. Under the 1988 Education Reform Act the governors of any school with a delegated budget may choose whether to delegate their entitlement to control spending to the headteacher. Here any authority accruing to heads is clearly delegated by the governing body, as was the case in the schools in our research. Even where heads adopt a team approach to management, delegation by the governing body is to the head, not the SMT.

Legislation tends to consist of general statements which often leave room for divergent interpretations about the relative degree of authority, delegated or otherwise, held by individuals and about the way in which this authority is or is not exercised. In LEA-maintained schools, headteachers' conditions of service include the obligation to 'consult, where this is appropriate, with the [local education] authority, the governing body, the staff of the school and the parents of its pupils'. Who decides where it is appropriate and, if so, how widely to consult? In one of our study schools several staff with middle management responsibility outside the SMT complained that they should have been consulted over the deadline dates for a series of major decisions. SMT members regarded it as their prerogative to set these dates.

The exclusive amount of authority of headteachers to manage the school enables them to choose how much delegated authority to distribute within the team. Yet perceptions may differ within the SMT according to the beliefs and values of their members. In one school several members perceived that the head did not delegate enough for the team to operate effectively. The head was reticent to delegate further because of the risk of colleagues doing things of which she might not approve and yet for which she alone could ultimately be held externally accountable.

The SMT was generally perceived as the group holding the highest status within the school management hierarchy. Members other than the head held considerable delegated authority linked to their individual management responsibilities and the expectation that they should contribute as equals in the team, although the head retained the legal authority to override other SMT members, make a unilateral decision, or take back what had been delegated. Delegated authority as team members was at the behest of the head and therefore there was little recourse to formal sanctions if the head temporarily rescinded that authority by, say, unilaterally withdrawing a decision from the SMT arena. Beliefs and values about differential status within the management hierarchy were directly associated with levels of delegated authority: in one team the head was responsible for the SMT; a deputy was responsible for the curriculum; and an allowance holder was responsible for maintenance of the building.

Potential for contradictory perceptions of relative delegated authority arose from SMT members' involvement in different groups or their overlapping responsibilities. Both the SMT member responsible for staff development and the headteacher tended to engage in personal counselling of individual colleagues. While on the surface, the distribution of authority may appear as clear cut as Bacharach and Lawler imply, beliefs and values may differ on how much is delegated within the school, to whom, and how it should or should not be used in particular situations.

UP FRONT OR BEHIND THE SCENES?

Influence, by comparison with authority, is the informal use of resources to achieve desired ends where individuals perceive there is no recourse to sanctions linked to the delegated authority accompanying status within the management hierarchy. A wide range of other sanctions may exist, such as refusal to contribute to SMT debate. The less delegated authority is held by individuals, the more influence is likely to be the main type of power. Yet the constraints placed upon the use of headteachers' authority mean that they, along with other staff, have recourse to extensive use of influence, more or less overtly deploying the various kinds of resources outlined earlier. A common example of the overt use of influence within SMTs was where individuals asked colleagues to do favours such as covering their teaching when they were particularly pressed.

A more covert use of influence in one SMT occurred when the deputies agreed to a decision during an SMT meeting, discovered afterwards in conversation that each deputy was uncomfortable with it, subsequently met to discuss this decision, and only then went to the head to ask if the decision could be altered. The theme of several organisational myths concerned assertions of covert use of influence either by the SMT (as where consultation exercises were held by other staff to be a sham) or individuals within it (as when one SMT member was claimed to be manipulating others without making his or her intentions explicit). Perhaps not surprisingly, we were not aware of observing any instances where influence was fully covert.

The term 'micropolitics' is often restricted to covert use of influence, following Hoyle's (1986) usage. Although he defines micropolitics as covering a continuum from conventional management procedures to 'almost a separate organizational world of illegitimate, self-interested manipulation', he confines description of micropolitical strategies largely to those which are covert. Bargaining is referred to as 'more micropolitical to the degree to which it is implicit rather than explicit, outside rather than inside formal structures and procedures, and draws upon informal resources of influence'. Hoyle's definition belies the distinction between implicit and unofficial, and the explicit and official that he wishes to explore. In this study, we have eschewed the term micropolitics because its use has been so varied and we wish to emphasise how power is endemic to interaction, whether overt or not.

While accepting that there is a continuum between the two extremes of overt or covert use of resources within interaction to achieve particular ends, it is important to distinguish between them. We suggest that action (or refraining from acting) is *manipulative* either where it is a conscious attempt, covertly, to influence events through means or ends which are not made explicit; or where it is illegitimate, whether overt or not. The analysis of interaction is complicated by the fact that implicit or explicit means and ends may be regarded by either party to interaction as legitimate or illegitimate. Reitzug and Reeves (1992) analysed the leadership actions of an elementary school principal according to how far the means and ends were manipulative, but designed to empower teachers by stimulating them to reflect on their practice and try new methods:

> Perhaps the closest example to manipulative behaviour is provided by the incident where Mr. Sage placed an 'out of order' sign on the copy machine that was still operating so as to force teachers to consider alternative means of instructional delivery. Although this action could be interpreted to lack straightforwardness and certainly promoted Mr. Sage's personal instructional beliefs, it provided an opportunity for teachers to improve their educational situations by examining and critiquing their methods of instructional delivery.
>
> (p. 208)

The principal's action was manipulative, since his intentions about the means were covert. Yet it was also legitimated for the principal because his intention was to stimulate teachers to explore avenues beyond the copying of worksheets. The researchers do not tell us whether the teachers ever found out, and if they did, whether they also thought it was legitimate manipulation, in so far as the end justified the means! Depending on the perception of the actor or the person on the receiving end, an action may be:

- overt and legitimate;
- manipulative because it is covert, yet still legitimate;
- manipulative because it is illegitimate, whether overt or covert.

Within a team, legitimacy of action is defined according to the norms that make up the culture of teamwork. Several heads in our study attempted to create a climate which was conducive to collaboration, perhaps by offering food and drink at the beginning of an SMT meeting. Their aim was not made explicit to colleagues yet, for the heads, it was a legitimate element of their work as team leader.

Individuals attempt to realise their *interests*, seen as outcomes that facilitate the fulfilment of their wants. In other words, use of resources in action to realise interests reflects individuals' efforts to give expression to their values which, in turn, are framed by their beliefs.

POWER AS A RELATIONSHIP

Individuals in a relationship of power are each partly autonomous and partly dependent on the other, however asymmetrical the relationship. Each person is thus implicated in a multidirectional *'dialectic of control'* (Giddens, 1984) manifested in interaction between individuals or groups. Interaction in schools is a complex network of interdependencies, depending upon the individuals involved at any point. Everyone has access to some resources. Conversely no individual has a monopoly on power: it is distributed throughout the organisation, albeit unequally. There is no sense in which heads, despite having exclusive authority in respect of colleagues' work, have exclusive control in practice over what their colleagues do.

Rather than assuming that some people have the power to determine the actions of others, we may instead conceive them as being able to *delimit* these actions. Heads may create conditions which open up the possibilities for SMT colleagues to take initiatives, yet at the same time attempt to keep these possibilities within boundaries that they define. The idea that control within interaction is dialectical implies a sequence of action and response where each party enables the other to choose what to do – but within limits. SMT members other than heads may also enable the latter to operate as team leader as long as the heads' actions lie within the bounds of acceptability to other members of the team. If a head was to step beyond the boundary, other members could potentially use their influence to persuade the head to step back, perhaps by indicating that they might withdraw their commitment to implementing a team decision.

A full analysis of staff power within a school entails investigating how individuals and groups across the organisation use resources in relation to each other, rather than concentrating upon, say, the accounts of teachers about the power of heads (Ball, 1987). If power is conceived as a relationship, the question arises about how far SMTs control other staff and how far the other staff control the SMT.

This point is illustrated by the research of Barnett (1984) into 'subordinate teacher power' in three secondary schools in the United States. He demonstrated how teachers had power based on their access to people, information and material resources on which senior staff depended to carry out their managerial tasks. Teachers with certain responsibilities, such as department chairs or members of school committees, were 'gatekeepers of information' who had an impact on senior staff through being assertive and persistent in pushing for what they wanted. The dialectic of control in our research schools operated across many levels, whether it was between two members of the SMT, between all SMT members, between the SMT and governors, or between the SMT and the rest of the teaching staff.

The relationship between power and conflict is contingent upon individuals attempting to realise different and irreconcilable interests. *Conflict* refers to struggle between people expressed through their interaction. It does not necessarily arise when actions are taken to realise *contradictory interests* as long as action according to one interest is separated from action according to the contradictory interest (Wallace 1987, 1991b). Mutual incompatibility between interests may be an enduring feature of social life and may not breed conflict where people are either unaware of their interests or the consequences of their actions, or are unwilling or unable to act on these interests. Where gender-related interests of women, for example, go unrecognised by women or are not acted upon, potential conflict with men within SMTs may be avoided.

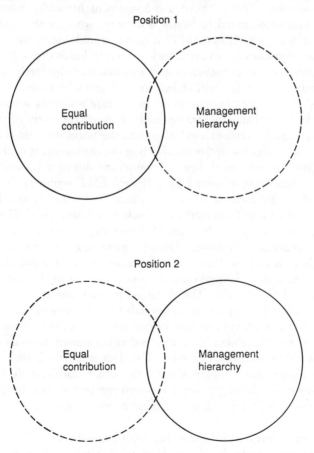

Position 1

Equal contribution

Management hierarchy

Position 2

Equal contribution

Management hierarchy

Figure 2.1 Contradictory norms expressed in interaction within SMTs

Figure 2.1 suggests how actions reflecting the contradictory norms of contributing equally as team members to school management and a management hierarchy entailing the authority to direct the work of colleagues were kept separate in much interaction. While SMT members continued to adhere to both norms, usually only one was expressed at any time. When SMTs engaged in a debate, members generally acted according to the norm of contributing as equals (Position 1). The opposing norm relating to a management hierarchy remained largely latent, though it might be expressed in the way heads chaired the meeting. If the heads were to use their authority to direct their SMT colleagues, the norm that there was a legitimate management hierarchy linked to status would be manifested, overriding the norm of equal contribution as team members (Position 2). The norm of equal contribution would now recede into the background.

The potential for conflict would arise if some members acted according to their formal status while others acted as equal contributors within the same interaction, as might happen if other SMT members refused to accept heads' authority to act unilaterally within an area that they perceived to lie within the SMT's jurisdiction. The norm of a management hierarchy was potentially backed by sanctions linked to heads' authority, whereas the norm of equal contribution was not. Other SMT members could use influence by withdrawing their commitment to teamwork, on which heads depended. However, the participation of other members in teamwork was ultimately at the invitation of heads and conflict would be likely to result in reversion to a more hierarchical approach to management. In the rare instances where heads did act in this way, other members temporarily forsook the norm of contributing as equals by (equally temporarily) accepting the norm that the head held the overarching authority for decisions affecting the management of the school.

This contradiction came to light in one school during a team-development activity. The head was informed by colleague SMT members that her occasional use of her authority in a manner which they perceived as arbitrary was an aspect of her style as team leader of which they disapproved. The contradiction had persisted until now because SMT members other than the head were unwilling to transgress the norm related to the management hierarchy that she had the right to withdraw decisions from the realm of the team, although they still held to the norm of equal contribution in respect of the areas where the head had acted unilaterally. The different groundrules of the development activity gave them the opportunity as equals to raise the issue of contention.

Figure 2.2 is a simple illustration of our hypothesis that a tension between the norms of a management hierarchy and equal contribution as team members within SMTs endures over time. The degree to which one norm is expressed in interaction compared with the other corresponds to different positions along the shifting balance between the two norms. Interactions are framed, in turn, by factors relating to these norms, including:

- the number of levels of formal status among members;
- the parameters set by heads, such as who is involved in selecting SMT members;

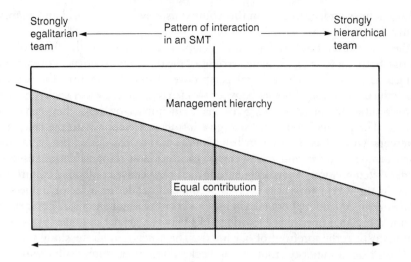

Figure 2.2 The shifting balance of contradictory norms within SMTs

- the degree to which members with lower status within the management hierarchy perceive that they should defer to those with higher status;
- who contributes to setting the team agenda;
- what is excluded from the agenda and by whom;
- how far all SMT members are committed to teamwork.

SMTs may differ in the degree to which the *overall pattern* of interaction within them expresses one norm or the other.

The left-hand extreme represents the most hierarchical team situation, where heads make maximum use of their authority to direct the work of other SMT colleagues. The right-hand extreme represents the position most strongly associated with the norm of equal contribution within a team, where heads largely refrain from directing colleagues or restricting the SMT agenda. The research evidence discussed in the previous chapter indicates that SMTs operate in very different ways and so we may expect to find SMTs at different positions between these extremes. Any SMT may shift gradually over time in the balance of the two norms it reflects. The pattern of interaction may become more hierarchical or egalitarian as the *team history* within the wider institutional history unfolds. A new head may introduce parameters for teamwork reflecting a greater emphasis on the norm of contributing as equals; where an SMT member other than the head does not accept a commitment to teamwork, the head is likely to be more directive with respect to this person, interaction between them becoming more hierarchical.

THE GENDER DIMENSION

We were concerned not to perpetuate the 'androcentrism' that characterises so many discussions of educational management in Britain (Hall, 1993). Hough

(1986) defines androcentrism in this context as viewing the world and shaping reality through a male lens.

The separate cultural and political perspectives which are the focus of our critique both fail to take adequate account of the different experiences of men and women as managers. The cultural perspective (Table 2.1) ignores the ways in which the distribution of power between women and men in wider society, as well as their different interests and goals, have an impact on how they behave in schools. The political concepts listed give insufficient emphasis to the culture of teamwork which has its roots in behavioural norms that cut across hierarchies based on male power and management structure and responsibilities based on gender differentiation. A challenge to our dual perspective combining culture and power is the extent to which it takes account of gender as a factor influencing teamwork in educational organisations. Our focus was not specifically on gender, but the associated questions exploring links between gender and teamwork were continuously at the forefront of our minds. The absence in all the study teams of members from a minority ethnic group background made it impossible within an observational study to focus on race as a factor influencing teamwork.

Other research in non-educational settings (e.g. Hearn *et al.*, 1989; Coleman, 1991) suggests that the experience of women in organisations is different from that of men and that the beliefs and values underpinning their behaviour may also be different. Our study of teams included both men and women who had made a commitment to teamwork. It emerged that they shared common professional values about collaboration, equity and collective responsibility that dominated their separate, private beliefs about men's and women's behaviour at work. We would be naïve to accept the almost total denial by most respondents (women and men) of the influence of gender on team behaviour as evidence that gender differentiation did not exist. On the other hand, the value that teamwork places on equal contribution appears to make it more likely that individuals will try to suppress or refrain from acting on values that subscribe to gender inequalities or differences in the workplace. We will show that the greatest threat to the value of equal contribution was an acceptance of the management hierarchy represented in our case study schools, by both women and men. What emerged was the potential that teamwork offers for a new model of leadership in which neither men nor women prescribe the dominant characteristics and to which both have equal access.

This possibility does not mean there were no instances in teamwork of gender-related behaviour. It was manifest at times in the type of language used to construct the meanings that frame teamwork. The three woman team leaders counted 'the need to protect against isolation' among their reasons for adopting a team approach. Men referred often to sports metaphors to highlight the value of teamwork. One female allowance holder recalled how she was learning to work in the initially rather foreign context of imagery and banter enjoyed by her five male SMT colleagues because of

the different behaviour patterns of men and women in groups. One of the things that I identified amongst them was the huge use of male sporting imagery, like the head will say, 'right, we'll pull a flanker on this' and lots of playing straight bats or kicking at an angle or letting out a lot of line, and all sorts of sporting imagery from sports I had never played. And the jokes, the wit and the repartee are pretty male, I think. Whereas there is a total awareness that I am there and nothing offensive is ever said, and there is nothing I can take exception to, men use patterns of language and modes of behaviour socially that are very different from those that women use. And sometimes I feel at a disadvantage. On the whole, women don't shout jokes at one another across the room, which is what men tend to do. And I find it difficult to join that sort of repartee.

Generally we found the discourse of teamwork to be supportive of it as a cooperative rather than competitive activity. Research into language and gender (Corson, 1992) suggests women use talk for cooperative rather than competitive exchange more frequently and easily than men. In so far as teamwork reflects a commitment to collaboration with facilitative rather than directive team leadership, then we might expect the language of teamwork to be less 'masculine' than is common in male-dominated groups (which all six teams were numerically). On the other hand, we did not find significant differences in gender-related language between the three teams headed by men and the three headed by women. The decision to adopt a team approach seems to signify a shift in leadership style towards an 'androgynous' model which posits the possibility for leaders to exhibit the wide range of qualities which are present in both men and women.

We consider describing teamwork as androgynous more useful than aligning a team or collaborative way of working with either 'masculine' or 'feminine' approaches. We suggest that teamwork undercuts gender-based behaviour by proposing different norms and rules that make some behaviours legitimate, particularly those stressing collaboration, equity and consensual decision making. Some conflicts may have their origins in gender-influenced responses but are unlikely to be articulated in these terms. Indeed, as we suggested earlier, not recognising or acting on gender-related interests is a way of avoiding potential conflict between team members. In the teams studied, women and men were equally committed to collaborative values, both as team leaders and team members. Individual responsibilities and status were defined in terms of the management hierarchy and team membership rather than gender, as some earlier studies of school management hierarchies have shown (e.g. Richardson, 1973).

There was little difference in participation by women and men in the rituals and ceremonies that helped affirm the values of their culture of teamwork. Both had allegiances based on faculty or departmental membership rather than gender affiliation. Politically, both men and women drew idiosyncratically upon resources associated with their personalities, skills and status. Although there were differences in delegation by individual headteachers, patterns were not gender specific. Nor were women any less likely than men to use power overtly or covertly in interaction.

The focus of our study was upon culture and power within the SMT, not the school as a whole. The culture of the SMT was not necessarily that of the other staff groups, where the behaviour of women and men may have reflected the androcentric universe of secondary school cultures. What we have tried to do is ensure that our dual cultural and political perspective addresses any gender-related teamwork issues that came to our attention.

Having set out the main elements of a cultural and political perspective and considered how sensitivity to gender-related aspects of interaction within SMTs may be sustained, let us now take a look at what we learned from our initial case studies of SMTs.

3

Team Structure and Role

We open our discussion of the six SMTs with a look at common features among their structures and the role of the team. They all exhibited a strong commitment among members to a team approach to management and the incorporation of responsibilities related to the national reforms. Yet there was also considerable variation in their composition and working practices, reflecting parameters set by the heads; past team history including the legacy of their predecessors' choice of senior staff; the heads' own appointments; the wider institutional history going back as far as comprehensivisation; and, more or less obliquely, certain LEA policies. While the opportunity for expression of heads' idiosyncratic beliefs and values in creating teams existed, it was both facilitated and bounded by school-level, local and national factors. Here we set the six SMTs in context by considering significant aspects of the local context and introducing the schools. Then we examine the profile of the teams themselves, and build up a picture of their role in managing the schools and the structures for carrying it out.

LEAS IN THE BACKGROUND

Our hunch at the outset of the study was that the influence of LEAs on the approaches to teamwork adopted by senior staff would be less significant than school-level factors such as the beliefs and values of the head. The findings indicated that, while such school-level factors did indeed have the greatest impact on the study SMTs, they were variably affected by three aspects of past or present LEA policy: first, the legacy of comprehensivisation; second, the degree to which the promotion of equal opportunities in staff appointments had been emphasised; and third, the type of investment in management de-velopment and training of senior staff related to central government arrange-ments for funding in-service training.

Table 3.1 Local context of the schools (summer 1991)

Contextual factor	Middleton	Longrise	Northend	Drake	Oldlea	Underhill
LEA	Westshire	Westshire	Westshire	Eastshire	Eastshire	Eastshire
Age range, school type and governance	11–18, comprehensive (county)	11–18, comprehensive (county)	11–18, comprehensive (voluntary controlled)	11–18, comprehensive (county)	13–18, comprehensive (voluntary controlled)	11–16, boys secondary modern (county)
Number of pupils and socio-economic status	1000, mainly working class	735, mainly working class	1050, mainly lower middle class	1000, working and middle class	760, working and middle class	475, mainly working class
Gender of full and part-time teaching staff	36F, 28M	25F, 26M	32F, 34M	42F, 34M	27F, 30M	10F, 24M
Gender of head and number of years in post	Male, 3+ years	Female, 6+ years	Male, 3 years (2nd headship)	Female, 6 years (2nd headship)	Female, 7 years	Male, 13 years
Location	Inner city	Inner city	Small town close to city	Suburb of medium-sized town	Suburban council estate in city	Suburbanised village near city
Type of site, age of buildings	Single, 1950s and 1970s	Single, 1970s, Victorian 6th form block	Single, 1970s	Single, 1970s	Single, 1950s	Single, 1950s

Table 3.1 *Continued*

Contextual factor	Middleton	Longrise	Northend	Drake	Oldlea	Underhill
Local history affecting SMT	Falling rolls in 1980s led to surplus capacity	Closure of 3 of the 4 original sites	Ex-grammar school, emphasis on continuity with past status, link with foundation	Created from secondary modern school, grammar school on adjacent site also became comprehensive	Created from girls' and boys' schools. Grammar schools remain in city	Roman Catholic school and girls' secondary modern on same site. Grammar schools nearby
Competition with other schools	Surplus capacity in all local schools, city technology college to be built nearby	Surplus capacity in all local schools	Very successful in attracting pupils from nearby city	Creation of shared catchment area increased competition with adjacent comprehensive	Competes against grammar schools which 'cream off' most able pupils	Competes against grammar schools in attempt to attract comprehensive intake
Curricular management and pastoral care	Faculties, tutor groups in each year	Faculties, tutor groups in each year	Departments, tutor groups in each year and houses across year groups	Faculties, tutor groups in each year	Departments grouped into three curriculum areas, tutor groups in each year	Departments, tutor groups in each year

Aspects of the local context of each school are compared in Table 3.1. Three were situated in Westshire: a densely populated county, created through the reorganisation of local government boundaries in 1974. A large and a medium-sized city were ringed by small towns and villages. Middleton School and Longrise School were within a few miles of the centre of the larger conurbation. Northend was located on the edge of a small town facing the green belt that divided it from this major city.

Comprehensivisation of all secondary schools had been completed in the 1970s, entailing many amalgamations. It was followed by a decline in pupil numbers during the 1980s which resulted in some school reorganisation. The local authority was committed to providing equal opportunities, reflected in LEA in-service training provision for senior staff in schools and staff appointment procedures. In 1991 about 20% of the heads of secondary schools were women (close to the national average). During the 1980s LEA staff had provided or supported a range of management courses for individuals. The LEA response to the increasing need for training support for senior staff arising from the central government reforms was to invest heavily in short residential training courses run by the Coverdale Organisation. Heads and deputies were strongly encouraged to participate in these off-the-job courses, where they were placed in teams consisting of individuals from different schools. They were given individual and team tasks and feedback on their performance.

The other three schools were in Eastshire, a much longer established rural county dotted with towns and a few small cities. Drake School was in the centre of a market town. Oldlea lay within a large estate on the outskirts of a city, while Underhill was a few miles away in a village which had been engulfed by city expansion.

Comprehensivisation had not been completed in this city, one half of which contained a mixture of comprehensives such as Oldlea, while the other half contained selective secondary modern schools for less able pupils, like Underhill, and grammar schools for the more able. Primary phase schools included primary schools with transfer to secondary schools at age eleven and middle schools with transfer at thirteen. The LEA designated catchment area for Oldlea included three middle schools. The county council embraced the central government policy of more open enrolment to increase competition between schools, enhancing further the ability of grammar schools to attract able pupils who might otherwise have gone to the less prestigious comprehensives. Equality of opportunity for school staff had a lower profile in Eastshire, with less evidence that equal opportunities issues had been taken into account in making appointments. Just 10% of secondary heads were women.

In contrast with the emphasis in Westshire on off-the-job management training for individuals, LEA staff in Eastshire made provision for the support of intact SMTs. The LEA funded a residential meeting for SMTs each year, where team members could review their work, make plans, engage in structured development activities, and use the opportunity for socialising together to consolidate the culture of teamwork. In addition LEA staff encouraged senior staff in schools to use distance-learning materials produced by the Henley

Management Centre, which included a team-building component incorporating the work of Belbin (1981), and supported attendance by individuals at off-the-job training courses.

THE SIX SCHOOLS

Middleton lay in a predominantly working class area of mixed housing ranging from Victorian terraces, through 1930s council estates to high rise flats. The buildings were a mixture of 1950s system-built blocks, newer blocks constructed in brick after a major fire in the 1970s, and a few temporary classrooms. Behind the compact site was a large playing field, recently enhanced by the construction of an all-weather playing surface. There were about 80 pupils in the sixth form. The school faced increasing competition from other local schools, partly a legacy of a decline in the secondary school population in the area. Nearby was a city technology college under construction, which senior staff expected to increase the existing level of surplus pupil places in local schools.

A couple of miles away, surrounded by similar housing, Longrise had also faced falling rolls. The school was opened in the early 1970s through the amalgamation of four smaller schools, and consequently began with four sites. It was intended at the outset that the school would eventually be located on one site. Three had been closed, leaving a single site with the sixth form on the other side of the playing field from the main buildings. Another legacy of contraction was two senior staff on protected salaries, whose major school-wide management responsibility had gone with the site closures. This was the only study school with a substantial proportion of pupils from minority ethnic groups (30% of Asian origin). There were 78 pupils in the sixth form. A major concern for the SMTs of both Longrise and Middleton was how to sustain pupil numbers and so minimise staff redundancies.

Northend, in contrast, was flourishing under open enrolment: the second most over-subscribed school in the county whose intake of pupils was predominantly middle class. Formerly a grammar school, the present comprehensive was created in the early 1970s and housed in brand new buildings on a large semi-rural site. In marketing the school to parents, the head emphasised continuity with its selective past. A substantial minority of pupils came from outside the old catchment area and were brought to school by a fleet of buses. Pastoral care was provided primarily through tutor groups for each year, but there was also a system of houses, the names of which commemorated figures closely connected with the history of the school. This was the only one of the large study schools which had retained a departmental structure for managing the curriculum. Northend benefited from a charitable foundation connected with the former grammar school, which provided some financial support for school projects. Although the total number of pupils was little more than at Middleton, the sixth form of 180 pupils was over twice the size.

Drake was situated in a leafy suburb, at one time the secondary modern school of the market town. Both Drake and the grammar school on an adjacent site became comprehensive schools in the 1970s. A recent county council decision to create a shared catchment area for both schools had resulted in increasing competition between them for pupils, heightened by the fact that they were the only secondary schools in this town. Pupils were from a wide range of social class backgrounds, some being bused in from surrounding villages. The site was spacious, with 1970s buildings supplemented by temporary classrooms.

Oldlea catered for pupils from a similarly varied social class background, but more able children were under-represented in the school. Although Oldlea was a comprehensive, grammar schools in the city 'creamed off' some able children who lived within Oldlea's catchment area. The school's status as a comprehensive was strongly emphasised in the prospectus:

> Oldlea reflects the community we serve. To select our pupils on the basis of ability, sex and race would be to divide one person from another, and to split families. Such divisions frequently cause unhappiness. Life outside Oldlea is in a mixed environment; life inside Oldlea is in a mixed environment with boys and girls of all backgrounds working extremely well and naturally together.

The context of a city split between two education systems based on contradictory values, exacerbated by open enrolment, led to a particularly strong emphasis within Oldlea on the value of comprehensive schooling. The present school had been formed in the early 1970s by amalgamating adjacent girls' and boys' schools built in the 1950s. Its voluntary controlled status related to the original church school founded in the eighteenth century. The school was in a council estate within the city suburbs, bordered by owner-occupied mixed housing.

Underhill was across the city in a suburbanised village. The school had been designed to cater for less academically able boys; most came from working class backgrounds. Here also, the head was strongly committed to comprehensive values, stating in a letter to parents included in the school prospectus:

> Educational justification for selection at eleven died long ago. The Local Authority Education Committee, supported by the full County Council, decided to end the Eleven Plus [examination on which selection was based] in 1964. But, in [the city], it still survives today – like the last of the dinosaurs.

With surplus pupil capacity in local schools, under open enrolment Underhill stood to lose pupils to other institutions. SMT members adopted a strongly competitive stance, striving to attract a more comprehensive intake. The governing body had just decided to consult parents on whether to opt out of LEA control, so paving the way in future years for possible redesignation as a comprehensive. The school was built in the 1950s, with a substantial number of temporary classrooms added since.

Despite the marked differences in their local context, a common issue on the agenda of the study school SMTs was how to compete against other local schools for pupils. New central government policies including open enrolment, coupled with the strictures of LMS meaning that staff redundancies would follow a substantial decline in pupil numbers, had interacted with the local effects of comprehensivisation (or resistance to it) and a decline in the second-ary school age population. The need to gain and sustain a favourable niche in the educational marketplace had influenced the head at Oldlea to emphasise the type of school it was, the head at Northend to emphasise what the school was in days gone by, the head at Drake to emphasise how the school was different from its adjacent competitor, and the head at Underhill to emphasise what he would like the school to become. Each head addressed the issue through the SMT.

COMPOSITION OF THE SMTS

All six heads were deeply committed to teamwork, reflected in the exercise of their authority to choose whether to have an SMT. Details of SMT member-ship in each school are summarised in Table 3.2. The largest SMTs contained seven members, there being no direct relationship between the size of the school and the number of senior staff in the team. Three or four status levels within the management hierarchy were reflected in the range of posts: all SMTs extended beyond the deputies to include one or more senior teaching staff on the highest grade of incentive allowance available within the school. At Drake not all members of staff with this grade of incentive allowance served on the SMT; in the other schools the grade was directly associated with SMT mem-bership. An officer responsible for finance had been appointed in two schools: the senior administrative officer at Drake headed the office staff, whereas at Underhill the bursar's work was confined to administering LMS.

Several principles governed how the composition of the SMTs was deter-mined, including the need to ensure coverage of major areas of school-wide management responsibility; recognition of existing senior post holders; a con-ception of what constitutes a 'balanced team' in terms of personalities, qualities, skills and expertise; and the desirability of fluid membership bound-aries to allow the interests of other staff to be represented through inclusion of members with 'their ear to the ground'. If we exclude heads, the gender bal-ance within the other status levels in all six schools was variably weighted towards men. Only Drake had an equal balance between female and male deputies; only Middleton had an equal balance between female and male incentive allowance holders. There were no women in the Underhill SMT, reflecting the fact that it was a boys' school, only about a quarter of whose staff were female. Important factors affecting the gender balance were:

- the balance among senior staff inherited by the present heads;
- the number of opportunities there had been since they had taken up post to make new appointments (reflecting, in part, how long the heads had been in post);
- the priority given by those involved in selection to appointing women to senior posts, relative to other criteria;

Table 3.2 SMT membership (summer 1991)

Membership factor	Middleton		Longrise		Northend		Drake		Oldlea		Underhill	
Size of SMT	6		7		6		6		7		5	
Gender balance and range of formal status	F	M	F	M	F	M	F	M	F	M	F	M
	Head; E allowance holder	3 deputies; E allowance holder	Head; D allowance holder	2 deputies; 2 E allowance holders	Deputy	Head; 2 deputies; 2 E allowance holders	Head; Deputy; Senior administrative officer	Deputy; 2 E allowance holders	Head	2 deputies; 4 E allowance holders		Head; 2 deputies; D allowance holder; Bursar
Range of external and internal appointments to present post	External	Internal	External	Internal	External	Internal	External	Internal	External	Internal	External	Internal
	Head; 2 deputies	*Deputy; *2 E allowance holders	Head; *2 F allowance holders	Deputy; *D allowance holder	Head; *Deputy	2 deputies; E allowance holder; *E allowance holder	Head; *Deputy; *Senior administrative officer	*Deputy; Deputy; *2 E allowance holders	Head; *Deputy	Deputy; *E allowance holder; *3 E allowane holders	Head; *2 deputies; *Senior administrative officer	*D allowance holder

* Appointments to SMT made since head in present post.

- the low proportion of applications received from women for many senior posts.

Table 3.2 illustrates how some heads had made more appointments to the SMT than others. The three heads in Eastshire schools had brought virtually all of the other SMT members to the present SMT. The head at Oldlea had appointed solely men to the SMT over the seven years of her headship, having failed to find female applicants of sufficient quality and experience:

> I do believe that women should be there because they are the best person for the job, not just because they are women . . . such women have not come to the fore in any of the appointments I have made.

The Westshire heads had not experienced the same scope over appointments as their counterparts in Eastshire.

The beliefs and values of the heads in respect of gender were a critical influence on the gender balance among SMT members because of their authority (tempered by the governing body) within the staff selection process. Their views varied, the head at Underhill justifying an all male SMT on the basis that: 'a member of the SMT in a boys' school has to be able to go anywhere and any place'. All six heads, their chairs of governors and most staff interviewed argued that the number one criterion should be to appoint 'the best person for the job', irrespective of gender.

The heads and many other SMT members within the three schools in Westshire, the LEA which had laid stronger emphasis on equal opportunities, indicated greater awareness and concern about the issue. The number one criterion had an additional component: if a female and a male candidate were judged equally competent to do the job, a woman was to be preferred. Several respondents mentioned the low proportion of female applicants for senior posts who demonstrated what was judged to be appropriate experience.

At Longrise, a female deputy and a female D allowance holder had been internally appointed by the present head, giving rise to the comment from one male teacher outside the SMT that she was creating 'jobs for the girls'. At Northend, a female E allowance holder had just been appointed who would replace a male member of the present SMT next term. The head reported that there had been an implicit consensus among those involved in the selection process that, other things being equal, a woman would be appointed. He had recently engaged with staff in discussing the issue of equal opportunities in staffing. There had been widespread agreement that some form of positive action was needed if more women were to succeed in being appointed to managerial positions.

Institutional history was a key factor in the selection of SMT members at Middleton. The head had inherited a situation where most senior staff (all men) were in acting positions. He began with a small SMT consisting of the two male deputies in permanent posts. A man was appointed to the vacant pastoral deputy post who had acted competently in this capacity for the previous two years. The head was instrumental in creating a senior post for staff development linked with SMT membership, to which a woman in the school was appointed after advertising nationally. The advert had included a statement that women were under-represented within the SMT. He expressed concern to create a more equal gender balance but pointed to the constraints of recent institutional history.

The proportion of external and internal appointments to the SMTs varied widely, depending on the heads' priorities and their perception of the quality of staff within the school. At one extreme, the head at Underhill took the opportunity to bring in 'new blood' when appointing the present deputies; at the other, six of the seven SMT members at Longrise, including the head herself, had been appointed from within the school. One site-specific factor here was the two male senior staff on protected salaries who were not committed to shouldering a commensurate level of responsibility. As a compromise measure, the head brought them into the SMT to encourage them to accept a school-wide responsibility which would match their protected status and remuneration. This was the only instance where appointments to an SMT were made where the new members had not put themselves forward and indicated their enthusiasm for SMT membership.

An implication of changes in membership for each SMT was that individuals with varied personal histories in the school, gender, and status within the management hierarchy were expected to form a positive working relationship with other team members. They had to compromise enough of their personal style to work well within the group as a key component of team development.

HIERARCHY AT THE LEVEL OF INDIVIDUAL RESPONSIBILITIES

Distinctions between levels of individual management responsibility variably reflected the formal status hierarchy within each team, heads standing out most clearly in all cases because of their overall responsibility for the work of the school and, within it, the SMT. Generally, along with greater management responsibility went more non-contact time and its corollary of a lighter teaching load. There was also some diversity over major management task areas that heads perceived should be included among SMT members. The main management responsibilities of team members at different status levels are summarised in Table 3.3.

Each team covered the traditional areas of curriculum (including timetabling), pastoral care and general administration, with the addition of staff development. Several other areas reflected the point particular schools had reached with phasing-in central government reforms including LMS, the associated responsibility for building maintenance, and staff appraisal. Curriculum and pastoral support were generally given to deputies, although at Oldlea oversight of pastoral care was divided between the head, deputies and an E allowance holder.

There was little indication of a formal hierarchy among deputies except at Drake, where the 'senior deputy' label was sometimes used. A system of

Table 3.3 Major individual management responsibilities of SMT members within each status level (summer 1991)

Status level	Middleton	Longrise	Northend	Drake	Oldlea	Underhill
Head	Overall responsibility	* Overall responsibility, LMS	Overall responsibility	* Overall responsibility, LMS, buildings and environment	* Overall responsibility, pastoral year 11	Overall responsibility
Deputy	Curriculum and learning support, TVEI Pupil support Administration, LMS	Curriculum and staff development * Pastoral organisation Administration, appraisal, staff cover (Deputies' duties rotated)	Curriculum, staff cover * Pupil support Resources, staff development	Academic and pastoral curriculum * Staff development, appraisal, community links, staff cover	Curriculum, external relations, one curriculum area, pastoral years 12 and 13 Staff development, appraisal, staff cover, second curriculum area, pastoral year 9	Curriculum Pastoral, staff development, staff cover
E or D allowance holder	* Staff development Resources, exams, staff cover	Resources Head of science exams * Head of sixth form	Head of year Head of science	Resources, TVEI Systems, monitoring, assessment	Third curriculum area, TVEI, pastoral year 10 Head of sixth form, records of achievement Head of maths, assessment Head of technology	Head of science
Senior Admin Officer/Bursar				* LMS, office staff		LMS

* Refers to members who are women.

rotation of deputies' major responsibilities had been introduced by the head at Longrise, ensuring that, if any task was perceived as more or less prestigious, it was shared out equitably between the deputies over time, and gave each the same developmental experience. She gave her rationale for this arrangement:

> I think that it's crucial for all sorts of reasons, not least that the school is effectively managed; secondly that their professional development is enhanced; and thirdly, if they are aspiring to headship I think it is important that they have an opportunity to take on the major generally accepted responsibilities of deputy headship . . . the management structure that we have is designed to enable them to get a taste of the major work of the school.

The possibility for a perception of hierarchy remained in arrangements for deputising in the absence of the head (including taking over the chairing of SMT meetings). At Middleton, the shared expectation was that the longest serving deputy, who had been acting head for two years, would be first in line. The job descriptions at Underhill spelled out the order whereby one deputy would normally deputise. The other would only undertake this task if both the head and colleague deputy were out of school. The D allowance holder was third in line of succession. In contrast, when the head at Oldlea had had to be absent from the school for several months the previous year, she ensured that there would be no hierarchical differentiation between the two deputies by giving them joint responsibility as acting heads and equal salary enhancement: 'The statement I made to each of them was, 'You are equal to me'' '.

How far there was a hierarchical distinction between the task areas of deputies and E or D allowance holders varied between the schools. In four cases, deputies had school-wide responsibility whereas allowance holders had a more 'parochial' responsibility, mainly for a faculty or department. In Middleton and Drake, allowance holders undertook school-wide responsibilities, such as resources, staff development, and arrangements for covering staff absences. Most of the teachers with middle-management responsibility were appointed to the SMT because, as well as specific expertise, they were in closer contact with other staff outside the SMT and could represent their views to the head and deputies. As the allowance holder at Underhill put it:

> This year I've spent more time in the staff room than I ever have, talking to staff. I feel I'm quite often putting the staff point of view in my management meetings. It's almost three to one: it's very weighted on the SMT side.

Another way in which a hierarchy could be manifested or avoided was through the inclusion or exclusion of individuals from meetings. The only 'two tier' team with a built-in hierarchy between deputies and allowance holders was at Longrise, where the head met alternately with the deputies alone and with them plus the allowance holders, with a different range of items on each agenda. The head had created this arrangement as part of the compromise solution to the problem of encouraging the two allowance holders on protected salaries to commit themselves to school-wide responsibilities.

The head at Drake had tried meeting with the deputies each week to discuss issues such as sensitive matters concerning staff, but the idea had soon been dropped because there proved to be no grounds in practice for excluding the allowance holders. This failed attempt to continue a formal recognition of hierarchy did not, however, lead to open discussion of staff issues by the whole team but pushed it into the informal arena of exchange between the head and deputies. The allowance holders were aware, and remained uncomfortable.

One deputy at Longrise (internally appointed a year before) commented how, in her previous post as head of post-16 education, she had occasionally been called into SMT meetings, the first part of which had been closed to her:

> Very often, I can understand why now, that first half didn't get through the business. I would be waiting outside and then I'd be called in, and there was the whole sort of status thing – like being kept waiting while the big grown ups are not ready for you.

The inner group of head and deputies at Longrise had operated as a team for some years and, in these members' view, continued to work effectively. The two allowance holders in the wider 'senior management group', who had been drafted in by the head, expressed dissatisfaction with not being involved with the 'inner cabinet' of head and deputies, wishing to contribute on a more equal basis. One commented on the importance of face to face contact for his sense of belonging to a team:

> Team is as team does. If you are not together then you can't pretend to be a team. The physical togetherness is as much an assertion of teamship as the particular tasks we are dealing with at the time.

Yet from the perspective of the head and deputies, these allowance holders had not made a full commitment to the SMT despite having been given an opportunity to do so through incorporation in the wider group.

The hierarchical team structure appeared to reinforce the diffidence towards the SMT displayed by the allowance holders because it constrained the possibility of inducting them fully into the SMT culture of teamwork. So too did the role conflict for some team members arising from their middle-management responsibility. One head of science felt his first loyalty was to his faculty: 'When do you defend the faculty and when do you defend the general policy?' His desire to serve partisan faculty interests, according to his beliefs and values about his role as faculty leader, clashed on occasion with the expectation of other SMT members that he should adopt a 'school-wide' perspective within the SMT culture of teamwork whose interest lay in determining what was best for the school as a whole.

Working out their primary allegiance was a significant issue for allowance holders in most other SMTs. Their problem of identity was either over the degree to which they were 'of the staff' or 'management', or, if they had middle-management responsibility, whether it or the school as a whole came first. There was some question over how far allowance holders with middle-management responsibility could develop a whole school perspective, since the bulk of their individual work was directed to a particular area of the school. The head at Northend commented that participation in the SMT was inevitably more 'part time' for allowance holders than for deputies and heads. A concern for several allowance holders was the relative lack of non-contact time compared with other SMT members to enable them to contribute fully to the SMT as well as carry out their middle-management responsibilities. At Underhill, the allowance holder commented:

> The deputies and head do have time off during school time and sometimes they meet formally, and I'm never able to get to these meetings. And quite often I miss out on certain tit-bits.

The allowance holders at Middleton had substantial school-wide management tasks to carry out yet the deputies had more non-contact time than them.

Deputies at Oldlea were allocated 'line management responsibility' for allowance holders within the SMT. Uniquely among the case study schools, the responsibility of one allowance holder for managing an area of the curriculum put him in the position of being technically the line manager of other allowance holders in the SMT responsible for faculties within his curriculum area. This element of hierarchy among holders of the same grade of incentive allowance contradicted the assumpton of their equal status within the SMT. He commented:

> I try to treat that situation delicately. I try to stress that I work with them, not order them around . . . the people I am working with are adult enough to change roles as the situation changes.

Potential conflict over who had greater authority in respect of the curriculum area was apparently avoided. The style of interaction enabled the legitimacy of the hierarchical ordering of responsibility to be accepted simply because the equal status of the three people concerned was acknowledged. As we suggested in Chapter 2, contradictory sets of beliefs and values may not lead to conflict where action according to each set is kept separate. In this case, the interaction itself reflected the norm of equal status but its initiation reflected the line responsibility within the management hierarchy.

The most clear cut hierarchical distinction operated between the senior administrative officer at Drake, the bursar at Underhill and senior teaching staff in these two SMTs. They were not members of the teaching profession, they were paid less, and their contribution to the SMT was mainly limited, as we mentioned earlier, to the administration of LMS. They did not attend all SMT meetings and their involvement in major policy decisions was largely restricted to considering the financial or administrative implications of proposals for action.

The five female SMT members other than heads (whose individual management responsibilities are marked in Table 3.3 with an asterisk) were all appointed since their present head was in post. Four had responsibilities emphasising caring: pastoral support and staff development. Yet all reported being fully on a par with colleagues, with no hint of being either seen as a 'token woman' or constrained into fulfilling menial and stereotypically women's tasks. The staff development coordinator at Middleton reported that:

> It has been a very positive experience and I am quite sure that I have equal status and I am taken as seriously as everybody else. And I certainly don't make the tea and coffee! There's no sense in which I am regarded as inferior.

Their job descriptions did not differ from those of their male counterparts in other schools responsible for the same task areas. It may not always be a mark of male stereotyping for women to occupy 'caring roles' as senior managers – much depends on the extent of their responsibilities in practice and the way their male colleagues relate to them. In these cases the best person for the job available (as a result of team history or awareness of the strategic importance of staff development) happened to be a woman.

As part of adopting a team approach to school management, most heads made some attempt to play down elements of hierarchy within it. Where the management structure of the school was represented within a diagram, it did not match the traditional management pyramid of line accountability with the head at the apex. At Longrise a matrix 'collaborative management structure' for the school was about to be implemented. It was developed to 'move away from a hierarchical structure', even the 'collaborative' label being chosen to convey the importance of cross-hierarchical links. Deputies were each to be responsible for working with certain faculties and year groups, a structure with affinities to that adopted at Oldlea. This distribution of linkages was designed to ensure that SMT members would have knowledge of curriculum and pastoral issues faced by middle managers.

The head at Middleton had changed the name of the SMT from 'senior' to 'school' management team, giving his reason as: 'I don't like senior as a label. I think it attracts to it undeserved notions of wisdom, or it's unfairly geriatric, or it's a sinecure – the old senior master at Harrow.' The Middleton school management structure is portrayed in Figure 3.1 (some labels have been altered to preserve anonymity). The hub was the curriculum, the *raison d'être* for the individual SMT members, depicted in the ring around the hub. The next ring represents the groups inside and outside the school to which the SMT had to relate. Each sector of the outer two rings represents the management responsibilities of each SMT member. The head was responsible for managing the SMT. Both the label and the diagram may be interpreted as symbols intended to get away from the notion of hierarchy. In practice, this SMT did retain a major hierarchical distinction between the head and the rest of the team.

The distribution of SMT members' offices around the school affected the ease of informal contact between them. The design of the buildings, dating back to before the current team approach was adopted, generally allowed limited room for manoeuvre. In most cases one or more deputies occupied rooms close to the head's office, with other team members' offices dispersed around the school. One allowance holder at Oldlea noted how he missed out on much informal contact between SMT members because his office was some distance away from theirs. However, at Drake the head had been able to

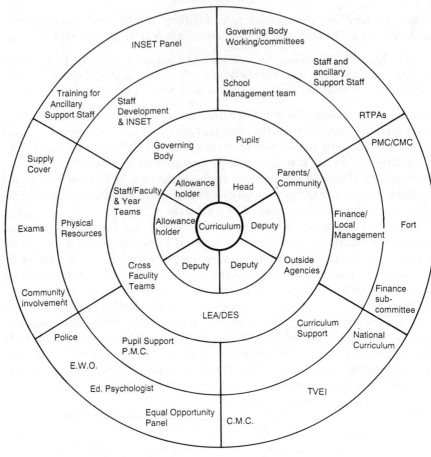

Key: CMC = curriculum management commitee
       EWO = educational welfare officer
       INSET = in-service training
       Fort = field studies centre leased by school
       PMC = pastoral management committee
       PMC/CMC = joint curriculum and pastoral management committee
       RTPA = representatives of teachers' professional associations

Figure 3.1   Diagram of the management structure at Middleton School

ensure that all members had rooms adjacent to her office, facilitating mutual contact and symbolising that the whole team was a single entity. This arrangement appeared to reinforce a perception among staff outside the SMT that members formed a group who worked together, but it was also seen by some to symbolise their separation from other staff.

THE ROLE OF THE SMT

If, as we suggested in Chapter 1, teams are more than the sum of their parts, managing schools through teamwork must consist of more than the sum of individual SMT members' responsibilities. Team members' perceptions of the joint role of the SMT were broadly similar across the six schools. Although not every SMT member who was interviewed mentioned all aspects of this role and there were differences of nuance, it is possible to build up a reasonably representative composite account.

The perception of chairs of governors and other staff was consistent with the account given by SMT members, although some viewed the SMT more as individuals with specific responsibilities than a group with a joint role. Apart from middle managers who might occasionally attend part of a team meeting to discuss an issue related to their responsibility, other staff (and governors) rarely witnessed SMT members working together as a group.

In essence the role of the SMT was to *manage the school within the leadership of the head, supported by the governing body.* As a deputy at Middleton put it: 'The team approach is essentially to support and counsel the head and the governors – the people where the buck stops.' The head, however, was in the team; the governing body was not. The management role of the teams was complex because it was in no sense exclusive: it was linked through individual SMT members' responsibilities and through communication structures to staff with middle-management responsibilities (such as heads of faculty or heads of year) and to the rest of the teaching and support staff. Communication structures extended to parents through such linkages as the governing body, parent–staff associations, and arrangements for pastoral support.

The educational purpose of the SMT's role was highlighted by several SMT members, a deputy at Northend stating that:

> The basic aim of the management team is to maximise the potential of the students and staff. Everything we do is geared towards that end including, for example, making sure that the fabric of the building is OK. You need a team to do this because no one person could do it; no one person would have the time and skills to do everything.

The core of the team's joint endeavour was connected with the process of making, implementing and evaluating policies. This work entailed making a stream of decisions relating to change and to the maintenance of existing practice. Decisions covered school-wide issues ranging from major policies (such as staffing the curriculum in the coming year, or the adoption of a school uniform) to detailed administrative matters (including what was to go in the school handbook for staff, or how the SMT could support other staff facing particular problems).

Sharing decisions relating to the responsibility of individual members meant that heads and other SMT members were accountable to the team, so reducing the likelihood of decisions of poor quality. According to a deputy at Middleton:

> By using a team, however small or large, you cut out arbitrary decisions, whimsical decisions, impulsive decisions, decisions based upon a whole host of background reasons . . . that introduces an element of accountability. You are in a sense called upon by the team to justify yourself, or you can be.

This deputy had responsibility for the LMS budget, and would occasionally ask the head to think twice about the financial implications of decisions. At least one allowance holder in each SMT mentioned how she or he habitually checked ideas for their practicality and acceptability among other staff.

While SMT members were key players in the policy process, their major joint decisions were generally informed by the views of staff and ratified by the governing body. Not all policies emanated from SMTs. Within the broad policy framework of school development plans set by the SMTs, policies covering areas of the school such as a particular faculty were developed by other staff and fed into the SMT for ratification.

Ultimately, the implementation of most decisions depended on the efforts of other staff. Feedback might, on occasion, lead to decisions being reversed or rethought within the SMT. An allowance holder at Drake stated that 'we have changed our views, we have sought to ask people in so that we can draw upon their strengths'. He gave an illustration where staff had asked individual SMT members if the SMT would rethink a decision on the number of classes of pupils for the coming year and create a larger number of smaller classes. The SMT had modified the original decision in accordance with this request.

Decisions are only meaningful if it is feasible for staff to implement them. An allowance holder at Oldlea described the SMT's role in these terms:

> Its responsibility should be to make the school run smoothly and make the job of the shop floor teacher as easy as possible. I think it's important that SMTs are not always coming up with ideas that simply mean more work. We should be looking at any initiative as something that actually makes life easier for the shop floor teacher.

The essence of a team approach to decision making was the provision of multiple perspectives on issues relating to the individual tasks of one or more SMT members. Often a member would lead a debate centring on some aspect of her or his individual responsibility. In the words of a deputy at Longrise:

> Although you might allocate responsibilities, there is a process whereby when you are discussing whole-school issues you need the different contributions and perspectives of that team to take the issues on as fully as they need to be . . . if you share things with people and tap their resources you get a better product at the end.

These perspectives were often informed by views expressed by other staff, primarily through the formal communication structure. An allowance holder at Oldlea commented that the SMT must

> respond to a ground swell of opinion that is coming up from any of the groups within the staff. The senior policy committee in the school, that is made up of heads of faculty and heads of year, is one such group to which the SMT have listened carefully.

The perspectives of SMT members were seen to relate to certain values which several respondents described in terms of a shared vision, most markedly at Underhill. According to a deputy there:

We are here to create a vision for the future of the school and to do everything we possibly can to guide the school towards that vision. The vision is
created through our own personal philosophies, through awareness of legislation, through knowing our staff and distilling all of this into a vision that
our boys are going to benefit from. We have to plan strategically to achieve
this and we have to carry this vision to the governing body and help them to
manage the school.

At Middleton, in contrast, the emphasis lay more on pragmatism within values
about the content of the issue that were only expressed as far as was necessary
to reach a decision. Although in most cases heads were reportedly a significant
source of the values that might underpin a vision, there was some variation
over the relative contribution of others inside and outside the SMT.

The multiplicity of perspectives that might lead to deciding that a decision
was needed or to informing the decision itself was not necessarily confined to
the team. A central part of the SMT joint role was to generate and sustain an
overview of the school and its context so as to inform the need for decisions
and their content. These decisions should provide support for staff to carry
out their individual responsibilities. According to an allowance holder at
Drake:

Our aim is to make this a purposeful, better institution for all by being able
to provide an overview to the institution, encourage others to see the overview but also give them the facilities to be able to concentrate on their own
area, so we don't have seventy or eighty managers all trying to operate.

Informally, SMT members gathered much information, including staff concerns and opinions, by making themselves accessible to staff so that they could
be used as a 'sounding board' for staff views. More formal means included
attending and often chairing regular meetings such as committees of middle
managers and governors' subcommittees. SMT members provided opportunities for issues to be brought to their attention; for consulting on issues
about which an SMT decision was to be made; and for seeking views on the
outcome of a decision. In addition, SMT members sought and fed in information gathered from outside the school, including details of LEA policies or
national requirements. Equally, arrangements were made to inform others of
SMT deliberations and decisions.

The implementation of decisions was generally led by the SMT members
responsible for the area in question and the progress of others with implementation was monitored through the usual means of gathering information.
Monitoring of individual SMT members' progress with their tasks was carried
out largely through reporting back within the team meetings.

The commitment of SMT members required if they were to contribute fully
to the joint SMT role was encapsulated by the head at Middleton within a
conception of 'whole-school awareness'. He expected SMT members not only
to view the school as an entity, rather than confining their attention to areas
connected with their individual responsibility, but also to adopt a range of
values within this perspective that were congruent with the stated aims of the

Whole-School Awareness

Middleton School is committed to a whole-school view of which the following are central:

- Encouragement and maintenance of harmonious working relationships and a sense of professionalism amongst teaching and ancillary support staff.
- Awareness of the staff development needs of teaching and ancillary support staff.
- Readiness to support and to listen to teaching and ancillary support staff.
- Willingness to direct comments/observations/suggestions/criticisms of the school to the appropriate places for discussion.
- Involvement in the selection and interviewing of staff.
- Involvement in the establishment, review and evaluation of all administration, curricular and pupil support systems within the school.
- Readiness to work with the governing body, parents, feeder primary schools, FE and HE sectors, and the LEA whenever appropriate.
- Commitment to the highest standards of learning and achievement and of self-esteem amongst all pupils regardless of age, gender, race, health or ability.
- Maintenance of good order and discipline of all pupils within the school.
- Encouragement of good practice in all classrooms by being seen in classrooms as teachers, supporters and observers.
- Involvement in the rewards and sanctions that are given to pupils.
- Care and concern for the environment of the school.
- Commitment to the best presentation of the name of Middleton School.
- Presence at parents' evenings and other school functions.

Figure 3.2   Components of 'whole-school awareness', Middleton School

school. The components of whole-school awareness were listed in a paper he wrote to accompany SMT members' job descriptions, portrayed in Figure 3.2. They imply that all SMT members place a high value on relating positively with other staff and gathering their views, and on supporting SMT colleagues in carrying out their individual responsibility. The list amounts to the head's vision of managerial values that the SMT should share, a summary of professional aspects of the culture of teamwork that he wished to promote. Here the head used his position of authority to establish key elements of the culture which the SMT was to adopt.

An account of a more restricted part in SMT decision making was given by two allowance holders at Longrise, who both stressed how information was shared and policies discussed, but excluded the making of policy. Their perception reflected the two-tier nature of this SMT, in which policy decisions were mainly made within the 'inner cabinet' meetings of the head and deputies, which the allowance holders did not attend. The head noted that this arrangement had been made because they had not fully embraced opportunities presented to them in the past to participate in making policy decisions.

EXTERNAL LINKS AND INTERNAL COMMUNICATION

Parameters for the role the SMTs were able to play rested, in part, on the approach of the governing body. We noted in Chapter 1 how authority to manage secondary schools is legally divided between heads and governors, the latter being able to decide how far to delegate responsibility to the former. Governing bodies generally supported major decisions made within the SMTs, rather than initiating policies. The chair at Middleton underlined the formal position of the governors in setting parameters within which the professional staff operated. He implied that governors were more concerned with delimiting the work of professional staff than directing it within narrow confines. The governors must

> keep control of all aspects of the school. You can't do it from day to day; that we have delegated to the headteacher. So it's overall control of what they [the professional staff] do. To make sure they don't move outside guidelines laid down by the policy makers.

The chair of governors at most schools highlighted how policies were mainly initiated within the school but approved by governors. The chair at Oldlea perceived that policies were moulded 'by the dynamism of our headteacher . . . she sows the seeds, then the SMT evolve what is going to happen, and the governors would then support virtually anything they suggest'. At Longrise the chair drew attention to ensuring that policies were in accord with the views of other staff who were to implement them:

> I very much want the staff to feel that we value their opinions and, as far as possible, we try to support what the staff want for the school . . . for the governors to formulate a policy and say to the staff, 'Here you are, sort this one out!' is just ridiculous because in the end it is the staff that have to actually work the policy.

Governing bodies were closely linked to the headteachers, with whom chairs drew up the agenda for governors' meetings. They did not have formal contact with the SMT as a group, although members other than the head attended governors' meetings as observers in the three Eastshire schools. In the Westshire schools contact was generally with individual SMT members: at Longrise the deputies each chaired a working group attended by some of the staff and governors.

Alongside the structure of SMT meetings, the main arena for carrying out the core of the joint SMT role, there were less frequent meetings between either the whole SMT or individual members and other groups. They were designed to facilitate communication between SMT members and others, so informing SMT deliberations and disseminating the outcomes. The structure of the main regular meetings where SMT members attended as senior managers is also depicted in Table 3.4. While all SMTs met at least once a week, there was variation in the amount of time spent together (ranging from two and a half to four hours) and in the scheduling of meetings, reflecting the site-level priorities of the SMT members. Only at Longrise were all SMT meetings held during individuals' non-contact time; elsewhere there was one after-school meeting which could be extended if necessary without being constrained by teaching and other commitments. On occasion, other staff would be invited to attend a particular item in these meetings.

Arrangements for meeting with middle managers were made in each school, Underhill – the smallest institution – being the only one without a formal

Table 3.4 Structure of regular meetings involving SMT members as senior managers

Type of Meeting	Middleton	Longrise	Northend	Drake	Oldlea	Underhill
Formal SMT meetings each week	Monday, after school Tuesday morning	Full SMT: Tuesday afternoon Head and deputies: Thursday afternoon	Wednesday morning Thursday, after school	Monday, after school 3 days, before school	Tuesday, after school	Wednesday, after school Daily, before school
Major regular meetings between SMT members and middle managers or other groups of staff	Joint curriculum and pastoral management committee Curriculum management committee Pastoral management committee In-service training panel Full staff meeting	Cross-curricular consultative groups Programme (curriculum) management group Community (pastoral) management group Full staff meeting	Joint curriculum and pastoral management group Pastoral group Full staff meeting	Senior staff (curriculum and pastoral) group Curriculum group Full staff meeting	School policy committee (curriculum and pastoral) Full staff meeting	Pastoral group Full staff meeting
Major regular meetings between SMT members and governors	Head attends governing body meetings (+ one SMT allowance holder is a teacher governor) Individuals attend sub-committee meetings	Head attends governing body meetings Deputies each chair working group involving governors	Head attends governing body meetings Head and deputy attend each sub-committee meeting	Head attends governing body meetings, deputies attend as observers A deputy attends each sub-committee meeting	Head attends governing body meetings, others attend as observers Individuals attend subcommittee meetings	Head attends governing body meetings, deputies, allowance holder and bursar attend as observers Bursar attends finance sub-committee meetings

arrangement for meeting with heads of department or faculty. Five schools had a joint curriculum and pastoral meeting, resulting in a very large group, especially at Northend which did not have a faculty structure. All the SMTs were represented by one or more of their number at governing body meetings and subcommittees. The entire SMT at Oldlea attended the main meetings, members other than the head having observer status. As the head was not a governor, no SMT member had voting power. At all schools, the head was clearly distinguished from other SMT members in being either a full member of the governing body or acting in an *ex officio* capacity. There appeared to be a hierarchical differentiation of SMT members' participation in meetings with governors in three schools: deputies were involved in subcommittee meetings whereas allowance holders were not.

The structure of regular meetings was supplemented by temporary task-related groups such as staff or governors' working parties, often with SMT representation, which were set up as the need arose. Two or more SMT members would occasionally meet to tackle particular tasks and individuals would have varying informal contact; the head and deputies at Oldlea also shared transport to and from school.

Apart from the formal meetings between the head and deputies at Longrise, Oldlea was the only other school with a regular meeting of a subgroup of SMT members, where the two deputies and the allowance holder with responsibility for a curriculum area met to discuss issues connected with their curriculum responsibilities. The head did not attend but was kept fully informed of their discussions. The other three allowance holders perceived that the members with curriculum responsibility and the head formed an 'inner cabinet' in practice, although such a differentiation was not part of the SMT structure. A deputy commented that the group did sometimes discuss issues in confidence which were connected with the performance of staff members, and had also attended a residential meeting this year in addition to the one shared by all seven members of the SMT.

Similar perceptions of a hierarchy occasionally emerging in practice were voiced by allowance holders at Drake and Underhill. One allowance holder at Drake commented:

> There have been times when I have felt that there is a senior senior management team in the team. Sometimes I feel I come rather late in on discussions and the decision has already been made.

The head and deputies here could easily meet informally as they had a lighter teaching load. The high degree of acceptance of lower status within the SMT among allowance holders in four schools contributed to the ability of the teams to operate smoothly while retaining an element of hierarchy between deputies and allowance holders. Only at Middleton was there no hint of an inner and outer group within the SMT.

It is clear that there was room for some variation in the membership of SMTs and the structures created for carrying out their role as a team, although there appeared to be no radical differences in their role at the level of generality revealed through our interviews. The hierarchy of status levels connected with salaries and conditions of service was interpreted in all the schools as a management hierarchy, with a clear distinction between heads and other members in all cases, and more variable differences between the responsibilities and the level of participation in teamwork amongst deputies and allowance holders (and the senior administrative officer or bursar in two schools).

We suggested in Chapter 2 that SMTs may reflect a variable balance between contradictory norms (Figure 2.2). This point may be illustrated tentatively on the basis of the 'snapshot' evidence about individual status and responsibilities and the SMT structures presented in this chapter. In the summer of 1991 the Middleton SMT appeared to be placed furthest towards the egalitarian end of the balance. There was the lowest number of hierarchical levels in terms of structure and reported practice, the one clear distinction lying between the head and other SMT members (although allowance holders had a heavier teaching load than the deputies). Longrise, because of its additional strong distinction between deputies and allowance holders expressed in the meetings structure, was perhaps furthest towards the hierarchical end. The other SMTs seemed to lie somewhere in between, each revealing a degree of hierarchical distinction between deputies and allowance holders in practice, if not in structure.

However, even the 'extreme' positions were far from extreme. We noted earlier how the head at Longrise was unique in rotating deputies' responsibilities, ensuring an equitable distribution over time of any that may have been perceived as reflecting higher or lower status. The inner group of head and deputies operated less hierarchically than the wider group taken as a whole. All the SMTs embraced norms connected with a management hierarchy and equal contribution as team members. It seems unlikely that a team approach to secondary school management can buck the present system of differential status within the management hierarchy. Yet the notion of a shared management role implies that a team approach cannot constitute simply a reflection of that hierarchy either.

Whatever the position of any SMT at the time of our fieldwork, there was also evidence that the balance might shift over time. The focus here on structures and the role of the SMT has given a more detailed picture of how the management hierarchy was expressed within the SMTs, than the ways SMT members at different levels in this hierarchy operated as equal partners. We found the norm of equal contribution as team members to be expressed more through working practices of the teams, especially in connection with decision making, as we will highlight in the next chapter where we look at the dynamics of team development and operation.

4

Team Dynamics

Here we continue the story of the six SMTs, considering the part played by heads, with support from other SMT members, in creating and developing the teams. Headteachers are shown to have used the power accompanying their status in the management hierarchy to adopt a team approach and to work on shaping the culture of teamwork that underpinned its operation. Next, we look at the process of teamwork, focusing on shared decision making within SMT meetings. We discuss the significance of the norm that decisions must be made by consensus and examine how heads delimited the boundaries of joint work. Finally, we examine briefly the criteria used by team members, other staff and chairs of governors in judging the effectiveness of the SMTs.

CREATING A TEAM APPROACH

At any time, the teamwork process represented the 'state of the art' within the unfolding of each team history, a pattern of working practices in which the heads had been prime movers. As a deputy at Underhill acknowledged:

> You cannot just wave a management wand and say you've got teams. It doesn't happen that way. You have to do everything you can to create as much of a team as possible.

All six heads had been through significant experiences which had moulded their beliefs and values about teamwork. The head at Underhill had turned to teamwork after a difficult period in the mid-1980s when teachers had taken industrial action. He had experienced a 'one term training opportunity' (OTTO) where the course leader had advocated a collaborative management style:

The OTTO was most useful as an opportunity to recuperate, rethink, and replan the future of the school. I realised how much I had been wound up at that time when most heads were under considerable stress. I was able to realise that a lot of the problems in my school were not my problems, that I had to shift ownership of problems. That was a weakness in the previous system when the head had to take over responsibility for any problem, even down to fixing a lock or looking after a case of child abuse. The system simply was not working . . . I became determined with the appointment of the new deputies to move towards a team approach.

He had since taken every opportunity to appoint senior staff committed to teamwork.

The other heads, who had been appointed to their present post more recently, adopted a team approach from the outset. Their previous experience in senior management positions and the circumstances they inherited affected their decision. The heads at Middleton, Longrise and Oldlea had valued their SMT experience when they were deputies, the latter referring to the benefit of support in dealing with adversity:

I would have gone home from here hitting my head against a brick wall every night if I hadn't had a team. The camaraderie and bonding of the SMT in my previous school stayed with me and I felt it was worth bringing and preserving . . . To actually build together with all the changes that were coming in education: that you could only do with a team structure.

The two taking up their second headship had different experiences as heads in their previous school. The head at Northend continued the style of 'collaborative decision making' he had developed in his first headship, assisted by the fact that his predecessor had adopted a consultative style of management and existing SMT members welcomed his approach. In contrast, the head at Drake decided that a change was required compared with her previous style as head of a smaller school, as she would be unable to deal with so many management tasks herself in a larger institution.

Each head therefore ascribed a positive value to teamwork, and it is notable that the values of the heads at both Drake and Underhill had shifted since first taking up this role. The head at Middleton was fascinated by the part played by leadership in developing teams:

The buzz is taking a group of people who probably would never wish to go on holiday with each other, find themselves in the same campsite and actually settle down around the same stove. And don't squabble about it but produce a good meal at the end.

The heads used their power to build towards their conception of teamwork within the current institutional context. Some activities were directed towards establishing a culture of teamwork, symbolising the values and practices that they wished others to embrace.

Unilateral action had been taken by the head at Middleton in expressing his values concerning fairness and openness, to which he expected other staff, including SMT members, to conform. He made public within the SMT what individuals had said to him concerning any SMT member, removing the potential for a form of manipulation that had existed in the past:

> It was possible under a former regime to play one person off against another. Access to information being a key factor. That's not possible now because [the head] . . . will actually start the meeting by saying, '[A deputy] came to me a moment ago and said x' – so instantly it's public.

The head had ruled out reference to past incidents or enmities, so paving the way for new alliances among the staff he inherited:

> There's a lot of historical memory within the school. I'm not actually that interested in it . . . there are some people who are very expert at keeping their skeletons in their cupboards and as far as I am concerned, in many cases, long may they stay there – or worms in the can. Because once they are out you can't get them back in.

Other staff had convinced the head at Northend that his personal style as leader had an impact on the school climate. In turn, he had worked to ensure that the SMT as a whole was influential in sustaining the professional culture of the school, convincing his colleagues that the SMT's top priority must be high academic standards, and that its operation should be a model for the rest of the staff. Modelling behaviour was not confined to managerial action. The head at Drake not only dressed very smartly herself but also made her expectation clear that other members of the SMT should also dress formally.

SELECTION OF SMT MEMBERS

All six heads used opportunities created by staff vacancies to appoint new members to the SMT according to what they believed was needed to build a strong team. Four had expanded the size of the group, either through new appointments or by inviting staff to become members of the SMT. Selection criteria included educational values, most strikingly at Oldlea, where the head was strongly opposed to selective and private schooling:

> I am only interested in people working with me who are completely committed to comprehensive education. I am not interested in those who come to work here and take their money, and send their children to private education. They've got to believe in what I believe in.

Competence in the individual responsibility to be undertaken and the ability to fit into the existing SMT and contribute effectively to teamwork were equally important. Four heads had been influenced by the work of Belbin on complementary team roles, and sought to achieve heterogeneity in teamworking styles within the SMT. The head at Underhill was unique in being able to create a team from scratch. He used a typology of complementary team roles to assess candidates during the selection process for both deputies, having become aware of his preferred team role as a result of his recent training:

I knew where I stood in the team and I wanted people not to be mirror images of myself but to have different qualities so that they could give different things to the team.

In contrast, the departure of a deputy at Northend had only recently provided the head with his first opportunity to make an SMT appointment. He sought to complement existing team members by appointing a 'completer/finisher' who would ideally be female, so reducing the present under-representation of women on the SMT. The successful candidate was indeed a woman, who commented:

I learned after I'd been appointed why I'd been appointed. In particular the fact that I was a finisher and completer and task oriented in the Belbin sense was important. I'm always willing to finish a job, get on with it and say, 'What's next?' So I think my personality fits in with personalities in the team.

At Drake, the head held an interview with each teacher to find out about staff concerns for the school, then invited an allowance holder into the team who was an ideas person and a good communicator. As existing SMT members left the school, she first invited another allowance holder who was long established and gave strong team support, then appointed a new deputy from within the school who was 'a very good curriculum thinker'. When the next opportunity to appoint a deputy came up she sought someone who had strong 'people skills', whose individual responsibility covered staff development and other personnel issues. This was an external appointment, where the new deputy perceived that the selectors were looking for someone with a 'human touch in dealing with people'.

An important element of culture building was the heads' involvement of existing SMT members in selecting their future team colleagues. SMT members were consulted prior to inviting allowance holders to join a team. Where there was a formal selection process, as in the appointment of deputies, existing deputies were more closely involved than their allowance holder colleagues in all cases except Middleton. They played some part in observing and initial interviewing of candidates. Questions about teamwork were frequently asked. At Longrise, one criterion used by existing deputies and the head when appointing a new deputy was 'Can I work with this person?'.

Some form of practical exercise entailing a team situation was reported in four schools, in three cases consisting of a simulation. At Oldlea, selectors observed a 'goldfish bowl' exercise where each candidate presented a topic for discussion. Criteria for judgement of their performance were not divulged to the candidates. A positive criterion was each candidate's ability to facilitate other candidates in the group in offering their views; a negative one was to identify individuals who dominated. Instead of a simulation, existing members of the SMT at Middleton (including an allowance holder) had a meeting with the final two candidates for the staff development coordinator post which included SMT membership. They were asked to comment on the school development plan and present their plans for staff development. The exercise was designed to represent as closely as possible the working situation which the successful candidate would join.

A deputy involved in this selection process and another at Longrise faced a test of their professional values when a friend on the staff proved to be a strong (and eventually successful) internal candidate for an SMT post. Both deputies took pains to separate their personal values from the professional criteria for the appointment.

An equally unintended consequence of SMT involvement occurred at Longrise and Drake, where the successful candidate was not the one preferred by an existing deputy. A difficult period of mutual adjustment followed, where the new SMT members had to work to gain these deputies' acceptance. It appears that in both cases it was difficult for a team member to accept the successful candidate (as teamworking norms required) having legitimately indicated at the selection stage that this person was not her or his first choice of team colleague, although the final decision rested formally with the governing body and was heavily influenced by the head.

By contrast, in the three instances where an SMT member was an unsuccessful internal candidate for promotion to another post within the SMT, no friction was reported between this person and the successful candidate. At Middleton, one deputy who had been acting head was interviewed for the headship. The head reflected how he could have been 'poisonous within the body politic', so reducing the potential for teamwork. The head paid tribute to the deputy's professional values, while the deputy emphasised how he had approved of the head's early demonstration of values concerning fairness and openness. The head's symbolic actions to build a culture of teamwork appear to have helped the deputy to accept him.

TEAM DEVELOPMENT

SMTs may go through a rapid period of evolution connected with changes in team membership, where old hands and newcomers go through a process of mutual adjustment. *Unstructured development* of the teams was largely subliminal, an outcome of working together. Interdependence grew with experience of support between the heads and their team colleagues. An SMT member (other than the head!) in three schools mentioned how the head's concern for them as people facilitated their own contribution to teamwork, echoing Halpin's (1966) contention that leadership includes attendance to personal needs. A deputy at Northend noted how the head would be the first to offer if she needed help, while an allowance holder at Middleton commented how the head showed concern about colleagues' personal interests and trials of life outside school: 'That actually has its place in SMT meetings. So that people are close as colleagues . . . that's part of the cement.'

The heads strongly appreciated the support of their SMT colleagues, since it was through them that much of the heads' work was achieved. We noted earlier how the head at Oldlea valued having colleagues with whom she could give vent to frustrations. Yet, for the heads, support did not always include development.

Two heads mentioned how few SMT members gave them positive or negative feedback on their performance. The head at Middleton commented:

> The one thing I never get from anybody – this isn't sob stuff at all – I never get any comment on my own performance, ever . . . I don't expect other staff to do that but even my closest team won't turn round – they almost feel you actually shouldn't say anything.

The head at Longrise perceived that lack of praise from SMT colleagues was gender related, stating how the female deputy

> will give me the emotional support if I need it. She will realise what a woman is feeling in some situations. The men probably realise but can't come and support me in that way. She'll come and tell me if she thinks I've done something well or if a parent said the head is from a rotten school – and the others wouldn't do that. The men wouldn't say, 'I thought what you said to the parents was very good.' They won't give the praise, but a woman will to another woman.

Members of three SMTs mentioned how enjoyment of teamwork was nurtured through humour. A deputy at Oldlea remarked that 'a team that can joke together can work together'. SMT experience also offered a diffuse learning experience for individuals. An allowance holder at Drake reported how his ability to summarise points made in meetings improved by his noting how the head did it: 'There are times when I think, "I wish I had said that." So simple, so clever and so effective.'

Structured development activities (especially those offered by LEA staff) were variably employed by the teams. One or more individuals from each SMT had attended a training course during the last few years where teamwork had been addressed. In Westshire there were courses for newly appointed deputies, and training delivered by the Coverdale Organisation was offered to heads and some deputies. This training did not extend beyond individuals, whereas the annual residential meeting supported by the Eastshire LEA was regarded as highly beneficial for development of the whole team. Residentials gave SMT members an unprecedented opportunity for uninterrupted debate and being in each other's company. As an allowance holder at Oldlea put it: 'Time together to thrash through philosophy and just to relax together on those weekends just brings you together as a team.' The residentials could also provide an environment where tensions within the team could be resolved.

Activities initiated in school which related to the teams' management role included review days for the Middleton SMT, sometimes with an external facilitator; a day's team training at Drake delivered by a management consultant from industry; and a seminar for the Oldlea SMT given by an industrialist on applying total quality management to schools. The head and one deputy at Underhill had attended a week-long leadership course offered by the Industrial Society which, according to the head, was 'all about working as a team, getting results, working hard and building team spirit'.

Formal induction of new SMT members was largely confined to instances where they were shouldering new individual responsibilities. The staff development coordinator at Middleton had received extensive support from the head, which included 'weekly meetings, very close monitoring, and complete availability if I needed him'. An allowance holder at Oldlea had found his first residential meeting an 'enormously valuable' induction into the SMT, while a deputy at Northend reported how her induction began prior to taking up post. It encompassed attending SMT meetings and participating in staff appointment panels, including one which had internally appointed a temporary member of the SMT. Her counterpart at Longrise had benefited from informal induction support from a deputy who was a friend and to whom she could turn for feedback and advice.

There was a marked contrast in how far the SMTs engaged in social activities intended as part of team development, reflecting different values among the heads and other SMT members. In all cases, socialising was an optional extra, rather than an obligatory part of the team approach. A criterion used by the head for selection of deputies at Underhill was participation in physical exercise:

> When I built up the management team, I was determined to be able to work with anyone who was appointed . . . Choosing candidates with an interest in physical activity is my own bias . . . I like outgoing people who are fit and healthy and are prepared to work hard and live hard. They have also got to have the right philosophy in that they believe in the potential of the boys in this school – a sort of muscular Christianity without a capital C.

The head and deputies occasionally met to pursue shared sporting interests, and the head and one deputy trained together for marathons. The head at Middleton reported how the SMT celebrated together as a group, a way of reinforcing the culture of teamwork:

> Once or twice a year we have meals together and so on. And they are enormously good humoured. They do a good function and help to smooth over historical memories. They are a way of giving people time as well.

At Oldlea, SMT members took turns to host a social event at their home for team colleagues and their families. Otherwise, the head avoided social contact with individuals to avoid being 'seen to be having any favourites.' She believed that team leadership entailed paying even-handed attention to other members. Socialising with certain individuals carried the risk of a social hierarchy being formed within the team.

The SMTs at Northend and Drake had very little social contact. The head at Drake perceived that socialising was not essential for effective teamwork, but would have added a desirable dimension:

> If we were the sort of group that could meet more informally, maybe socially, I think that would introduce a different element into the team. It continues to be . . . fairly formal I suppose. There is not the easy give and take, cut and thrust that I think might come about if you had a group of people who had more in common in terms of age, social life and family background.

Her view was confirmed by three other SMT members. Here the culture of teamwork included an implicit understanding about its limits: socialising was off the SMT agenda.

In sum, the process of team development was multifaceted: both subliminal and structured. The heads played a key part in nurturing their preferred teamwork culture, but it depended equally on the values of SMT members, only some of which were deemed to be appropriately the target of the heads' influence. This culture was strongly expressed within SMT meetings.

JOINT WORK

These meetings, held in the head's office, were the core of the SMTs' activity. All the heads attempted to create a setting and procedures for SMT meetings which symbolised the relationship between SMT members that they sought and which facilitated the process of teamwork they valued. There was considerable room for expressing their individual beliefs and values. Figure 4.1 illustrates the arrangement of furniture in three schools. At Middleton the head held meetings with team members sitting around a coffee table. He consciously avoided seating himself apart from his colleagues (and so possibly symbolising his differential position within the management hierarchy) by joining the circle away from his desk. The head at Underhill had a circular table grafted on to a corner of his desk, enabling him to remain there while SMT colleagues sat at the round table. At Oldlea the SMT sat at a large dining table. The head at Drake had moved the team away from the formality of sitting at a large table to the informality of a low table and easy chairs.

Rituals for provision of food and drink also reflected different values. The (male) head at Middleton habitually made coffee or tea and provided biscuits, occasionally celebrating by bringing in delicacies; the (female) head at Drake eschewed providing refreshments as an accompaniment to meetings; the head at Oldlea designed her office to be like an extension to her home. Crockery was displayed in a cabinet, and a small kitchen opened off from the room. SMT meetings held after school always started with a meal (prepared by catering staff) at the table, which was covered with a lace cloth. The head wished the setting for meetings to be symbolic of a family:

> I've always rationalised to myself that I spend more time in school than I do at home. I feel comfortable in it and other people think, 'How nice, how pleasant.' Hopefully it's warm, it's friendly. I start all management meetings with food because it matches Maslow's theory of satisfying basic physiological needs. No matter how difficult the subject you have to discuss or however personal it may be to some people, it's very difficult to be unkind to each other when you've actually eaten together. I suppose it's the idea of the last supper. It means I'm saying to them, 'Look, you've sacrificed your time away from your family. It may not be a real family, but we're a family together and we're married to each other.' It's the same if anyone comes in. We always have coffee on and biscuits on the table.

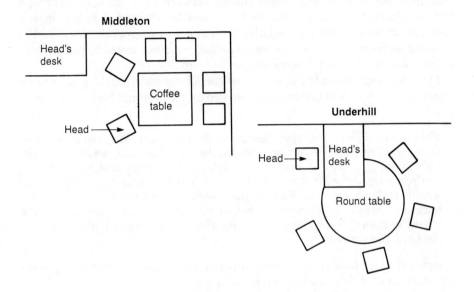

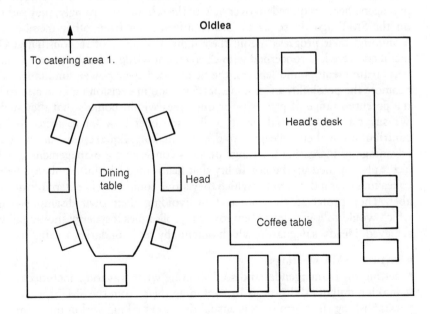

Figure 4.1 Settings for SMT meetings

The head had used her influence to promote a sense of community while inhibiting any hostility that might emerge between SMT members. Through the introduction of such rituals, the heads may be interpreted as legitimately (from their perspective) manipulating the culture of teamwork. Their aim in creating a climate conducive to collaboration remained implicit, yet was directed towards achieving synergy within the team.

SMT meetings provided a setting where all members could gain mutual support. One deputy at Longrise commented on the meetings between deputies and head:

> They are to do with therapy; they are to do with back slapping; they are to do with telling ourselves we are going in the right direction, we are doing the right thing . . . because a lot of the jobs that deputies and heads do are confrontational, quite stressful. Today I had to chase two thieves and wrestle stolen bikes from them in the middle of the road. It's nice to come back and have a coffee with the senior management team and say, 'Look what I've done!', have a laugh, be told, 'You're doing a good job', patted on the head and sent off.

Another stressed how team meetings offered individuals a safety valve, enabling them to vent their frustrations in confidence.

Team meetings fulfilled, in the main, two purposes connected with the SMT's role: sustaining an overview and decision making. Within their responsibility as managers, heads required an overview of the school. Accordingly, they put items on the SMT agenda so as to gather information from other members, and monitored their progress within their individual areas of responsibility. Other members were less concerned with detailed knowledge of colleagues' work.

As team creators and leaders, the heads used their power simultaneously to promote the possibility of genuine participation in decision making and to keep the potential range of processes or outcomes within bounds that they defined. We suggest that the heads faced a dilemma over how far to foster an equal contribution by their colleagues to decision making. Equal contribution gave the advantage of increasing the range of ideas concerning a management problem. Yet it also opened up the possibility that heads might be outnumbered by their colleagues over a decision for which they alone could be held externally accountable. They protected their interest in avoiding their own disempowerment, which would follow from the empowering colleagues if synergy should fail to be achieved. Heads' safeguards, which potentially set boundaries, related to:

- chairing SMT meetings;
- setting the team agenda, and so delimiting what was to be included;
- making unilateral decisions by excluding them from the SMT;
- establishing the norm of consensual decision making within the team;
- retaining the right to make unilateral decisions by withdrawing them from the SMT arena.

They all *chaired SMT meetings*. The head at Drake commented that 'I would feel very uneasy if I did not chair . . . I must have the control to accept that it is my decision, whatever comes of it'. Chairing was tied with *setting the SMT meeting agenda*, drawn up by the head in consultation with SMT colleagues. The head at Longrise drew up the agenda for the two types of regular meeting. Individuals could ask for items to be put on the agenda and she always included 'any other business'.

The head at Middleton had several times suggested to colleagues that they rotate the chair and agenda building task, in order to introduce a more equitable distribution of responsibility for the team meeting process. Other SMT members had resisted this proposal because they were comfortable with his performance and perceived that he was in the best position to do the work. A deputy noted that the head had the greatest access to information which might affect the agenda: 'Most stuff that goes onto the agenda goes on because it has come in through his desk. It's the only desk that everything travels across.' Another deputy added that he was trusted not to withhold items that should be within the province of the SMT. An allowance holder reported how the head informed SMT members about what he intended to keep off the agenda to save them time. Within the dialectic of control within the team, the head bowed to the influence of other SMT members, although he had the authority to compel his colleagues to take a turn at chairing and agenda building. We suggest that to have insisted would have run counter to the belief in consensus decisions, so might have undermined the culture of teamwork.

Chairing and consultative agenda building by heads was widely approved by other SMT members; there appeared to be no struggle for control of meetings through these means. An allowance holder at Drake commented on the head's chairing skills: 'She's just got this very quiet way of keeping you on target.' He was never aware that she was chairing.

Equally, heads excluded little from the SMT agenda apart from matters connected with staff members' personal circumstances divulged in confidence to the head alone, and issues connected with the performance of individual SMT members which were addressed outside the meetings. Five heads were reported very occasionally to *make a unilateral decision with school-wide implications without putting it onto the SMT agenda*. The head at Northend decided to have a school uniform but then invited SMT members to consider the detail of what it should be. Major unilateral decisions by the head at Middleton were largely confined to the early days of his headship, where he had defined the initial size of the SMT and interviewed each member of staff prior to announcing changes, including the transition from a departmental to a faculty structure.

There was considerable variation over how far the outcomes of discussions within SMT meetings were recorded or disseminated to other staff. At Middleton, the head or other SMT members wrote items for the weekly 'head-teacher's bulletin for staff'; the head at Drake wrote brief action minutes which were published on the staff noticeboard. Minutes for SMT consumption only were made at Oldlea and Underhill, while no formal record was made at the other schools. When the head at Drake had recently suggested that someone else wrote the minutes, she was met by unanimous resistance from her colleagues on similar grounds to those expressed to the head at Middleton over chairing and agenda building. Whether a record of meetings was made public to staff outside the SMT affected how far they felt informed about the team's work.

CONSENSUAL, DEMOCRATIC, OR UNILATERAL DECISION MAKING?

In all six SMTs, members subscribed to the norm that *major decisions must be made by consensus* even though, technically, the head might decide. Consensual decision making may be interpreted as expressing the norm within the culture of teamwork that each member had an equal contribution to make to joint work. Adherence to consensual decision making blurred the distinction between consultation (where the decision maker seeks others' views and then makes the decision alone) and shared decision making (where all parties share the making of the decision itself). If consensus could be found after various views had been put forward on a problem, it was immaterial whether the head was consulting SMT colleagues within the framework of a management hierarchy or whether individuals were contributing as equals to making a shared decision.

Consensus seeking as a model of decision making implies adherence to a second norm: that individuals should compromise their view where necessary to reach a 'working consensus' acceptable to all participants. Then unified commitment to implementation of the decision may be expected since implementation follows agreement reached before the decision was made. This model differs from democratic decision making in the point at which compromise is expected to occur. In the latter model, primacy is given to individual views before the decision, needing agreement amongst only a majority prior to the decision. The main compromise comes after the vote, where those holding a minority view are expected to commit themselves to implementing something that they legitimately rejected in contributing to the decision itself.

The major practical difficulty with consensual decision making is finding a working resolution of dissenting views prior to the decision where individuals are not prepared to subscribe to the norm of compromising their view. In democratic decision making, dissenting views may remain unsullied, but a major practical problem arises if those holding a minority view are not ready to commit themselves to implementing something in which they do not believe. Rather than revert to democratic decision making (and hence a vote) where agreement was difficult to reach on major decisions, other means were attempted in all the SMTs to find a working consensus – testimony to the strength of the norm of consensual decision making.

A deputy at Longrise expressed his belief in compromising to reach consensus, implying that the culture of teamwork placed a duty upon SMT members to seek it:

> I think one respects the views of other members of the team. I think one has to, and feel, 'I still have my worries, I still have my doubts, I still might think

it's wrong but we wish to try it this way; let's try it this way and see what happens.' Otherwise things would never move on. I think you run the risk of being seen and being tempted to be obstructive. In a place that has to be managed, has to be organised, things have to be moved on, decisions have to be made sometimes, however difficult they are.

According to a deputy at Middleton, this team had evolved a strategy for determining the extent of consensus as a way of focusing subsequent debate on areas where dissent remained: 'Quite a useful tool we have worked on is to decide how much we can decide. It is possible to go this far without compromising or prejudicing anything else.'

Where there was disagreement, heads could in principle resort to their authority within the management hierarchy to change the rules of decision making by allowing a majority decision (according to the democratic decision-making model). Where other SMT members advocated a course of action which lay outside the boundaries of acceptability to the head, the latter could *withdraw a decision from the SMT and make it unilaterally*. Both strategies would override the norm of consensus which, in turn, was allied to the contradictory belief that each SMT member should be able to make an equal contribution to the decision. Unless the break with consensual decision making was accepted by SMT members other than the head as a legitimate move for heads to make by switching to the perception of a management hierarchy, it risked undermining the culture of teamwork, with its norm of equal contribution to decisons.

The heads were reported as withdrawing a decision on very rare occasions. The head at Oldlea commented that, where she deemed it necessary, she had made the statement to her SMT colleagues: 'I hear what you say, but for the good of the school . . .'. She recalled overriding the unanimous view of the rest of the SMT when the deputies had led an argument that the SMT should respond to unfair press criticism of the school. The head felt it was more prudent to keep quiet. She noted that her colleagues 'had the good grace to turn round and say afterwards: "You're absolutely right".' Their response may be interpreted as an acceptance that in retrospect the head's view was the best, and that she had the right as head to overrule them. An allowance holder in this team commented: 'In some areas we all bow to [the head's] view because she is, after all, head of the school.' In contrast, a deputy at Drake noted how the head might 'put her foot down and go against opinion. When she does it – and it is very occasionally – it grates on everybody'. A deputy at Middleton remarked that

> if [the head] makes an *ex cathedra* statement on a matter of strong principle the composition of the group is such that they would accept it. I can't remember that happening on a major issue – except the shredder . . . He was heavily outnumbered about this. He had acquired for himself a shredder in the face of enormous opposition from the environmentalists amongst us who didn't want to waste electricity, but that's the only major area of contention!

A more common situation, where both heads and other SMT members had backed down when strong arguments had been presented against their view, indicated the strength of the norm of consensual decision making within the culture of teamwork. The head at Underhill had acquiesced when his proposal for a new name for the school was argued down by SMT colleagues. During a debate about staff smoking on the premises, a deputy at Middleton held out for a total ban, whereas colleagues wished to confine smoking to a designated room. Afterwards he spoke to the head, backing down from his position to enable progress to be made.

The example set by heads in backing down symbolised to other SMT members that they practised what they preached within the culture of teamwork. An allowance holder at Middleton commented how the head's behaviour influenced colleagues' willingness to contribute:

> The fact that we are very open in our discussions, the fact that [the head] doesn't totally dominate things, the fact that sometimes he is in a minority and is prepared to back down, change his view, modify it or say, 'I'm happy to accept that but I don't agree' sets the tone for everybody else.

The norm that the team should be involved in making major decisions did not inhibit only heads. A deputy at Drake noted how she held back from making certain decisions alone because colleagues might perceive that they should be team decisions. The culture of teamwork led to the creation of a boundary to be negotiated between individuals' delegated authority to make decisions within their area of responsibility and the authority which rested with colleagues as members of the SMT. Each member could legitimately have an input into the work of others in the team. This distribution of authority contradicted the management structure in so far as individuals (including, to a lesser extent, heads) perceived themselves as accountable to the team, rather than solely to a line manager or to the governing body.

Surfacing of disagreements over decisions, and consequently the need for their resolution, depended on the openness of the SMT debate. The degree of openness, in turn, depended on norms within the culture of teamwork that were to some extent contradictory, depending on how strongly they were held by each member. They included the norms that members should:

- state a view and express it frankly;
- listen to others' views;
- be willing to challenge where views differ;
- be sensitive to colleagues' feelings;
- refrain from making personal attacks;
- confine confrontation to the meetings, if personal animosity does arise.

An important part in fostering this aspect of the culture was played by heads. With the authority as team leader, the head at Drake had spelled out the norms she wished other SMT members to adopt:

> Within the confines of the meeting you can say anything you like to me as long as you do it politely. But outside of this room the team must be seen to act coherently. I think it is very unsettling and damaging for groups of people if they sense that their managers are at odds. So any differences can be aired but only between ourselves.

Frankness could lead to strong emotions. A deputy at Underhill commented: 'It isn't always a nice cosy little chat over a cup of coffee.' An allowance holder at Middleton mentioned how coping with the emotional consequences of open debate had not been easy for the group to learn: 'Some of the debates do get fiery and we get quite stroppy at times. I think we are getting better at leaving it in the room, no matter how stroppy it gets.' SMT members at Oldlea high-lighted the problem posed by an individual's confrontational style that did not conform with the norms of colleagues. They recalled how a past team member had been 'willing to listen and prepared to concede to effective arguments', yet did not appear to take into account colleagues' feelings. Emotional conflict generated in this way could distract team members from disagreement con-nected with the content of the debate.

Some inhibition about stating a dissenting view was expressed by a deputy at Longrise, who pointed to the discomfort that opening up a disagreement could imply:

> Because we work as a team we play down the conflict side. . . A case will be put and it will be greeted with a certain amount of silence. [Afterwards] somebody will go to the person and say, 'I wasn't too happy about that; can we look at it again?' It doesn't happen that often, but you may be able to readdress the issue. There's something about the formality of the meeting that prevents it happening.

We have seen how gaining a multiplicity of perspectives on management issues was an important part of the role of the SMTs. Yet the desired openness of debate in SMT meetings appears difficult to achieve where actions according to contradictory norms were expressed among team members. Another deputy at Longrise speculated whether the cordiality of relationships among SMT mem-bers narrowed the range of views brought to bear in decision making:

> Maybe at times we are almost a bit too much at one. While that's good for managing and good for the team approach, I sometimes wonder if we gener-ate enough provocative thought.

Being too ready to compromise might mean suppressing minority perspectives which, if included in the debate, might contribute to higher quality decisions.

Most individuals in each SMT perceived that they made a contribution to debate which complemented that of others. The teams were more than the sum of their parts because the combined contributions of their members were more diverse that that of any individual. In addition to perceptions of adopting a team role related to the work of Belbin, contributions included:

- acting as a devil's advocate and so challenging colleagues constructively (deputy, Middleton);
- promoting more openness of debate (deputy, Longrise);
- shaping decisions (head, Northend);
- being close to the staff and so able to represent their views (allowance holder, Drake);
- being a visionary for the team (head, Oldlea);
- adopting a conciliatory style (deputy, Underhill).

These contributions related to the perceived need for multiple perspectives, including the reporting of staff opinions, and working towards consensus.

COLLECTIVE RESPONSIBILITY

Consistent with the model of consensual decision making adopted in the SMTs, a norm variably reflected in their culture of teamwork was that all team members should share responsibility for making and implementing shared decisions. The norm carried the expectation that members' first loyalty on SMT matters should be to the team. In the words of a deputy at Oldlea:

> We share in the process of formulating policy and therefore through how we act consistently around the school we must ensure, as best we can, the implementation of policy. So loyalty, consistency, leadership – in whatever domain – are an important aspect and we share responsibility for that. The outcome would be, if you could not accept anything, that you would have to step down from the senior management team rather than to stand out in public against the senior management team. You can argue as much as you like inside the room but if the decision be that we would do otherwise [than you wish], you accept it.

Loyalty to the team was expected by the heads. It implied that a united front be presented to outsiders, the head at Oldlea stating: 'If they were to split ranks they would have my wrath. They are absolutely united to the outside world.' Unity gave the team considerable power through the command of information within the dialectic of control between the SMT and other staff. An SMT member could not be 'picked off' by lobbying and so enable other staff manipulatively to influence the work of the team. A deputy at Underhill reported how a teacher who disagreed with an SMT policy had confronted the deputies, saying:'I don't expect the two of you to disagree anyway; you are both clones!' Heads defined what information could be divulged to other staff and what must remain confidential to the SMT.

A few leaks were reported in two teams: either inadvertent, where an individual did not realise a matter was confidential, or when a team member expressed frustration about what had gone on within an SMT meeting where there had been dissent among members. A few team members other than heads occasionally experienced some conflict of loyalty when reporting back to the team about teachers' performance or when faced with the negative consequences of some SMT decisions. A deputy at Longrise noted how

> Although we are senior management we are not the boss. We do have a position of authority and you can't shirk that, but also we have friends out there. They are not people we go out and order around; they are people we work with in the classroom next to, share things with, meet socially. And inevitably conversations will come which will question decisions we made in senior management. And I suppose that occasionally you find yourself laughing at yourself, laughing at decisions you have made.

A colleague deputy pointed to the symbolic value of admitting to other staff when the SMT had made a mistake, as it exemplified the values that SMT members expected these teachers to hold. In addition, as we noted in Chapter 3, allowance holders with middle-management responsibility were most likely to experience conflict between their loyalty to colleagues for whom they were directly responsible and those in the SMT.

PERCEPTIONS OF SMT EFFECTIVENESS

Team members, a sample of other staff, and chairs of governors were asked about the effectiveness of the SMTs. Their responses reflected their different levels of familiarity with the internal workings of the teams. Chairs of governors worked most closely with heads. Staff outside the teams did not normally attend SMT meetings, but those with middle-management responsibility worked with the SMT in consultative meetings and were consequently more familiar with their mode of operation than main-scale teachers. Overall, the six teams were judged from within and without to be quite or very effective. There were no major discrepancies in the judgements made by insiders and outsiders, and areas perceived by other staff as being capable of improvement were matched by the concerns of SMT members. The evidence on which judgements were based was mostly impressionistic. The range of criteria used in making judgements is instructive, relating to many of the topics we have already discussed. It offers one starting point for considering what makes for effective SMTs (a topic to which we return in the final chapter). We have combined the responses from the six schools into a single list of criteria which is shown in Table 4.1.

The criteria are divided into those which are positive (linked with SMT effectiveness) and those which are negative (associated with ineffectiveness). They relate to:

- inputs to the teams – referring to individual members and the structure and combined talents of the group;
- the process of teamwork – covering the internal operation of SMTs and their external relationships;
- outputs from the SMTs – encompassing those that are a direct outcome of the process of teamwork (such as major decisions) and those perceived to have an indirect link (like the quality of pupil learning).

There was some overlap between criteria used by SMT members and outsiders. The criteria listed in normal type were emphasised mainly by SMT members; those in italics were primarily the concern of other staff and chairs of governors. Team members concentrated upon input, internal process and direct output – dealing with areas which were central to the teams' operation. Criteria employed by outsiders related to their experience of the SMT: especially to external relationships, to individual team members' performance (which included liaison with other groups in the area of their individual responsibility), and to indirect outputs. The chair of governors at Middleton was unique

Table 4.1   Criteria for judging effectiveness of SMTs

Positive	*Negative*

Input: Team members

Individual

- Competent in SMT role
- *Weak in SMT role*

Group

- *Complementary strengths*
- *Too large for discussion*
- Small enough for discussion
- Two-tier structure
- Single-tier structure

Process of teamwork

Internal

- Protect agenda from external pressures
- Inner cabinet
- Head shares information and decisions
- Full participation by all members
- Work hard
- Positive relationships

External

- *Communicate decisions*
- *Fail to communicate*
- *Encourage staff input and respond*
- *Some members inaccessible leading to 'them and us' perception*
- *All members accessible to outsiders*
- *Present united front*
- *Expression of dissent or leakage of confidences*
- *Positive relationships with outsiders*
- *Aloof, unpraising of staff*

Outputs for SMT

Direct

- Decisions made
- Fail to follow through
- Decisions implemented
- Full backing of SMT members for decisions

Indirect

- *School runs smoothly in difficult circumstances*
- *Good educational results*
- *Happy pupils*
- *High staff morale*
- *Within budget*

among the chairs at the case study schools in having attended several SMT meetings as an observer. On this basis, he perceived that it worked well as a team. He also indicated how impressionistic was the link he made between the team's work and indirect outputs:

> The school is being run very efficiently and the management of it is good. The education has progressed and the children seem quite happy, so I assume [the SMT members'] roles must be effective. The morale of the school seems to be high; in these days that's an added bonus.

Similarly, a teacher with middle-management responsibility at Longrise gave her impression that the SMT coped well in difficult circumstances and referred approvingly to team members' candidness in relating to the rest of the staff:

> They're handling a difficult situation pretty well. I feel there's a lot going on in the way of initiatives and we've actually taken on a lot of initiatives in the school, and there's talk of innovation overkill. And they are willing to admit they've made mistakes, and do face up to problems.

An example of an insider's view was given by an allowance holder in the SMT at Middleton, which complements the comment of the chair of governors by focusing on the internal process and direct outputs:

> It works excellently as a team I would say. Because all the important decisions relating to the running of the school are made via a procedure which invites consensus and they all have the full backing of the team. And all of the team feel responsible for implementing them.

Most judgements about ineffectiveness are consistent with the problems highlighted in the research discussed in Chapter 1, such as the perception that some individuals were more competent as team members than others, or the inhibiting effect of a team with a two-tier structure or 'inner cabinet'. Those relating to external relationships may be characteristic of permanent 'top teams' where a central aspect of their group role, as in the case of SMTs, is to work with and through the people in the institution who are accountable to them.

Effectiveness is mainly about instrumental ends. SMTs are ultimately concerned with promoting the education of pupils through the work of staff. Yet despite the perception of a large majority of team members that their team approach soaked up a large amount of precious time, most also reported a range of intrinsic benefits for themselves. We have already noted how mutual support was valued by heads and other SMT members alike. For several SMT members, teamwork was valued as a way of spending their professional lives. According to an allowance holder at Middleton the SMT was

> terrific fun to work in. There's lots of humour and lots of answers. It's always enjoyable. One always feels it has been a good hour or two hours [in SMT meetings]. You enjoy it, as well as achieve something, and relax with a good conscience.

In this and the previous chapter we have looked at six SMTs: continually evolving entities with varied structures and working practices, fulfilling a broadly similar role in managing the school. We have glimpsed how heads were instrumental in using their power to build a team, fostering the culture of teamwork that they valued. They may have been 'first among equals', but we have also seen how the first actually depended on the equals – other SMT members, who also used their influence to help shape this culture. We explored how the contradictory norms relating to a management hierarchy and equal contribution by members of a team, and certain gender-related factors, were built into each SMT structure and process of teamwork.

The story so far is based largely on interviews undertaken over a short period. In the light of these findings and according to the criteria outlined in Chapter 1, we elected to conduct our observational work over a year at Middleton and Drake. This strategy gave us direct access to the interaction that lies at the heart of teamwork and it is to these findings that we turn in the coming chapters.

5

Individual Contributions to Teamwork

Findings from the year's observation and interviews at Middleton and Drake were consistent with the account of the SMT role in Chapter 3. They revealed not only the detail of two contrasting ways of carrying it out, but also dimensions not apparent in the initial case studies. Our analysis of teamwork at Middleton and Drake begins with the people most directly involved. First, we set out a framework for understanding individual contributions within the two SMTs, elaborating on the notions of leadership and teamwork introduced in Chapter 1. We give names to the players who will feature prominently in the next chapters.

Second, we use our framework to analyse, with examples, the contributions of team members to fulfilling the role of the SMT in managing each school through the expression of their individual team roles. We explore how the teams were led and how members used their power to help create synergy, in part by enabling (or even persuading) leaders to lead. We also discuss the contribution of a key member of the administrative staff in each school who supported the SMT.

LEADERSHIP OF THE TEAM AND TEAM MEMBERSHIP

We distinguished two patterns of behaviour or individual team roles within the SMTs which were fundamental to teamwork: *leadership of the team*, and *team membership*. Neither team role need necessarily be the sole prerogative of a particular person or status level within the management hierarchy. It is important to note that the team roles we have identified are differently conceived from the more complex set identified by Belbin. We noted in Chapter 1 how his findings focus on idiosyncratic preferences in contributing to a single, pre-specified, shared task in a temporary, self-contained team with no predetermined structure. Our team roles are a combination of idiosyncratic preference and response to others' expectations about the behaviour of anyone occupying an individual role in the team. Like Belbin's team roles, ours were generated through observation within a particular context. The teams to which we refer were permanent and embedded within a large organisation; their members enjoyed the highest levels of status within a management hierarchy, and they decided upon their multiple-item agenda and the process of achieving team tasks.

Leadership of the team has two components incorporating all aspects of the definition of leadership offered by Louis and Miles (1990). Setting the course of the SMT for continuing existing practice and initiating change entails *setting parameters for teamwork by orchestrating team members' contribution*. Orchestration implies strategic planning (whether determining team membership, a vision for the team, working procedures or the SMT agenda); and stimulating, inspiring and creating conditions favourable for others to act (whether by encouraging or directing other members to contribute, through chairing meetings, deciding what to exclude from the SMT agenda, or leading through example). Parameters for teamwork imply both possibilities and their boundaries. For heads in particular, because they are accountable for the SMT, *ensuring that teamwork follows these parameters by scrutinising their boundaries* is the obverse of creating possibilities. It may entail monitoring team progress and taking action if boundaries are overstepped either by team members or by outsiders such as governors who may affect the SMT via the head. Action may be to direct the work of SMT members or protect their ability to operate within the parameters set.

The team membership role has three components which link with leadership of the team. First, individuals may make their *contribution as an equal* with other members to joint tasks (such as sustaining an overview and decision making). Second, they may express *leadership within the team* by setting the course for action on particular issues within the team agenda (by leading on matters connected with individual responsibilities or taking on other tasks). Third, they may display *followership within the team* in contrasting ways: enabling leadership of the team and team membership to happen by accepting the parameters set and keeping within their boundaries (whether by respecting the groundrules for chairing, leading within the team or contributing fully as an equal); or by persuading others to express leadership of the team or team membership by withholding from opportunities to contribute.

Both heads used their authority in different ways to delimit how and by whom leadership of the team and team membership were carried out. They varied in how far they carried out leadership of the team and operated through team membership, and the degree to which they encouraged colleagues to share leadership of the team or to take on particular aspects of the team membership role. Equally, all members exercised delegated authority or influence in choosing whether to take opportunities given them to fulfil either role. Heads were the main leaders of their teams partly because other members wanted it that way.

In Chapter 2 we discussed how power is shared between each party to interaction, whatever individuals' position in a status hierarchy. The ability of heads to develop a team approach to school management is heavily dependent upon other members using their delegated authority and influence to work towards the same ends for the team, so generating the mutual empowerment that synergy implies. Expression of team-membership behaviour in each SMT rested on the strength of commitment among all members, reflected in the extent to which they shared a culture of teamwork fostered and exemplified by heads.

Backing for both teams was offered by a member of the administrative staff who fulfilled a third team role: *team support*. In different ways they facilitated leadership of the team (focused on the head) and team membership (relating to all team members).

PEOPLE IN (AND BEHIND) THE SMTS

The profiles of the two teams and their key supporters are summarised in Tables 5.1 and 5.2 (elaborating on information in Tables 3.2 and 3.3. in Chapter 3). By the autumn term of 1991, all members of the SMT at Middleton had served in this capacity for over two years and perceived the team to be well established. A new deputy had recently been appointed at Drake, and members were concerned to develop their approach to teamwork. The spread

Table 5.1 Middleton SMT membership and support

		Profile component		
Name	Status level	Management responsibility	Teaching responsibility	No. years in present SMT (autumn 1991)
Peter	Head	Overall, managing SMT	English	3+
Jim	Deputy	Administration, LMS	Maths	3+
Nick	Deputy	Curriculum and learning support, TVEI	French, music	3+
Harry	Deputy	Pupil support	Science	3+
Julia	E allowance holder	Staff development	English	2+
Colin	E allowance holder	Resources, exams, staff cover	Maths	3
Jenny	Professional assistant	Head's assistant, managing support staff	Not applicable	2+ years in post

Table 5.2 Drake SMT membership and support

Name	Status level	Management responsibility	Teaching responsibility	No. years in present SMT (autumn 1991)
Kate	Head	Overall managing SMT	English	6+
Derek	Deputy	Academic and pastoral curriculum	History	6+
Marian	Deputy	Personnel (including development, appraisal, cover) community links staff cover	Science	1+
Greg	E allowance holder	Resources & TVEI	English, information technology	5+
Philip	E allowance holder	Systems, monitoring assessment, resources, exams	Modern languages	4+
Barbara	Senior administrative officer	LMS managing support staff	Not applicable	6+

of teaching responsibilities among SMT members at Middleton suggests that they could draw on their knowledge as teachers in most faculties. Although no member taught humanities or technology, the head walked round the school each day, visiting classes during lesson time. Harry also visited classrooms in the course of his pupil-support work. At Drake, the teaching commitments of SMT members gave them direct contact with each faculty, except physical education and mathematics.

A contrast not apparent from the tables is that Peter was the youngest member of the Middleton SMT, whereas Kate was the oldest member of the Drake team. Disparity in age concerned Kate more than the question of gender balance within the SMT, since she felt it affected the dynamic between herself and the rest of the team by creating a social distance between them. Team support at Middleton was offered by the head's professional assistant, Jenny, responsible also for managing office staff. She was not an SMT member and did not attend team meetings. At Drake, Barbara was officially a member of the team, with responsibility for the budget, and was in charge of support staff. Ambiguities surrounded her team membership: she did not attend all SMT meetings and was not involved in the team's development programme.

Another difference between members of the two SMTs lay in the relationship with governors. At Middleton, Julia served as a teacher–governor, having been elected prior to being promoted to her present post. She occasionally referred to this capacity in SMT meetings, as when reminding colleagues that the governing body must approve a newly formulated policy on information technology.

LEADERSHIP OF THE TEAM AT MIDDLETON

Peter was the exclusive SMT member demonstrating leadership of the team through a principled, dynamic and forceful style: the major stimulus for SMT activity. His educational and managerial beliefs and values were expressed in the way he stimulated action by generating work for the team, rather than merely reacting to pressures. The principle of fairness lay behind a drive to rationalise the structure of management responsibilities and associated incentive allowances among teaching staff. He encouraged governors to examine whether heads of year should continue to receive a smaller allowance than heads of faculty, and capitalised on the governors' response by launching a review of the pupil-support system. He viewed this initiative as the proper starting point for considering pastoral responsibilities, from which the salary structure should follow. Once the issue was placed on the SMT agenda, members organised the staff consultation exercise and made the resulting decision. Similarly, the principle of promoting equal opportunities for other team members within his leadership was reflected in the parameter he set for teamwork of downplaying the distinction between deputies and allowance holders within the management hierarchy.

While the work of the team lay within parameters of acceptability to Peter, his forcefulness took the form of a task-focused approach to orchestrating team members' contribution through the SMT meetings, where he worked continually to move through the agenda. He would ask SMT colleagues to contribute, in one meeting seeking views about the content of a letter he had written to another member of staff concerning underperformance. He would often ask team members to keep an issue confidential until it was announced through the head's bulletin. This typical style was contingent, indicated by his more directive approach on the extremely rare occasions where other team members overstepped the boundaries of acceptability to Peter, whether related to teamwork or their individual work.

As team members were assembling for one meeting, he checked with Jim about pupils due to visit a local higher education institution. The teacher responsible for the trip had been called for interview elsewhere at short notice and Jim had sanctioned the trip after she reassured him the pupils would be supervised by the higher education students. Peter insisted that a teacher must accompany these pupils; he held up the meeting until he and other SMT members had arranged for a teacher to go whom he was confident could control the pupils. Peter commented afterwards how he perceived that his colleagues did not fully share his priorities because he would be accountable if anything went wrong. The incident indicates how this head's concern about external accountability was strong enough for him both to monitor colleagues' actions and, temporarily, suspend the normal parameters for teamwork through the almost unprecedented step of halting proceedings.

Other members accepted both the head's view and his authority to direct them, expressing their followership by working collaboratively with him to rectify the error. They adhered to the norm connected with management hierarchy that the head could legitimately direct their work. Within the dialectic of control inside the SMT, they used their delegated authority as managers to work synergistically towards a shared aim.

Peter used his authority as head to sustain a comprehensive overview, continually monitoring the work of the SMT through items placed on the agenda. The fast working pace of this team and its heavy agenda were not due solely to externally initiated reforms. Peter's leadership of the team was directed towards his wider concerns as a proactive leader of the staff who felt a strong need to scrutinise the boundaries of teamwork and activity throughout the institution, so as to ensure that the work of staff lay within boundaries he regarded as acceptable. The SMT was his core means of addressing these concerns.

Through his everyday actions, Peter consciously orchestrated members' contribution to teamwork. He nurtured a harmonious and productive team, partly by modelling behaviour which he wished his colleagues to embody within the culture of teamwork he promoted. His concern for team tasks was complemented by attention to the needs of colleagues. Although nothing had been said in the meeting held up by Peter, he perceived that Jim was embarrassed by his uncharacteristic slip. Peter subsequently worked behind the scenes to help Jim re-establish any credibility he might have lost within the team. He made certain that a proposal Jim was due to put forward to the SMT the following day was given top priority for typing ready for the meeting.

His colleagues were aware of being monitored by Peter, Julia noting:

> He does that very closely all the time with all of us. He does it in terms of managing the school effectively, but he also does it in terms of our welfare because it is important obviously for the good functioning of the team. Our welfare is looked after, but I'm not meaning to imply that he doesn't also care about us as people. So if somebody appears to be overloaded or if somebody doesn't meet deadlines he is immediately into it.

Ways in which Peter's actions symbolised the culture of teamwork were manifold, demonstrated in the match between his behaviour and that which he encouraged among other team members. Such actions included:

● working hard – he committed as much time to teamwork as he perceived the agenda required, often working in the evening writing papers for debate;

- setting deadlines for the team and meeting his own – he endeavoured to produce the head's bulletin for staff on time each week;
- being prepared to admit mistakes – when he discovered he had missed an opportunity to bid for an initiative which turned out to be lucrative for the successful schools he put an item on the SMT agenda to 'eat humble pie';
- valuing colleagues equally – he frequently acknowledged the efforts of individuals and the team. On the other hand, he withheld from socialising with individuals to avoid giving grounds for a perception of favouritism;
- demonstrating concern for colleagues' professional development and job satisfaction – he initiated a round of confidential interviews with each team member;
- working to promote positive relationships within the team – once when antagonism between two members arose he held a separate confidential meeting with both, encouraging them to patch up their differences;
- displaying a sense of humour and enjoying the repartee of colleagues, often sending up himself and the work of the team – in going through his written proposal for the decision on the pupil support system (a draft for the head's bulletin) he commented on the team effort to get the phrasing right: 'Have we come up with a set of responses that are suitably anodyne, anaemic, apple pie?'

As leader, Peter protected the SMT. He tried to prevent colleagues being overloaded, so keeping demand on their contribution within parameters he found acceptable. Due to the movement of staff, temporary leadership was required for the staff responsible for pupils with special needs. He asked colleagues who should pick up this leadership responsibility and, after hearing how busy they were, offered to take it on himself since he had most flexibility to shift priorities. He also protected the centrality of the team's role in managing the school. When Harry's application for early retirement was approved at LEA level, he argued with governors who wished to keep consideration of any replacement to themselves that the SMT must contribute fully to making this decision.

Peter created conditions for other members to lead on issues within the framework of the team approach. He was concerned that part of the individual responsibility of all members should be developmental, so they could take initiatives as well as respond to demands. He also invited individuals to take on other initiatives. Opportunities were available for colleagues to put their own items on the SMT agenda and to contribute ideas in team meetings, and they chaired middle-management meetings and working parties. Peter judged when to give other members the space to lead. He noted how he had kept quiet at a difficult middle-management meeting because he believed he should trust his SMT colleagues to manage the situation for themselves, and that they had performed very competently. Here, power was expressed through non-intervention to empower other SMT members.

Although we did not observe other members displaying leadership of the team, we were aware from the interviews in the first phase of the research that when Peter had tried to persuade SMT colleagues to rotate the chair (a key means of orchestrating team members' contributions to teamwork) they had argued strongly against doing so. They had expressed the persuasive side of team followership, making sure that Peter remained the sole leader of the team. The already strong emphasis on leadership of the SMT at Middleton, because of the degree to which Peter stimulated action, was therefore reinforced by other members.

LEADERSHIP OF THE TEAM AT DRAKE

We mentioned earlier how the Drake SMT was developing rapidly. Kate had been building the team over the six years since she had taken up headship of the school. The appointment of Marian meant that in Kate's eyes the team was complete. She had brought together people with different but complementary skills and personalities to create a balanced team within which she could enact her evolving interpretation of headship. She had sought to develop a style as head that contrasted both with her predecessor's and her own in her previous school ('where I was fairly autocratic'). The changing educational climate encouraged her to adopt a team approach where problems were shared and decisions were the outcome of consensus. By the time of Marian's appointment, Kate had evolved a way of leading the team based on commitment to delegation and development, against a backcloth of her own very orderly and methodical approach to managing. In the face of multiple change the team approach for her was 'therapeutic and a safety valve; if there is anything on my mind I share it with them'. It was for her a high gain strategy inevitably accompanied by anxieties or high strain of the sort that more directive heads are unlikely to encounter.

Some anxieties came from the integrity and consistency of her style which made her unwilling to compromise on her interpretation of delegation. She led the team by setting a key parameter: encouraging equal contribution of all team members, including herself, and leaving each person to get on (and express leadership within the team on particular issues) once his or her area of responsibility had been decided. For Kate, continual close monitoring would deny the authenticity of the delegation, although she saw as essential her part in getting right the match between people and tasks. Her values connected with delegation led her to withhold from scrutinising the boundaries of other members' work: a form of non-intervention to empower others.

Kate used her leadership position to allocate tasks according to individual talents and interest and, most importantly, according to what was in the best interest of the school. It was the main area in which individual team members liaised directly with the head rather than exploring issues as a team. As a result, it was the only area where it was acknowledged that she had the sole overview and greatest authority. She gave Marian responsibility for staff development as part of her personnel function and, later, resisted Marian's attempt to drop cover duties and take over some of Derek's curriculum tasks, on the grounds that everyone in the team had to do humdrum tasks. She included herself, taking responsibility for the environment and offering herself as first call for cover whenever she was available. This arrangement was part of her strategy for acknowledging the value of equal contribution, including her own, and protecting team colleagues from overload.

In working out the boundaries of her leadership of the team and team membership roles, her concern was that:

> If it is right in terms of team management for the head to give up some autonomy, at what point on a continuum do you actually have to stop and think, 'I will actually have delegated everything and I will have become the sort of cypher head who is not really doing any real job at all'? At what point does the good team manager become the person who has off-loaded all the work and become a rather useless passenger? Could the team operate just as well without me? If I was run over by a bus tomorrow, how far would it be noticed?

Kate's attempt to be a team member and honour the principle of equal contribution did not always sit easily with her awareness that 'the buck does stop with me'. Although she gave team members continuous opportunities to take over leadership on various issues, and encouraged them to chair other management meetings, she retained the right to chair SMT meetings. She could retain some control through the chair by delimiting the boundaries of team decisions, which she was ultimately responsible for implementing.

At the same time she showed herself fully committed to consensual decision making, both in her style of chairing and her willingness to go along with SMT decisions emerging in this way. Consistent with her style around the school, she chaired the meetings quietly and efficiently: creating space for everyone's contribution and rarely giving precedence to her own. Other members were responsible for leadership within the team on most issues, with Kate coming in usually after everyone had responded, reacting to and summarising what had been said, rather than pushing the discussion along new avenues. Her actions reflected her belief that the school's goals and necessary action for achieving them should be the outcome of joint effort. She was willing to trade some loss of autonomy as head, for the opportunity teamwork provided to share worries and problems: despite her concern to extend ability setting in the school, Kate accepted the consensus of other SMT members that it was not appropriate.

She sought colleagues' acceptance, within the culture of teamwork, of the value she placed on sharing. Only on rare occasions did she seek to impose her view. When Drake appeared to be in danger of attracting fewer pupils than its competitor school, she insisted on confronting staff with the urgency of the situation. Standing apart from the team in this way was unusual. It contrasted with her behaviour as formal leader of the team that symbolised the beliefs and values she wanted her team colleagues to accept. Her conception of teamwork made interventionist strategies inappropriate. She chose to support and to create space for colleagues to fulfil their delegated responsibilities by:

- first asking for rather than giving, ideas on how to go forward – although responsible for premises, she encouraged a decision about alternative uses of space to emerge from each team member's identification of what was feasible and desirable;

- refusing to use divide and rule strategies or pre-meeting discussions to influence the outcomes of team decisions, because she wished to empower all team members equally – she kept nothing off the agenda, to which all contributed, and shared information so that all had ownership of decisions to be made;
- listening attentively to others' contributions and praising their efforts;
- encouraging team members to reflect longer on important issues, rather than reach hasty decisions – proposals to move away from integrated humanities to a single-subject arts curriculum generated heated discussion and Kate suggested giving the existing scheme more time before condemning it;
- reminding other members that, although they needed to have arrived at a clear joint view on issues, other staff should not feel they were being presented with decisions already made;
- standing back or sharing tasks to give team colleagues space for development – Kate shared with Marian the professional development interviews with all staff that she had previously done herself;
- allowing discussions to become heated but setting boundaries on open expression of conflict.

Through her own performance in the team, Kate modelled behaviour she hoped others would adopt: honesty, trust, respect for the value of all contributions, and reaching decisions through quiet reflection. She used her authority in setting parameters for teamwork that ensured all members had adequate space to carry out their responsibilities effectively, and identified herself as an equal member by giving her own views equal weight with others', and refraining from defining a framework for discussions. Above all, Kate was continually reflective about her own performance in the team.

Her attempt to express both leadership of the team and team-membership roles by playing down aspects of the former inevitably had an impact on her own and others' perceptions of her as leader of the school. Making the professional development interviews her sole responsibility, again was her acknowledgement of the need to reassert a school-leader identity separate from that of SMT leader.

TEAM MEMBERSHIP AT MIDDLETON

The cohesiveness of the SMT at Middleton reflected a strong culture of teamwork where leadership of the team and team membership were complementary, with most interaction between SMT members centred on the head. There was a conspicuous lack of evidence to support a contrary interpretation, such as the existence of enduring coalitions between factions or any disruptive action (say, refusing to contribute to debate). Team members other than the head reported their satisfaction with the way he decided unilaterally what to exclude from the SMT agenda. He would often inform them about tasks he was keeping for himself and his rationale for so doing.

Although at times debate was heated, team members generally used their delegated authority and influence to realise the potential for synergy. Peter's team colleagues contributed as equals in SMT meetings, helping to build the 'whole school awareness' he advocated in sustaining an overview of the internal workings of the school. They employed this level of awareness in working towards decisions. At one meeting Peter circulated his draft of the head's bulletin with an account of an SMT decision taken after consultation with staff over whether to continue with the timetable based on a thirty-five period week. All members vetted the proposal, assessing likely staff responses to the content and phrasing of the account to make sure the statement was unambiguous and represented their collective agreement.

Individuals also employed diverse expertise and knowledge, including:

- management responsibility – Jim pointed to implications of buying more computer hardware for the LMS budget;
- faculty membership – Harry suggested that a way of increasing the amount of time for science in the curriculum was to increase the human biology taught within the arts faculty under sports studies;
- informal contact with staff – Julia reported on how exhausted staff were towards the end of term;
- recollection of the institutional history – Colin highlighted the importance of arranging in-service training for staff if new information technology was introduced, referring to his past experience of coordinating this area.

Nick's commitment to making an equal contribution was illustrated when he could not attend the SMT meeting to reach a decision on the review of the pupil-support system. He wrote a paper with suggestions which were discussed in his absence within the decision-making process. There was unified commitment to guarding against individuals being unduly influenced when lobbied by other staff. During one SMT meeting, three members reported being approached by a teacher who asked them to approve a letter to parents. It became evident that, when each person refused in accordance with a previously agreed party line communicated to the teacher, the latter went to the next person with the same request. SMT members shared a perception that the teacher had tried to manipulate them. (On our definition of manipulation, the teacher's action was manipulative since its intention was not made explicit. From the perspective of SMT members it was illegitimate.)

Individuals took opportunities to lead on particular issues, Peter offering to take on implementation of staff appraisal. Other members led on matters related to individual responsibility, as where Julia and Harry organised the in-service training day to review the pupil-support system. Initiatives offered to anyone willing to volunteer included the 'summer school', taking place of the normal timetable for a week, which Jim organised. Where other members led, Peter monitored their work through progress reports appearing as SMT agenda items.

He contributed as an equal with his team colleagues to a relatively small degree, adding to the pool of knowledge that made up the shared overview and to the flow of ideas in debate. However his forceful approach to chairing, coupled with close monitoring, meant that he made most proposals for decisions and put most items on to the agenda. There was a strong element of followership in other members' behaviour both because of the extent of Peter's behaviour in leading the team and because they wanted him to lead. The effect was to reinforce his differential status within the management hierarchy. Other members accepted his interpretation of headship and had come to trust him to do the job effectively.

For several weeks, Nick experienced problems in negotiating with other staff over curriculum and staffing plans for the following year. The head spoke confidentially with him, suggesting he consult each middle manager with a curriculum coordination responsibility. Nick commented afterwards: 'He said it in a nice way but he made his intentions clear and it also helped my way forward.' Nick displayed followership in being ready to receive the head's guidance.

Conversely, other SMT members used their influence occasionally to block Peter's attempts to share leadership on certain issues. Nick demonstrated how humour could be used to forestall unwanted change in the process of teamwork:

> [Peter] actually tries to move the chairs in the room and we go round and say, 'Don't tell me any of these trendy management theories, leave it alone – I like sitting in my corner!' Or else if he changes it around too much we'll say, 'Ah, been on a course then?'

Peter reported at one SMT meeting how several staff had been late for pupil registration and he had spoken to them individually. He asked what strategy the team should adopt as he did not wish to be perceived as the only person chivvying these teachers. Nick argued that Peter should continue to chase up staff for the week and then inform the SMT how well this strategy had worked. Peter accepted the task.

We noted above how Peter continually monitored other SMT members and the performance of the team as a whole, in contrast to his colleagues. Their monitoring was limited largely to where others' work had implications for their individual management responsibility. Colin checked Nick's work on timetabling as it had consequences for his responsibility for arranging cover. Equally, Colin monitored Peter, reminding him of tasks he had agreed to do which were linked with Colin's work.

Jim indicated how the value of retaining some autonomy set a limit to the amount of monitoring that would be acceptable: 'We do like our individual patch which is individual to us. And one wants to be left to some extent to get on with it.' Close monitoring by Peter was legitimated for other team members because of his position in the management hierarchy.

Mutual support was freely given within the team. Nick and Colin volunteered to write a proposal on arrangements for the first day of term when it transpired that Nick was pressed for time. However, members other than the head acknowledged others' efforts only on rare occasions, as when Julia publicly thanked Peter and Harry for their inputs to the in-service training day on the pupil-support system.

Each team member made a unique contribution according to personality and professional values. Nick often cracked jokes, providing relief from the seriousness of the SMT's work. Julia was very aware of gender issues for staff and ready to challenge colleagues. She had arranged for staff without management responsibility to lead each discussion group during the review of pupil support. Team members subsequently discussed how to collate the ideas of each group without managerial bias introduced by the SMT. It was suggested that the group leaders be asked to do the collating work, and Colin noted that they were all women. Julia pointed out that the collating group was entirely female because there was 'a handful of men and a load of women' without management responsibility. (Peter responded by acknowledging the unacceptability of this situation in a school committed to promoting equal opportunities for staff.)

The strength of the culture of teamwork was demonstrated when Peter was out of school. As the longest serving deputy who had been acting head, Jim generally deputised, taking the chair at SMT meetings after being briefed by Peter. Their approaches to chairing were entirely consistent; Jim even upstaged Peter's ceremonial offering of food by providing chocolate biscuits, quipping that they were 'a cut above the norm'. Recommendations were made for discussion with the head, as opposed to taking decisions.

Both such meetings we observed were terminated by an emergency. The first time pupils set off the school fire alarm and SMT members went through the usual procedure, including the fire drill and search to identify culprits. The second time a secretary interrupted the meeting to state that a person with a young voice had telephoned, saying that there were two bombs in the school and they had an hour to vacate the premises. In similar situations previously, Peter had always responded to such a threat. Jim, as acting head for the day, was concerned to follow the procedure that the head would have implemented although he guessed it was almost certainly a hoax. Team members agreed that they they should err on the side of caution. Nick suggested staff should be warned, a fire drill called in half an hour's time, and the police informed. The drill was duly implemented. No bomb was found (nor was the culprit).

TEAM MEMBERSHIP AT DRAKE

This SMT demonstrated a cohesive culture of teamwork based on a shared commitment to working within parameters determined by the head and influenced by other members. Without these parameters, including providing considerable space for individuals to lead within the team, it is unlikely that members other than Kate and Marian would have chosen teamwork. Both Derek and Greg saw themselves primarily as individualists who preferred to carry out responsibilities in their own time and in their own way. Philip was less reluctant about working in a group but sometimes questioned the time-consuming nature of consensus decision making. Yet all three had discovered benefits in teamwork that outweighed their reservations and were committed to making it operate as they perceived the head wished. Only Marian, who had served in a very different SMT in her previous school, had no doubts about the superiority of teamwork in managing a school. She threw herself into the team wholeheartedly, adapting her personal style where necessary to work within the existing culture of teamwork and seeking opportunities (as we show in Chapter 8) to transform it.

The culture of teamwork at Drake was shaped by the head, though not centered on her. Her response to Marian's comment on joining the team regarding how lucky she was to have a collection of such good people was 'there's no luck in it. I've spent a long time on this'. Discussions were sometimes heated, but conflict was generally dealt with outside meetings by the people concerned. All members felt free to say what they wanted and to challenge when appropriate, but Kate would judge the point at which conflict needed to have the lid put on, to bubble outside. After one occasion when Greg challenged her, she pointed out her annoyance, not at the challenge itself, but at his use of the word 'absurd'. He commented afterwards on his tendency 'to go over the top' and his lack of training as a manager, but Kate's rebuke had the effect of 'shutting me up for two weeks'.

Team members were generally polite with each other; they worked well together professionally but kept their private lives apart. Other than Marian, SMT members were relieved that Kate never encouraged socialising as a team outside school. In Philip's view:

> One of the worst things that could happen to me if the head was run over by a bus or left would be someone coming in who wanted to make the team a big social event.

There was great respect for the parameters for teamwork set by Kate and for each person's contribution. In common with Middleton, there were no enduring factions or refusals to participate fully. Major decisions were to be taken by everybody, and all members accepted the need to make concessions for each other's personality type and preferences if they were to operate effectively as a team. They accepted too the need to compromise for the sake of consensus.

The experience could be painful, made more so by Kate's insistence on being a co-member, rather than leader, at points where agreement on a decision was not readily forthcoming. A minor clash occurred when Philip was initially uncomfortable with a decision about who should attend the annual school review. Since his priority was continuity of teaching, he felt that he should be fetched when needed rather than freed for the whole day. Derek disagreed, arguing that the status of the review demanded Philip's full attendance. After a lively discussion about whether pupils were more important than the review, Philip's point was conceded and cover arrangements made. In Kate's view the decision was reached by the group: 'I did not seek to be influential. It moved to a position where Derek was outnumbered.' Once he recognised the balance of opinion was going a particular way, Derek accepted the decision.

Resolutions were not so easily reached on issues such as the extent of an individual's time commitment to liaising with primary schools. Kate had created an opportunity for Marian to lead on this issue, but Derek was unhappy with the proposed strategy. Compromise was unacceptable and Kate was forced to take a firm line, creating temporarily some negative feelings which were not expressed openly in the team. The incident suggests to us that other members were ambivalent about whether the head should use her authority within the management hierarchy to revoke temporarily their delegated authority to make an equal contribution to the decision. Yet Kate had chosen this course of action only when colleagues, unusually, could not accept the norm of seeking compromise that was one of the parameters she set for teamwork. Here she had become aware that colleagues threatened to step beyond the boundaries of acceptability to her, and expressed leadership of the team in ensuring that they did not do so.

A culture of teamwork is delineated by transgressions of its boundaries. Ill feeling as a result of unacceptable strategies is one example. In developing a strategy for primary school liaison, Derek felt the team was 'shooting from the hip', a style that he perceived was encouraged by Marian and which he questioned. It left the SMT particularly vulnerable if members had not worked out an agreed strategy before making a public announcement. Philip recalled his blunder in repeating to other staff plans discussed within the SMT for moving to a thirty period week:

> I didn't realise we were on a three line whip. We learned from that that if there's a time when we have to act cohesively then someone has got to say it. Generally I don't think there is a party line. There is a sort of trust among us.

Here, a team norm about stating when something was confidential was made explicit after the boundary had unwittingly been overstepped.

Maintaining a united front constituted another team norm, necessitating some changes in personal style. Philip was uncomfortable with establishing a party line before going public: 'It's a bit like having to learn your lines before a play. I prefer to ad lib.' Kate, however, was uncompromising in her view that allowance holders in the SMT (like Peter) owed their first allegiance to it:

> If they have taken the decision to accept the offer to become part of the SMT and of course the money that goes with it, then they have to accept the less comfortable bits as well.

Against this background of respect, trust and politeness, members worked to create the synergy of which teams are capable. Separate responsibilities involved them in interactions with others outside the team or one or more individuals within it, but on any issue they always came together eventually to share progress and provide the information base for decision making. Derek gave as an example of the group's changing style the proposal to adopt the thirty period week:

> The first time I tried to bring about change it didn't go through, maybe because it was too new. The following year the SMT took a conscious decision

to be more open, so this time the heads of faculty were invited to come up with changes themselves, so that they would both see the difficulties involved but also feel ownership of the decisions taken. During that process we [SMT members] had hammered out the sense of direction that we wanted, kept an eye on the process and tried to guide it in that direction. In other words, it wasn't delegated entirely, but a lot of responsibility for decision making was left to those responsible for implementing the outcomes. And the scheme they [heads of faculty] came up with was the one implemented.

Four factors operated here: Derek's perception of his responsibility for managing the timetable and taking a lead on the issue; team agreement to involve middle managers more in decisions affecting them; team members' joint effort to agree a strategy for reorganising the week; and the head's contribution as a member, having delegated leadership on this issue to Derek. All members chaired working parties whose outcomes they would present to the team, leading on the discussion to arrive at decisions. They were all kept fully informed and were involved in all aspects of the school, thereby sustaining a shared whole-school awareness.

Greg would sometimes feed in staff discontent with SMT decisions, which members would then reconsider. All members had to make daily decisions about what was and was not team business, particularly when staff pressurised them for immediate responses. Marian's criterion as to whether something was a team issue was whether it would be useful and appropriate to discuss it within the SMT. This view meant that some things were seen to happen that had not been taken to the team, an indication in Marian's eyes that the team approach was not yet fully developed. Greg preferred doing some of his business outside SMT meetings as a way of stopping them being too lengthy.

The potential for synergy depended on the ability of team members to use each other's knowledge and expertise. Marian was considered to be expert on appraisal as a result of her previous school experience, though her tendency to draw on it at times grated on members whose histories were largely related to Drake. Although an SMT member, Philip, owing to his twenty years' experience on the school staff, still had one foot in the staffroom and regularly fed back staff concerns to the team. Faculty membership enabled each person to contribute subject specialism concerns, although members tried to separate their management and subject commitments at team meetings.

A barrier to equal contribution of all members was the impact of lower status within the management hierarchy upon Greg and Philip. Although Kate had worked to share team membership and created conditions for widespread leadership within the team, the allowance holders saw themselves (and were perceived by others) sometimes as followers. They accessed their delegated authority to make an equal contribution to teamwork but also perceived the management hierarchy as legitimately inhibiting them. They had formal line management accountability to Marian and Derek. When the SMT was present at staff meetings, they sat separately from the head and two deputies. They did not attend governors' meetings and there were different expectations about their attendance at evening events.

Philip shared Marian's closeness to other staff but they saw him as having less influence in the team. While a line management approach to appraisal was acceptable, team members knew that some people would be less happy with the allowance holders as their appraisers, even though they were SMT members. Greg noted that, for other staff, 'we're in parentheses'. Philip and Greg were conscious of their 'poacher turned gamekeeper' identity and sometimes withheld from contributing as a result. Occasionally aware of being excluded from an SMT discussion or, rarely, a decision, they were ambivalent whether the 'senior management team in the team' should allow this situation to occur. Greg wished to be kept informed only on school-wide issues. Philip also referred to a 'senior team':

> I do feel I'm on the third tier, not only from the point of view of pay and in a way I'm quite happy to still be there. I'm still governed by 1,265 hours. They're not.

The freedom he was left by his conditions of service, to choose when to be involved, counterbalanced any occasional sense of a less than equal place in the team. Although both he and Greg worked well in excess of 1,265 hours, they welcomed not having to attend events that did not directly concern them. Within the dialectic of control in the team, the allowance holders were constrained by the hierarchy built into its structure but also referred to it in finding room to manoeuvre when they wished to limit their contribution.

All members took opportunities to lead on particular issues and gave mutual support. Kate was explicit about not wanting to trespass on Marian's responsibility for setting up appraisal and, while she requested Derek and Marian to attempt to develop heads of year into a pastoral team, she did not otherwise intervene. Similarly Greg and Philip led on their areas. Supporting leadership did not necessarily mean going along with individuals' proposals and strategies, which would still be subject to the same SMT scrutiny that preceded consensus decision making.

An emerging pattern as the team developed was an extension of sharing leadership within the team on the same issue, not only by Kate but also by other members who had previously led individually. Formerly Derek had met with each head of faculty to review progress in his or her contribution to the school development plan. His proposal was accepted that all SMT members (except Kate) should be involved in the discussions as they had an interest in faculty proposals. As a result they all felt better informed when meeting to finalise details of the school development plan.

There was less emphasis on monitoring than at Middleton. Monitoring individual SMT members' performance was shared and rarely made explicit. Generally individuals were left to get on with their responsibilities on their own. The structured team development programme provided an opportunity to scrutinise the performance of the group as a whole.

A primary benefit in working as a team was the mutual support colleagues provided both in accomplishing tasks and dealing with problems. Through their actions each recognised others' unique contributions, taking care not to overstep boundaries of individual job responsibilities while using the team meetings to share and resolve concerns arising from them. It was not apparent that any of the unique contributions were related to gender. Derek and Philip shared similar styles of interaction with Kate and Marian respectively who, in turn, differed sharply from each other. Kate and her three male colleagues were happy to delegate equal-opportunities concerns to Marian, who never raised them in team meetings. The culture of teamwork can perhaps be described as a 'separate togetherness' in which the style of their willing collaboration reflected the strength of their individual contributions.

TEAM SUPPORT AT MIDDLETON

Support for SMT members from office staff varied with individuals' management responsibility. Jim worked with the bursar on the school budget and one secretary worked with Harry so that he could make a rapid response where necessary in his pupil-support work. Other team members worked through Jenny, the office manager.

As Peter's professional assistant, she worked closely with him in a managerial capacity which belied her formal status, helping to sustain smooth links between him and his SMT colleagues. Peter held a weekly briefing meeting with Jenny and also communicated during the day. Jenny was highly respected throughout the team, members other than the head assuming that she shared many confidences with Peter. They approved of her working relationship with the head and her integrity in respecting confidences. She was regarded as a facilitator for the SMT, Nick remarking:

> She's almost like a minister without portfolio; she becomes part of the school management team without actually sitting in on all of the meetings. Jenny has access, I imagine, to really all the material that the head has. Because of her personality and how she carries out her professional job it doesn't threaten anybody . . . I am sure she would have the complete confidence of the group [the SMT] without it ever being questioned.

Team members appreciated her understanding of school management which enabled her to support their individual work effectively. Julia perceived that she was underpaid for the level of work she had proved herself capable of doing, commenting: 'However complex the task I give her she is able to understand it. She has the sort of whole-school perspective of a deputy head.' This level of awareness derived significantly from the confidential dialogue between herself and Peter. As professional assistant, Jenny gave leadership support to the head as his confidante on professional matters, extending to the work of the SMT. Colin assumed that she worked in this way, commenting that Peter could not have such support from another SMT member because it would be divisive to favour one person in the team. Jenny's contribution complemented ways in which members other than the head operated in the SMT, including:

- acting as a sounding board for Peter's ideas – he would check out first thoughts before taking them to the rest of the SMT;

- listening to Peter's concerns about staff, including SMT members, offering her own ideas and taking initiatives in this area – when Peter asked her to type up a draft summary of the development concerns and aspirations of SMT members, he had excluded his own (which he had discussed with her). She put them in, suggesting that, to be fair, all team members' concerns should be shared;
- showing interest in Peter's professional development – when he mentioned his intention to interview SMT colleagues she asked who was doing the same for him;
- monitoring and offering both criticism and acknowledgement of his work;
- giving moral support – he could let off steam about frustrations that were not shared within the SMT;
- acting as a buffer between staff, outsiders such as parents, and the head – individuals would tell her things about which they wished Peter to be informed but did not want to address face to face. Equally, she acted as Peter's ambassador, once being asked to explain to a teacher why he had been unable to keep his promise to attend an assembly;
- facilitating the smooth operation of the SMT – she arranged for members other than the head to have access to Peter whenever necessary. She frequently saved them waiting because she was aware of his correspondence and current activities and could tell them what they needed to know;
- acting as clerk to the governors, facilitating Peter's work with the governing body.

Jenny's team support work was complex. Within the management hierarchy her duty was to support the head as his professional assistant and all members through management of office staff. Like SMT members she also contributed as an equal, but in a different arena: through her confidential dialogue with Peter, and especially her input to maintaining positive staff relationships and her monitoring of his work.

Her management responsibility gave her authority in respect of support staff and her close working relationship with the head gave her considerable influence in the school. She employed this power synergistically to facilitate the work of both the head and other SMT members. While not officially a member of the team, the professional beliefs and values she expressed through her actions were consistent with the SMT culture of teamwork. We suggest she played a significant part in sustaining the culture on which synergy within the team depended. The head had empowered her; in turn, she empowered the SMT. Mutual empowerment within the dialectic of control between head, other members of the SMT, and professional assistant resulted when all were working towards congruent ends.

TEAM SUPPORT AT DRAKE

The nature of team support at Drake challenged the notion of equal contribution that underpins teamwork in two ways. First, Kate had her own 'head's secretary', a title Jean (the incumbent) described as having an archaic ring. Team members were unaware of the issue of its appropriateness ever having been discussed in the SMT. She was responsible for all Kate's administrative needs but also supported the two deputies. Both her title and her tasks thereby contributed to others' perceptions of hierarchy within the team, unlike at Middleton where Jenny provided support for all team members' individual work. Kate's style also set parameters for Jean's involvement in any discussions of team matters, confining it mainly to business:

> Although she will sometimes make comments off the cuff that would be very confidential, she wouldn't sit me down and talk things through. She doesn't use me as a sounding board, nor do other members of the team.

When Kate was asked how she saw Jean's role in relation to the SMT, she commented 'I can't imagine how the head's secretary would have a role'.

As bursar, Barbara was a team member, and so potentially entitled to make an equal contribution. Yet her role was fraught with ambiguities, raising the question: when is a team member not a team member? Although she was counted as being in the team, the extent of her participation was bounded by both her own and other members' interpretation of her position. All other team members had access to the support staff whom she managed, apart from Jean. Barbara's SMT brief was to work with Kate on financial matters (with little involvement of other team members) and contribute to team decision making. Unlike other team members, she chose not to attend SMT meetings concerned with issues where she could contribute little, or which did not affect her areas of responsibility. She occasionally excluded herself and at times felt excluded:

> I am part of the group; I am referred to on some items, obviously; I have expertise in quite a few areas but I don't think some of the other members of the team would even ask me questions about some of the things because in a sense I feel that, although I am there, they don't really include me in it.

Her presence on the SMT was the result of the previous head's intention to give status to her bursar's role. In developing her own team, Kate supported Barbara's continued membership. Barbara felt she had proved her worth to Kate and that they had developed a partnership on financial matters that was mutually supportive. Her one area of substantive responsibility, finances, combined with overall responsibility for managing office staff, gave her less involvement in whole-school matters. She was still expected to contribute to SMT decisions. Inevitably, because of the frequency of meetings between Kate and Barbara and their control over financial information, she was separated from other team members. Concern at the potential exclusion of the rest of the SMT from financial decisions only became apparent when the school was allocated its own LMS budget. Before that:

> In terms of finances, staff will either come to me or go directly to the head. She will always check with me first though, before she gives any decision to a member of staff on financial issues. On the whole, staff are unlikely to go to

anyone else on the team regarding financial matters. They might mention it to a deputy who might then bring it up at a meeting but in the end it wouldn't be for the deputy to make a decision. It would be up to myself and the head.

Initially their interaction was formal, influenced both by Kate's style and Barbara's respect for her as leader, but 'as I got to know her we could talk more freely'. She found it difficult to call the head Kate in any group, and preferred to use Mrs Smith or her title. She did not in any way consider herself Kate's confidante. Kate agreed that her self-contained nature precluded anyone from that role although on occasions 'I might have a word with Barbara who is utterly professional and who wouldn't reveal confidences'.

Barbara's support for the team was therefore focused on Kate and confined to her area of responsibility. She was constrained as an equal contributor by her limited knowledge of curriculum, and her concern that not all other members saw her presence as legitimate. On the other hand, when she needed to influence the team she could be assertive:

> When the SMT wanted pupils to sign in and out we talked it through in the office and came up with a system we thought we could manage. Then I was quite firm with the team about how we were going to do it and they accepted it. As it was something that had come up in the team I didn't go to Kate first but fed back to the whole team.

Her language reflects her ambivalence; sometimes the team are 'we', sometimes 'they'. Other SMT members never referred to the team as 'they'.

Unlike other team members, she felt relatively isolated in her job because she alone had the necessary knowledge. She had little sense of other members trying to shape how she did her job, perceiving that she had sole influence on her sphere of responsibility in contrast to team colleagues.

Barbara emerged as someone who was both a member of the team and outside it; who at times used influence to exclude herself but also felt excluded. Issues surrounding her contribution both to team process and to her areas of responsibility were dealt with mainly either between her and Kate, or when she was not present.

DIVERSITY, COMPLEMENTARITY AND SYNERGY

We observed both teams to operate smoothly, most of the time, in working through the agenda set by their members, a finding consistent with the view widespread among team members and others that the SMTs were quite or very effective. The different constellation of individual contributions to teamwork in the two SMTs suggests that there is unlikely to be one best way of achieving synergy. A significant characteristic of each constellation was the *complementarity* of the patterns of behaviour expressed within individual team roles (echoing Belbin's view of team roles as complementary).

At Middleton, the considerable amount of activity through which the head displayed leadership of the team was complemented by team membership

among SMT colleagues which included an equally strong element of followership within the team. Part of the behaviour expressing followership was directed towards persuading the head to remain the exclusive team leader. The
head's leadership of the team covered both setting parameters for teamwork
and close attention to their boundaries, to safeguard against the actions of
other members falling outside the limits of acceptability to him. His conception
of delegation required action within the role of leadership of the team to
monitor the performance of those to whom responsibilities were delegated.

A different constellation of individual team roles was evident at Drake. A
lower proportion of the head's behaviour expressed leadership of the team,
and consequently less followership within the team was evident. Her own
behaviour emphasised team membership in contributing equally with other
members. Team membership expressed by members other than the head included a strong element of leadership within the team on particular issues,
running to development of the team itself. In setting parameters for teamwork,
the head put her belief into effect that delegation of responsibilities should not
include close monitoring of colleagues' performance. She assumed that they
would operate within her parameters and so did not seek the safeguard of
continually scrutinising their boundaries closely.

There was also a contrast in team support roles. At Middleton, the professional assistant was almost in the team, but not quite. She gave assistance to
the head in his exclusive role expressing leadership of the team, but did not
participate in SMT decision making. At Drake, the senior administrative officer was in the SMT, but only just. She mainly assisted the head within her
individual responsibility for LMS, and her contribution to team decisions was
largely restricted to financial implications. In both cases, team support was a
valued extension to the roles expressed within the teams.

The evidence of these two SMTs leads us to speculate that *complementarity*
between the individual team roles of team leadership and team membership
could prove more important for achieving synergy in SMTs than, say, a particular pattern of behaviour within either of these team roles. Complementary
individual contributions were reflected in SMT meetings (where most teamwork took place), which we explore next.

6

SMT Meetings – the Central Forum for Teamwork

At the heart of the team approach adopted in Middleton and Drake lay regular SMT meetings: the major setting where all team members engaged face to face in joint work within a largely private arena. Earlier we discussed how interviews (and brief observations) in the initial case studies indicated the importance of SMT meetings as a means of sustaining an overview, making decisions connected with policies, and offering mutual support. Meetings not only enabled joint work to be conducted; they also constituted the key ritual through which the culture of teamwork was developed and reinforced.

Here we take up the inside story, offering examples of interaction drawn from our observation of team meetings. We focus on how their process reflected different interpretations of teamwork and their content reflected the role of the SMT. First, we examine the meeting process, building on the account of individual contributions to teamwork in the previous chapter. Although the aspects of the process of meetings varied there was a clear pattern. Second, we explore how this process was directed towards a range of management issues: the aggregate of what SMT members perceived to be priorities in fulfilling their shared role. We note how the SMT agenda consisted of a flow of items whose profile continually evolved as the team dealt with some business while new business emerged. Lastly, we look briefly at interaction within one team when working towards an example of a major decision, a key occasion when individuals could contribute as equals.

THE MEETING PROCESS AT MIDDLETON

The two weekly SMT meetings were scheduled a day apart. The agenda for both meetings was typically compiled between the Thursday meeting of one week and the Wednesday meeting of the next. This arrangement provided some flexibility as items which were not addressed in the first meeting could be carried over to the following day. It also allowed SMT members to mull over proposals prior to finalising a decision. After spending some time considering who should be invited to serve on a working party to develop an assessment policy for the school, and which team member should lead it, Peter suggested that SMT members should leave the discussion, 'sleep on it', and finalise their decisions at the meeting the next afternoon.

Peter's chairing role was a key means by which he provided leadership of the team, with the approval of other SMT members. Chairing encompassed writing the agenda, taking responsibility for chairing the meeting itself, and publishing a record of decisions or other statements that SMT members wished to disseminate through the head's bulletin to all staff. The agenda was generally circulated to SMT members the day before a meeting, consisting of items put forward by Peter alongside a few supplied by colleagues. He decided which items it was the highest priority to address and put one or two asterisks beside them. He sometimes wrote people's initials beside items he expected them to introduce. Occasionally a paper he or a colleague had written accompanied the agenda or was tabled at the meeting.

Team members assembled in Peter's office, choosing to sit in the same place each time, while he served coffee or tea. Julia was occasionally delayed for a few minutes by problems connected with her teaching role. Once she commented that four English faculty staff were absent, leaving her to ensure that the work of the faculty went as smoothly as possible. Julia's teaching load, which was the heaviest of all team members, appeared to pose a larger constraint on her managerial work than that of the others (a disparity which was later addressed in the team restructuring exercise).

Members used the opportunity to talk informally about issues connected with their individual management tasks or exchanged jokes until Peter started the proceedings. He led the team from the chair, taking responsibility for checking out the maximum duration of meetings which went on after the end of the teaching day, selecting the order of items, setting the normally brisk pace of the meeting and timekeeping. Typical actions in working through the agenda included:

- introducing an item or asking others to do so – he asked individuals who were due to chair a middle-management meeting to report on progress with preparation;
- putting forward a procedure for tackling complex items, especially those relating to a major decision – Peter asked colleagues to go systematically through his draft proposal for a decision on the review of the pupil-support system, accepted their wish to look at particular parts of it but, after a few minutes of inconclusive discussion, insisted on following the procedure;
- keeping colleagues to task if in his view humour became too prolonged or the discussion became unproductive – he intervened to curtail a debate between Julia and Colin over costing the release time for staff who were to collate the outcome of the in-service training day on pupil support;

- very occasionally blocking off suggestions which threatened to divert attention from priorities he had established within the agenda – towards the end of a Wednesday meeting when Jim reminded Peter that they had not yet discussed arrangements for planning the summer school (a priority for him), Peter deferred the item to the meeting next day;
- inviting team members to state a view in checking their agreement on a decision or in sharing perceptions – he asked each colleague, in turn, to evaluate the in-service training day on the pupil-support system;
- summarising the debate – when the SMT had met the information technology (IT) coordinator to discuss the draft IT policy, Peter made a concluding statement of each individual's comments and concerns;
- publicly acknowledging colleagues' contributions – he thanked Colin for his skilful chairing of a middle-management meeting;
- putting forward proposals to which others could respond – he suggested that the SMT met the IT coordinator a second time to finalise the IT policy and that relevant information was given at the next meeting of middle managers;
- stating when debate on an item was to remain confidential within the SMT or suggesting an SMT 'party line' where information was to be made public – often the account to be published in the head's bulletin.

Peter asked colleagues to supply material for the head's bulletin and after meetings wrote an account where he had led on particular items. He asked other SMT members to check anything he had written which might be contentious. If necessary to get through the agenda, he would occasionally call an extra SMT meeting before or after the school day.

In his chairing role, Peter operated within the boundaries of the parameters for teamwork he had established within the team. The high degree to which these parameters were accepted within the culture of teamwork was indicated by the fact that it was extremely rare for an individual to attempt to step outside them. We observed one incident which indicates how the culture of teamwork was extensive but still limited, and a product of ongoing negotiation between all members of the SMT.

During a discussion about the temporary leadership of staff responsible for pupils with special needs, Peter had argued that a member of the SMT should take on this role. Nick pressed for the staff concerned to be consulted about selecting their own leader although they had earlier requested that the decision be made by senior staff. Julia and Colin supported the head's view but no one volunteered to do the job. Peter then proposed that he should do it. Nick responded by noting that the leader of the team was accepting a task which he should be delegating. He was faced with compromising his stated view in order to reach a working consensus unless the ground rules for SMT decision making were changed. Nick suggested that the SMT should hold a vote on Peter's proposal. A majority decision would enable him to stick to his view, even if he lost the vote. However, Julia immediately replied, 'We don't have votes here!' Voting lay outside the normal parameters for SMT decision making and we interpret Julia to have used her influence as a team member (supported by other team members) to prevent Nick from altering these parameters, so reinforcing the value within the existing culture of teamwork that decisions should be reached by consensus.

Jim expressed support for Peter's offer but was concerned whether he would be able to drop other work in order to make room for the new task. Peter stated, 'It will be your job to monitor me.' In the previous chapter we noted that, despite Peter's willingness, colleagues' monitoring of him was confined to his contribution to their individual tasks. Although Peter had used his authority to invite colleagues to monitor him more closely they had, tacitly, not accepted. Through inaction we suggest that they had used their influence to reject a parameter that Peter had promoted, so excluding it from the culture of teamwork.

Peter asked colleagues to give their view on his proposal and all supported it except Nick, who reiterated his disagreement but acknowledged that he was in a minority of one. Peter stated that at his first meeting with the special needs staff he would seek their views on temporary leadership. Peter's compromise was accepted by Nick and, having checked whether colleagues had any other comment, Peter pronounced the decision made. Both Peter and Nick were prepared on this occasion to compromise in order to reach a working consensus. The fact that dissent over the meeting process was so unusual also indicates how, by participating fully within the parameters of Peter's leadership of the team, others in the SMT normally used their influence as followers to enable the meeting process to work smoothly.

Leadership within the team on particular issues complied with the meeting process. Whoever was responsible for leading typically introduced or reported on progress with the issue when the relevant item came up on the agenda compiled by Peter. Individuals sought the views of the rest of the SMT and their contribution to shared decisions connected with the process of addressing the issue (Jim initiated the idea of holding the summer school, asking Peter to include it as an item on the agenda, and discussing how they might involve staff in its organisation), or a major decision to resolve the issue (Nick presented his draft curriculum plan for the next academic year for amendment and approval by the SMT). Through his approach to chairing, Peter framed the way colleagues led within SMT meetings.

Julia had agreed to take the lead on establishing a working party to develop the policy on assessment. At one SMT meeting she reported that she had a list of nominees from staff and presented three options for working party membership. She asked for two decisions to be made: who the SMT member on the working party would be and whether the group should be enlarged to represent a wider range of staff. Colleagues offered views on membership, Colin suggesting a new option within the list of nominees which would enable any SMT member to serve on the working party, as he or she would not have to represent a faculty interest. Peter intervened, as chair, to ask which SMT member wished to be on the working party. Julia was the only person keen to do so but she stated that she would need some remission from her teaching load. He suggested that the team consider the issue overnight and make the decisions the following day.

Unlike his colleagues, Peter was able to use his authority as head to ask others to lead on his behalf, within his overall leadership of the team. Disagreement had emerged in SMT discussions about the timing of various major decisions to be made during the autumn term of 1991. Peter had asked Jim to put forward his ideas for the sequence of consultations with other staff and deadlines for these decisions as a starting point for team debate.

Prior to the next SMT meeting Peter sent a memo to SMT colleagues, outlining the rationale for adopting a 'critical path' approach to mapping the relevant consultation arrangements and decision points for the remainder of the term. The memo was accompanied by a flowchart drawn up by Jim, with his preferred option and two others. Peter introduced the item in the meeting by explaining that it was imperative to get these decisions made on time. He asked Jim to take colleagues through the flowchart, and all members contributed suggestions about components of the critical path. They accepted a suggestion from Peter that Jim's first option be taken up. After the meeting, Jim revised the paper to take into account the suggestions which had been agreed among SMT members. Peter introduced the revised version at the SMT meeting the next day and more refinements were put forward. He stated that he would prepare a final draft of the critical path and asked colleagues to meet early the following day before teaching started, to check that it reflected accurately what they had agreed. He published the final version, together with the rationale for the critical path, in the head's bulletin.

THE MEETING PROCESS AT DRAKE

The normal pattern of SMT meetings at Drake was one a week after school on a Monday afternoon, lasting two hours. For one year team members experimented with an additional meeting of forty-five minutes in the penultimate period of Friday afternoons. The intention had been to expand the time available to cover an increasingly demanding agenda; and to allow more room for 'creative thinking'. The team also made use of two extended periods of meeting: at a teacher training day, when they met for four hours, and at the residential where they met for thirteen hours. Both these events provided, in SMT members' view, the space to arrive at decisions away from school demands after all the necessary information had been collected and consultation had taken place. This strategy took some pressure off the weekly meeting as a decision-making forum.

Holding SMT meetings after school also reduced some pressures since, although team members aimed always to finish by six o'clock, the constraints were less than a mid-afternoon period, after which individuals had to teach. This arrangement allowed room for informal sharing of member's concerns that might later need a team discussion or decision. It also reflected the importance Kate attached to allowing space for everyone's contribution and for ideas to emerge rather than be imposed. On a decision about changes to arts at Key Stage 4, she commented: 'I would like us to take time to reflect on this. These are big questions and we should not rush in.' SMT members' concentration on the development of the team meant that they kept their meeting patterns under review as they strove to find those that were most efficient and effective. This chapter will focus on the weekly meeting and residential two days as the normal pattern during the fieldwork period.

The agenda for the weekly meeting was generated at the twenty minute briefings held before school three times a week. Kate would propose items for inclusion and then ask each member in turn for suggestions. There were no regular items other than minutes and matters arising, and any other business (AOB). Issues that were of continuing concern would reappear, rather than decisions being taken in haste.

Kate's interpretation of chairing emphasised acting as a facilitator, rather than giving a strong lead on the process or content of the meeting. After full consultation, she drew up the agenda (no colleague member had known her to keep issues off the agenda or put them on unexpectedly), chaired the meeting itself, and took minutes which were posted on the noticeboard in the staffroom. She took great care to secure unanimous agreement as to how each item in the minutes should be worded in the report back to staff. The agenda was circulated to members on the day of the meeting with initials by items on which individuals were expected to lead. Individuals were responsible for circulating or tabling papers supporting their presentation and most items were led by members other than Kate. The only evidence of prioritising items was in shifting an item forward when someone from outside the team was responsible for its presentation.

The team always met in the head's office, usually sitting round a large square table with Kate at one end and the others down each side. It was a seating arrangement that reflected team members' preferred businesslike ambience for the meetings. When Kate's room was redecorated, she chose to exchange the large table for a small coffee table around which easy chairs were grouped. Her office was adjacent to those of other team members and to a small kitchen where individuals would make tea as they arrived. It was rare for anyone to be late or to miss a meeting, or for a meeting to be cancelled. Barbara would attend for those items where she felt she could make a contribution or where budgeting issues were clearly involved.

As they arrived, individuals exchanged immediate concerns about their work or events in school that day. Once the meeting began, Kate kept it strictly to business, reminding the group of the task in hand if the discussion diverted too far or hilarity threatened to take over. There was an unspoken agreement that meetings should end at six o'clock. Sometimes Kate, Marian and Derek would continue talking after that time, often because there were evening meetings for which they had to stay on. Kate kept a close eye on the time spent on issues, but only rarely intervened to speed up the pace of the meeting. Typical actions on Kate's part in working through the agenda included:

- asking others to introduce an item, often consisting of feedback from the working parties for which each team member had responsibility and which constituted an important forum for the genesis of ideas to be considered by

the SMT – Derek presented the School Development Plan Working Party's proposals for revamping the structure of the plan;
- allowing others to lead the discussion, listening to them first before coming in, often as devil's advocate;
- asking questions (e.g. 'What if . . .') in response to others' presentations, rather than making statements – during the team's deliberation about a context statement, she acted as facilitator, using a flip chart to record and summarise as it developed;
- occasionally leading on issues about which she felt strongly – each time news arrived about the competitor school's apparently enhanced position, Kate moved to a more directive style in relation to this issue. Other team members' attempts to rationalise 'bad news' had little impact: 'I think we've got to do some hard thinking to say why they have got the edge and what we are going to do about it';
- setting the pattern for the process (rather than direction) of discussion – she invited other members to brainstorm ideas about how the pastoral system might develop;
- checking out with the rest of the team how 'we want to go forward on an issue' – finding alternative uses for the lecture theatre was a controversial issue among the team, each advocating different options, with Greg believing he had a prior claim. Each person was asked to contribute ideas with Kate stressing 'It is not for me to determine';
- thanking and praising others for their presentations and successful task achievement;
- requesting volunteers and occasionally allocating tasks arising from discussions – after a long debate about the content of the school's context statement, Derek responded to her query 'Right, where are we now on this?' by offering to draw up a draft statement on the basis of their discussion;
- checking timing, drawing items to a close, summarising and writing down what SMT members had agreed should be reported to staff, as well as action to be taken – Philip asked for confidentiality for feedback from staff in one faculty that he had reported to the SMT meeting.

Team meetings rarely deviated from either the atmosphere or practices described above. When outsiders were asked to contribute to an item on the agenda, they had also been prepared for how to perform. This opportunity was seen as part of their management development. They were given ample space for their presentations and supporting papers to be considered and treated as the team members treated each other: with respect and consideration for the fact that at that point they were leading the discussion. They were to be challenged but within the boundaries of politeness. They were expected to accept the boundaries set within the SMT for its own operations. Kate commented to other staff attending for an item on liaison with primary schools: 'I wouldn't want to speak in the same way to the whole staff group.'

The boundaries of teamwork within SMT meetings were continuously reaffirmed by team members' expectations of each other's individual behaviour.

If anyone acted uncharacteristically, the team's joint work in the meeting was temporarily thrown off balance. Marian or Greg's silence, Kate's directiveness, Derek's annoyance, or Philip's emotions would all have been contradictions of how they usually behaved in the team and were therefore rarely evident. The three men described their behaviour on the team as contrasting with that at home, whereas Kate and Marian considered their personal styles consistent across both domains. The pressure was always to behave as expected.

Any transgression of normal procedures, agreed by the team as fair and efficient, could create dissatisfaction. Once Kate introduced under AOB at the end of a very long meeting an item that was close to Greg's heart. This action did not reflect a strongly held norm within the culture of teamwork that any item should be given whatever time members perceived it required. The unwitting offence this action caused was dealt with outside the meeting, when she apologised and ensured at the next meeting that his concerns had sufficient space on the agenda. We suggest that this incident also shows how, although Greg held lower status within the management hierarchy than the head, within the SMT he could contribute as an equal in keeping teamwork within the bounds of acceptability. Both Greg and Kate accepted that her behaviour had inadvertently failed to comply with a key parameter for teamwork which Kate had been instrumental in establishing and all members accepted.

Team members at Drake were concerned about the image the SMT presented to the school, which included a commitment to hard work and recognition of the endeavours of other staff. They often reminded themselves of the need to show through the minutes of their meetings that they were addressing important matters and that they recognised the value of what staff were doing. Less easy was finding a balance between identifying the SMT and its meetings as a decision-making forum and wanting staff to feel fully consulted and influential in decisions made. They agreed that only that part of the discussion relating to the training aspects of appraisal should be fed back to staff, not the policy debate, since there was not a firm agreement among SMT members about who should appraise whom. Similarly, in deciding what should go into the context statement, they vacillated between their own decisions about what was appropriate and the desire to incorporate proposals from the rest of the staff. The groundrule here for the team's operations was not always clear: did they make the decisions or did they arrive at consensus on their own views which were then shared and modified in the light of staff responses?

Although the ways in which the SMT could most effectively lead the school were often under review, leadership within the team was well established. Members other than the head knew exactly what was expected of them as a result of the process that had evolved under Kate's leadership of the team. Often they had checked first with Kate what they wanted to say before presenting it to the SMT. All complex issues were accompanied by a paper, usually tabled, from whoever was taking the lead. The procedure was so routinised that (as we discuss in Chapter 8) team members were sometimes anxious that it stifled creative thought. Parameters for others' thinking tended to be set by their respect for proposals from the person with special responsibility for and particular expertise in the area in which the issue fell. Although presentations usually indicated a range of options, there was scope for the presenter to influence thinking. At the same time, Kate created plenty of space for the diversity of responses represented by each member's contribution.

Each offered expertise and knowledge, often from outside the school. Members had different grapevines: Greg's included TVEI; Kate's, other heads; Marian's and Derek's, other deputies; and Philip's, other staff in the school. The different and predictable styles of their contributions also shaped discussions, so that Marian was often proposing, Derek cautioning, Kate questioning, Greg innovating and Philip checking. It all contributed to the synergy of team meetings; that was Kate's intention.

Kate had asked Marian, whose brief was for staffing and staff development, to lead on introducing an appraisal system into the school. The SMT had previously agreed a policy for using working parties whenever possible to involve staff in decisions. Marian's task was to report to the SMT the planning group's proposals for the training day and her outline plan for who was to appraise whom, when and how. Marian had already had experience of appraisal in her other school but it was new to the rest of the team. After her presentation, Philip commented: 'Fascinating. It's the first time we've touched on this. It's a minefield.' Although SMT members were mainly willing for her to lead on the issue, her proposal for heads of year as potential appraisers was greeted with silence. She had, Kate said, given them 'something unpalatable'. In introducing an idea from her previous school, she had clashed with the wider staff culture of Drake which, in this case, other SMT members saw themselves as protecting.

At the next meeting, Marian stressed she needed confirmation of the policy the team had agreed, as staff would ask about it at the end of the training day. The discussion still concentrated mainly on the mechanics of appraisal so that Marian, when confronted by staff at the end of the training day, emphasised, 'I want to start by saying what I feel ought to happen next'. This ploy met the desire of SMT members not to be seen to impose policies as a team (since Marian was only representing an individual view) though the way the team operated could sometimes be uncomfortable for individual team members when up front, as on this occasion.

THE SMT AGENDAS AT MIDDLETON AND DRAKE

The range of agenda items reflected the balance sought by each head between sustaining an overview, monitoring internally and externally, consulting staff about school policies, and making policy decisions. The large areas of school management covered by the SMT agenda reflected their managerial beliefs and values. We noted earlier how Peter used the SMT at Middleton as a means of monitoring internally and was proactive, seeking to take initiatives to improve the school. Kate's priority was to use the SMT at Drake less for monitoring and more for creative decision making. What could be kept off the agenda was a continual concern for both heads because of the time SMT meetings

Table 6.1 Types of agenda item for SMT meetings at Middleton and Drake

Category of agenda item	Contribution to SMT role	Range of content	Examples
Staff/staffing	Mainly monitoring for overview, some decisions	Individuals causing concern	Ill health, underperformance
		Good practice	Competence of new head of year
		Staffing complement	Forthcoming appointments, staff likely to leave
		Redistributing allowances	Creating a new post**
		General	Staff requests for leave of absence
Check	Mainly monitoring and process decisions related to policy making	Preparation immediately before events	Arrangements for open day for parents
		Preparation for meetings of outsiders where SMT involved	Agenda and party line for selected items within meeting with middle managers
		Operation of routine procedures	Effectiveness of emergency support for staff experiencing pupil discipline problems
Shared awareness	Mainly monitoring for overview, a few decisions	Information from outside school	Head summarised letter received on computerised administration/fed back LEA discussion on grant-maintained status**
		Information from inside school	Pupil's misbehaviour during wet lunchtimes
Policy making	Policy decisions and related process decisions, monitoring for overview informing these decisions	Initial consideration of issue	Discussion of Jim's proposal for summer school*/Marian's proposals for an appraisal scheme**
		Process decisions for managing issue	Deciding how to implement critical path approach to decision making*/ deciding on inviting pastoral heads to morning meetings**

Table 6.1 *Continued*

Category of agenda item	Contribution to SMT role	Range of content	Examples
		Consultation with other staff	SMT meeting with middle managers over provision for pupils aged 16–19
		Decision making and preparation for dissemination	Major: evaluation of 35 period week*/minor: procedures for Health and Safety
		Update on progress with implementation of SMT decisions leading to process decisions	Arranging to meet deadlines for decisions within critical path*/finalising arrangements for individual staff contracts with local primary schools**
Review/ development	At Middleton mainly monitoring for overview, a few decisions	Engagement in development activities/implementation of SMT	Review of team members' satisfaction**/review of critical path approach to decision making*
	At Drake review of team process and progress for development purposes	Activities with implications for school management	Outcomes of review of technology faculty by LEA advisers*

* Specific to Middleton; ** specific to Drake.

required. At Middleton up to six hours might be needed in a week where a major decision was to be made. There was consequent pressure from Peter to work at a rapid pace in order to get through the team's business. The pressure on team meetings at Drake appeared less intense, partly as a result of Kate's style, their timing and team members' knowledge that they had the extended period of the residential to make many key policy decisions.

Another factor influencing the pace of meetings was the size and range of content of the agendas. The categories of agenda item we identified, their main contribution to the SMT role and the range of content covered by each category are summarised in Table 6.1, illustrated by examples from Middleton during the autumn term 1991.

'Staff/staffing', 'check' and 'review' were categories used by the Middleton head to identify regular items on his team's agenda. These categories were not defined as such at Drake but items relating to staff and check items did appear. Review items were evident but in usually a different guise from Middleton. At Drake they embraced review of team process as part of the development programme. The 'development' category applies therefore mainly to Drake, where team members incorporated it into their team meetings. Two other categories used at Drake did not appear on Middleton's agenda: minutes and matters arising, and AOB. They constituted an important feature of the Drake's team's approach to teamwork, since they allowed mutual monitoring as part of 'matters arising' and equal contribution to the agenda via the opportunities offered under AOB. Peter's emphasis on close monitoring of the Middleton team led him to add items to the agenda which would allow him to check on progress, thereby also extending its length. His desire to keep the agenda within bounds, and the reluctance of colleagues to contribute additional items once the agenda was drawn up, made AOB redundant.

In both teams, meetings during most weeks included agenda items to do with shared awareness, checking and policy making. The Drake SMT included staffing only when there was a specific issue, whereas it was a regular item on Middleton's agenda, intended to sustain an overview. At Middleton monitoring was a major emphasis of all categories, and decisions connected with the process of managing an issue were also a significant feature in dealing with the check items. Decision making was central to the category of policy making, which reflected a variety of content according to which part of the policy-making process was being addressed at any time. This process included up to five areas of activity:

- considering an issue for the first time;
- making process decisions about how to manage working towards a decision, usually entailing consultation with other staff;
- going through the consultation process itself;
- making policy decisions and preparing to disseminate them and their rationale;
- monitoring progress with SMT process and policy decisions, often leading to new decisions connected with implementation.

The rapid flow of decisions which characterised many SMT meetings was partly a consequence of the need to make detailed decisions on the process of managing policy making, in addition to making the major substantive decisions which often constituted the climax of policy-making effort within the team.

Each SMT addressed a multiplicity of agenda items every week, some more onerous than others. Figures 6.1 and 6.2 provide examples of an agenda from each SMT, illustrating both similarities and differences in length and categories covered.

The Middleton agenda is an extract (slightly modified to preserve anonymity) from one containing all categories. The agenda is listed on the left hand side of Figure 6.1 and includes two items marked by asterisks, indicating their priority for Peter. He directed colleagues to begin with item 2, where Jim introduced his first draft of the critical path for major decisions to be taken by the end of term. When meeting time ran out, Peter deferred other items, including the second priority of considering whether to replace the normal timetable for a week with a summer school, until the meeting the following day. Several agenda items consist of more than one component. The category and more detailed content of each agenda item or component within it are listed on the right hand side of Figure 6.1.

School management team meeting 16.10.91	Category and content of agenda item
1. Staff/staffing – leave of absence (VW, LM)	staff/staffing – general – staffing causing concern
** 2. Organisation for November/December JK – critical path/opportunities for discussion/consultation	policy making – decision making
3. Organisation of computerised administration	shared awareness – information from outside school
4. Review of: In-service training day on pupil support LEA review of technology faculty	review: – implementation of SMT process decisions – activity with implications for school management
5. Information technology policy	policy making – process decisions for managing issue
6. Check: Pupil support middle managers' meeting 16.10.91 Curriculum middle managers' meeting 30.10.91 Full staff meeting 31.10.91 Emergency staff support	check: – preparation for meetings " " – operation of routine procedure
* 7. Summer school	policy making – initial consideration of issue
8. Speaker on records of achievement (for future in-service training session)	policy making – process decision
9. Pupil underachievement	shared awareness – information from inside school

(A few additional items were connected with detailed administration)

Figure 6.1 Extract from SMT meeting agenda at Middleton and analysis of items

The brevity of the agenda at Drake compared with that at Middleton belies the time spent on each item and the importance given to minutes and matters arising, and AOB. The tendency to put 'check' items first, as here, meant that policy or development items were often dealt with in the second half of the meeting. The order of items was rarely changed and the agenda always completed by the end of the meeting, although decisions might be deferred.

While individuals within both SMTs were responsible for leading on certain items within the team, it is important to note that SMT members elected to have a major input *as a group* into all these agenda items so as to fulfil the extensive role in managing the school adopted within the team. The team agenda reflected how much power lay with the group rather than with individuals, some of whose individual autonomy was sacrificed for the sake of mutual empowerment within the team. The time-consuming nature of employing a team approach to such a role followed from two sources: the variety of areas subject to monitoring or intervention by the SMT; and the close involvement

Meeting of senior management team 21.10.91	Category and content of agenda item
1. Minutes of last meeting and matters arising	Check – action or developments since last meeting a) Completion of appraisal training day programme Praise to working party b) Success of prospective parents evening. Thanks to staff. Necessary changes noted.
2. Awards Evening: review of arrangements (MZ)	Check – final decisions on conduct of the evening
3. Upper School Curriculum: consideration of possible future developments Briefing paper to be tabled by DY	Policy making – Considering issue for the first time
4. Any Other Business	Shared awareness – input of information regarding costing of a bus service for pupils to school Policy making – agreement on action to be taken before making a decision on bus service

Figure 6.2   An SMT agenda at Drake and analysis of items

of the whole team throughout the course of major issues, whoever held individual responsibility for them.

The latter point is illustrated in Table 6.2, which records the sequence over a term of agenda items at Middleton connected with one major policy issue: the review of the pupil-support system. Most items lay within the category of policy making, portraying how this core SMT activity was often evolutionary, building towards a decision over a considerable period. The review process was managed by Julia, yet she both consulted SMT colleagues and was expected to report on progress repeatedly through the term as the consultation exercise unfolded. SMT involvement is likely to have been even more frequent than the table suggests, because we did not observe all SMT meetings and have only recorded relevant activity in the meetings at which we were present.

It is also noteworthy that in Table 6.2 agenda items for the whole term related to policy making. Even the check items were concerned with events within the consultation process. The policy issue had been initiated almost a year earlier when a governors' subcommittee began a review of staff incentive allowances. Heads of year were consulted about the future of their role and, as governors felt that the issue was of school-wide importance, they wished to broaden the consultation to all members of the teaching staff. Policy making within a wider culture which emphasises consultation with outsiders affected by policies can be a long drawn out affair; a team approach may additionally take up the time of the group of senior managers at almost every step along the way.

Table 6.2 Addressing review of pupil support within SMT meetings at Middleton School

SMT meeting observed (autumn 1991)	Activity in SMT meeting	Category and content of agenda
25.9.91	Julia announced arrangements for in-service training day and sought advice on discussion groups	Policy making – process decisions (for managing consultation with staff)
16.10.91	Reviewed in-service training day and considered next steps	Ditto
17.10.91	Considered how to complete consultation within critical path for decisions	Ditto
30.10.91	Finalised arrangements for full staff meeting to consult further and made arrangements for collation of group responses at in-service training day	Check – preparation for meeting with staff Policy making – process decisions
31.10.91	Discussed how to consult within pupil support and curriculum middle managers' meetings	Policy making – update on progress of SMT decisions within critical path
6.11.91	Julia sought advice on collation after full staff meeting	Policy making – process decisions
20.11.91	Discussed progress of group collating staff responses from in-service training day	Ditto
4.12.91	Debated in his absence Peter's proposal for SMT decision	Policy making – making major decision
5.12.91	Decided on Peter's proposal and checked wording for inclusion in head's bulletin for staff	Policy making – making major decision and preparation for dissemination
11.12.91	Checked staff response to decision	Policy making – update on progress with implementation of SMT decision

The SMT decision took over three hours to reach during two meetings on consecutive days. Like most policy decisions we observed, the length of time needed to make this decision and prepare it for public consumption was a result of its complexity. The overall SMT decision actually consisted of a set of more detailed and interrelated decisions. Deliberation from the multiplicity of perspectives among team members on one decision of detail might entail consideration of implications for others. The involvement of the SMT did not end there as, a week later, the team checked staff reactions to the announcement of the overall decision and its rationale in the head's bulletin. The SMT decision had the status of recommendations to the governors' subcommittee, which gave its approval at its next meeting.

SMT involvement in policy making encompassed several policies at any time. The profile of policies at different stages of development and implementation changed continually as the policy-making process for each policy

Major policy issue \ Time	September	October	November	December
Curriculum & staffing plan	– – – –	– – – –		* –
Evaluation of 35 period week timetable	– – – –	– – – –	–––– *	
Review of pupil support	– – –	––––	– – – –	* – –
Information technology policy	– – – –	– –––––	––––– *	
Summer school	– – – –	– * –	– – – –	– – –
Special needs policy		– – –	––––––*	
Critical path approach to decision making		– *––––	––––––	–––– *

(Vertical band labels: Summer Holiday before September; Half Term between October and November; Christmas Holiday after December.)

Key: – – – – – – – = minor focus for SMT
_____ = major focus for SMT
 *   = major process or policy decision

Figure 6.3 Flow of SMT policy-making activity during autumn 1991 at Middleton School

progressed. Another consequence of both these teams' approach to school management was to engage the entire SMT in keeping tabs on this evolving policy profile and attempting to move forward while at the same time addressing a range of agenda items within the other categories. Attention of all team members was therefore split between an ever changing variety of issues. Teamwork meant each person in the team having a finger in each other's pie, rather than just the individual who led on a policy or the headteacher who had oversight of all policies. This finding is consistent with the research we examined at the beginning of the book that all members of an SMT where there is a strong commitment to teamwork are likely to have a multifarious individual role paralleling that long associated with headteachers.

The flow of SMT activity in each school relating to major policies tackled during the autumn term 1991 is portrayed very impressionistically in Figures 6.3 and 6.4. Throughout the term, work continued on a variety of policies, building up towards a series of major decisions in the latter months. By this time, at Middleton, SMT members were grappling with a new policy decision every week. Team members at Drake deferred some of their decisions to the residential the following January. Process decisions were about whether and how to proceed with a policy (as in the case of the summer school at Middleton or the appraisal policy at Drake); policy decisions were about staying with the *status quo* (at Middleton it was decided to retain the thirty-five period timetable for one more year prior to a probable change dictated by the introduction of the national curriculum), or implementing changes (at Drake the SMT revamped considerably the format of the school development plan, the process

Major policy issue \ Time	September	October		November	December		January
School development plan		– – – – – –					– *
Marketing and primary school liaison	Summer Holiday	– – – – – –	Half Term		*	Christmas Holiday	
Appraisal					*		
Upper school curriculum					*		
Year ll underachievers		– –		*			
Staffing structure		– – – – –					– *

* The time is extended beyond the end of the Autumn Term in order to take account of the SMT's use of the January residential for policy decision making.

Figure 6.4 Flow of SMT policy-making activity September 1991 – January 1992* at Drake School

of consultation with faculties, and the nature of their contributions to it). One very significant source of strain for a team approach to school management seems to be the time (and mental effort) needed by each member to keep abreast of a wide variety of issues, only some of which are a central part of any individual's role.

AN EXAMPLE OF DECISION MAKING AT MIDDLETON

Our observations of interaction within both SMTs when making a major decision confirmed how the contribution made by team members as equals led to a much wider range of factors being taken into account than was likely to be considered by a manager working alone. We will illustrate this finding through the example of the SMT decision concerning the review of the pupil-support system at Middleton.

Peter, in his role as leader of the team, analysed the account of discussion group responses made at the in-service training day which had been collated by discussion group leaders, together with the relevant minutes of middle managers' meetings. He wrote a draft proposal for the SMT decision as a starting point for SMT debate which consisted of the context of the decision, a summary of staff responses, the set of detailed SMT decisions, and a short conclusion acknowledging the effort of staff and expressing confidence in the pupil-support system.

On neither day when the draft proposal was debated by the SMT were all members present. However, as we noted earlier, other team members used their authority and influence to ensure that all voices were heard. On the first day, Jim chaired the meeting in Peter's absence according to the brief they had agreed. Nick wrote a paper that evening responding to the draft, which Peter ensured was circulated, read and referred to during the final debate the following day when Nick was unable to be present. He, Peter and other SMT members collaborated to ensure that Nick was able to make a contribution which, as far as possible, equated with that of any other member.

During the initial debate, Jim invited colleagues to respond to the draft in general terms. Their comments indicated how individuals

- drew on their experience – Colin reported on majority opinion among staff;
- used expertise linked to their individual responsibility – Jim reported on the financial implications of the proposed decision to recommend that all heads of year should have a D allowance, on a par with heads of faculty;
- offered ideas – Harry pointed to the implications of increasing salaries within a fixed overall budget for any chance of increasing the amount of non-contact time for staff.

Peter chaired the final meeting and began by asking Jim for feedback on the initial debate and by making time for colleagues to read Nick's paper. He used his authority as chair to argue that they should work through the draft systematically so that it represented a team interpretation, not merely his own:

> This [proposal] is SMT responding. At the moment this is me responding on your behalf and I may have missed things out and I may have got it wrong. And following your response there could be entirely different conclusions.

Peter was concerned that team members made an equal contribution to what was an SMT (rather the head's) decision. The group went through the draft, sentence by sentence, making a number of modifications. Individual contributions included:

- checking for accuracy of the interpretation of staff responses – Julia examined all the written evidence to see if it matched the statements in the draft;
- making sure that all views were taken into account – Peter asked colleagues to refer back to Nick's paper to check that they had not missed any of his points;
- establishing which detailed decisions were most fundamental and should be dealt with first – Colin pointed to the importance of deciding how far the present pupil-support system was to remain or to change;
- offering ideas for new detailed decisions – Harry argued that the SMT should make a commitment to reducing the size of tutor groups;
- checking for phrases that might be open to misinterpretation by staff – all members clarified statements.

When the whole draft had been examined, Peter read out the revised proposal, checked that all members were in agreement, and acknowledged colleagues' efforts. Julia acknowledged his work in producing the draft. The final document contained a considerable number of modifications compared with the original: a joint statement reflecting the input of all SMT members.

The degree of synergy the team achieved rested upon mutual commitment to contributing on an equal basis towards a consensual decision within Peter's leadership. His interpretation of the chairing role in team decision making suggests to us a compromise between contradictory values through which he may have made a marginally more equal input to the content of major decisions than other members, despite his insistence on their contribution. He sought the gain of a high-quality decision which had benefited from a range of perspectives; but he also wished to minimise the strain posed by the time it could take to reach a decision by this means and to ensure that its content lay within the boundaries that he found acceptable. Consequently he used his authority in leading the SMT to draft proposals as a means of funnelling colleagues' contributions towards the decision. His contribution was offered first and provided a framework for colleagues' subsequent contributions. Nevertheless they were at liberty to step outside this framework, as Harry did by initiating a new detailed decision which became incorporated in the final document.

CONTRASTING APPROACHES, SIMILAR WORK

The analysis of SMT meetings indicates how they fulfilled their purpose of combining the talents of all members in managing the school. In both cases, individuals were given extensive opportunities to contribute as equals by leading on particular issues, helping to sustain an overview and making an input into shared decisions. The meeting process contained similar elements which reflected the culture of teamwork. The high degree to which it was shared was highlighted by the rarity of occasions when individuals transgressed its norms and the way they were swiftly brought back into line by their colleagues, whatever their position in the management hierarchy. Elements included a regular setting, a formal agenda, chairing by the head, groundrules for working together, and a selective record of outcomes.

The main differences between the two team processes lay within certain elements, consistent with the contrast in individual contributions to teamwork that we have already explored. The heads set parameters for each element of the team meeting process which allowed expression of a different balance of complementary team roles. The greatest contrast within any element lay in the approaches to chairing, from which groundrules for working together followed. The lists of actions by each head show that they did similar things in working through the SMT meeting agenda. Yet one head used the chair to orchestrate teamwork and scrutinise its boundaries through an emphasis on *intervention*; the other, who believed that boundaries should not be actively scrutinised, operated with a stronger reliance on equally deliberate *non-intervention*. Both heads employed intervention and non-intervention at times, but the balance of emphasis differed markedly.

The head at Middleton was proactive in working through the agenda; the head at Drake generally refrained from intervening until colleagues' input on an item dried up. The head at Middleton habitually intervened to shape the way individuals led within the team on particular issues, whether by monitoring their progress through check items on the SMT meeting agenda, or by putting forward proposals for managing an issue or for a team decision. The process of reviewing the pupil support system was led by Julia, but Peter wrote the draft proposal for the final decision. The head at Drake gave individuals more scope in leading within the team on particular issues. She withheld from monitoring them, leaving them to take the initiative to report on progress through the regular agenda items of minutes and matters arising, to manage the issue, and to propose decisions. Different approaches to chairing therefore resulted in some variation over groundrules for working together. At Middleton it was accepted that discussion of most issues could be of limited duration, Peter taking responsibility as chair for keeping colleagues to time. At Drake, individuals did not expect discussion to be time limited to the same degree.

The relatively small amount of variation in the meeting process was matched by diversity in the range of content addressed within each SMT: differences were largely restricted to emphases within types of item, reflecting primarily the interests of the two heads. While staffing and check items were a regular feature of the Middleton SMT agenda, they were covered, although less regularly, under different headings at Drake. Similarly, in this SMT, keeping track of progress with ongoing issues was formalised in the minutes and matters arising whereas, in the other case, it was more likely to be placed on the agenda by the head in the form of a check item. The main distinction within categories appeared to lie with review: it was largely confined to the team process at Drake, encompassing a range of substantive issues at Middleton (but excluding the team process).

National reforms, which we highlighted in Chapter 1, had a heavy direct and indirect impact on both SMT meeting agendas. The team approaches to management constituted the means of addressing the innovations associated with these reforms, most of which were imposed on the schools:

- implementing current innovations included planning to introduce appraisal at Drake and increasing the amount of science at Middleton to meet the demands of the national curriculum;
- coping with the consequences of innovations included discussion at Drake about how to meet increasing competition for pupils from the school on the adjacent site;
- operating within the parameters of institutionalised innovations included considering the implications of most initiatives for the LMS budget and for staff development in both schools;
- adapting existing arrangements to meet new requirements following from innovations included reviewing the number of periods per week in the timetable at Middleton;
- keeping abreast of the range of innovations while maintaining the rest of ongoing work included adopting the critical path approach to short-term planning at Middleton and work on the school development plan at Drake.

The national reforms therefore had a profound effect on both schools, contributing in no small part to the heavy agenda that took up so much of senior managers' time.

7

The SMT Within the School

In focusing on the internal workings of SMTs it is important not to lose sight of the fact that they existed within a wider school setting which it was their members' shared role to manage. We have noted how much of the work of our study SMTs took place in the privacy of the headteacher's office. There was a clear distinction between interaction inside the team and contact with those outside, giving rise to the possibility that the inner world of the SMT might have been isolated from the outer world of the rest of the school, especially that of other staff. Just as a consequence of creating a two-tier SMT was to exclude some members from the 'inner cabinet', a result of creating a team approach to school management was to create the potential for those beyond the SMT to perceive themselves as an 'out-group' to the extent that they were excluded from the inner world of the team.

So as to avoid this danger, SMT members tried to bridge the gap between the SMT and colleagues throughout the school as far as possible while still retaining a private SMT arena. Here we investigate how the team approaches to school management at Middleton and Drake were affected by the need to work with and through other staff and (much less frequently) with governors, whose awareness of how the SMT operated was very largely limited to what happened in public.

The articulation between the SMT and other staff partially paralleled the complementary individual team roles within the SMT. The teams were ultimately as dependent upon the contribution of other staff in attempting to achieve synergy across the school as the heads were upon their colleague SMT members in achieving synergy within the work of the team. This parallel was limited, however, by the extent of the demarcation between the two groups. Since links with other staff were so central to the day-to-day work of the SMTs, we will focus mainly on this insider–outsider relationship.

We first examine the partial parallel we have highlighted between roles within the SMT and links between the SMT and other staff (adapting the framework discussed in Chapter 5). Second, we consider two issues arising in both schools which were connected with providing leadership of other staff. Finally, we touch on the way the governing body gave equal status to representatives of different interest groups within the school, providing a potential means of shaping the work of the SMT should it overstep the boundaries of acceptability to the majority of governors.

THE RELATIONSHIP BETWEEN THE SMT AND OTHER STAFF

What was the parallel with patterns of behaviour we identified among individual contributions to teamwork within the SMT? In carrying out its shared role in managing the school within the leadership of the head, each team offered *leadership of the other staff*. The head was supported by other SMT members in *setting parameters for the managerial and teaching work of other staff by orchestrating their contribution to the work of the school*. A strategic managerial task for the team was to create conditions for other staff to take initiatives within the bounds of school-wide policies, over most of which they were consulted in some way, while delimiting the boundaries of their work. We saw in Chapter 3 how each SMT interacted with other staff through a system of regular meetings where the interests of different groups of staff were represented. SMT members' individual school-wide responsibilities gave them the delegated authority to manage aspects of the work of other staff, coordinated through the deliberations of the team. In the last chapter we discussed how the SMTs had a major hand in setting the agenda for consultation with other staff related to school-wide policy making.

They also variably *ensured that the work of other staff followed these parameters by scrutinising their boundaries*. We noted how the emphasis on monitoring other staff within the SMT at both Drake and Middleton brought to light instances where staff had stepped beyond these boundaries (as where teachers at Middleton had arrived late to register their tutor group of pupils).

The legitimacy of this role in leading other staff was enshrined in the management hierarchy, SMT members enjoying higher managerial status and remuneration than other teaching or ancillary staff (except for one E allowance holder at Drake who was not a member of the SMT). Lines of accountability were established whereby other staff were supervised by SMT members within their individual school-wide management responsibility.

The decision by the heads to adopt a team approach meant that their authority to manage the school was variably delegated to other SMT members, and so rested to some extent with the team. As part of their *staff membership*, other staff could be expected to contribute to the work of the school within parameters which were backed by the authority of the SMT. *Contributing as equals* to the management of the school was much more restricted than within the SMT because of the multiplicity of hierarchical levels of responsibility across the staff and retention by the SMT of the exclusive authority to make major decisions. While middle managers could contribute as equals to consultative meetings with the SMT, or teachers with different formal status could contribute as equals to the deliberations of a working party, their influence within the school-wide-policy making process did not extend beyond representing the views of staff to the team. Other staff could be required to *express leadership within their area of responsibility* in the school, as when a head of faculty held a meeting with colleague teachers to determine details of faculty policy within the framework of school-wide policies. They were also expected by SMT members to display *followership within the staff* by participating fully in consultation exercises organised by the SMT, by implementing SMT decisions or by responding to encouragement to take initiatives.

We noted when considering contributions of SMT members to teamwork that SMT members other than the head were able in principle to use influence to resist compliance with the head's wishes. Similarly, other staff could resist the efforts of the SMT by withholding from full engagement in consultation or implementing SMT decisions superficially. Within the dialectic of control between the SMT and other staff, therefore, both groups had access to resources to realise interests which might not necessarily coincide. The possibility of mutual empowerment of the SMT and other staff depended on unified commitment to compromise between the sectional interests of different groups of other staff. Then a considerable degree of synergy throughout the school was achievable. However, it was not easy for the SMT to promote synergy across the demarcation zone between the team and a multiplicity of other interest groups.

The parallel we have drawn accounts for only a part of the relationship we observed between the SMTs and other staff. The individual team roles we earlier identified within the SMTs related to a single entity where, to a great extent, all members were party to team action. The demarcation between SMT and other staff meant that leadership of the staff and staff membership spanned two groups whose relationship was strictly hierarchical. The contrast between SMT and other staff involvement in school management is indicated in Table 7.1, where we have listed factors associated with the demarcation between them. The SMT side of the story will be familiar from earlier chapters, so we will concentrate on the other side.

Several differences between the two entities had significant implications for the SMT approach to leadership of other staff. First, other staff played a smaller part in school-wide policy making than the SMT. Since team decision making took place in a private arena, other staff had no direct experience of how decisions were made, and did not know to what extent any views they had expressed during prior consultation had actually influenced decisions. The credibility of the SMT with other staff, and so their willingness to express followership, rested in considerable measure on how far SMT members were able to convince them that consultation was genuine. Yet it could not be proven without compromising the privacy of the SMT decision-making arena.

Second, other staff did not have access to the overview of the school that SMT members worked to sustain, and their perspective on school-wide issues

Table 7.1 Factors relating to the demarcation between the SMT and other staff

Factor \ Staff group	Demarcation zone	
	SMT	Other staff
School-wide policy decisions	Make decisions and have authority to delimit contribution of other staff to decision making	Do not make these decisions
Consultation on decisions	Decide whom and over what to consult according to SMT norms including being seen by other staff to be fair	Consulted when SMT decide, but have access to SMT to request issues to be considered
Knowledge of how decisions made	Know how decisions made and range of views taken into account	Do not know how decisions made except through account disseminated by SMT
Breadth of perspective	School-wide perspective related to SMT overview	'Parochial' perspective since do not have overview except as disseminated by SMT
Breadth of responsibility	School-wide responsibility, primary concern with implications of issues for whole school	Sectional responsibility, primary concern with implications of issues for own area of responsibility
Status within management hierarchy	Senior status, responsible for managing other staff	Junior status, managed by SMT
Pattern of interaction	Strong face-to-face links within SMT, weaker links with other staff as a group	Strong face-to-face links with a proportion of other staff, weaker links with SMT as a team
Cultural allegiance	Strong allegiance to SMT culture of teamwork within wider management culture	Strong allegiance to teaching or ancillary staff culture

was less comprehensive. Consequently it was more likely that their sectional interest in fighting the corner that related to their work in one part of the school might not coincide with the school-wide interest of the SMT. Their individual responsibility as teachers and middle managers tended to reinforce this difference as it also covered a more restricted aspect of the school than the more global responsibility of SMT members. The more restricted responsibility of other staff reflected their lower status within the management hierarchy.

Third, other staff had most face-to-face contact with their immediate colleagues and fairly seldom interacted with the full SMT (as opposed to particular members within their individual management responsibility). In consequence, we suggest that other staff were affected only indirectly by the SMT culture of teamwork, retaining a strong allegiance to the culture of the colleagues outside the SMT with whom they had more contact. The exclusion of other staff from much SMT business limited their exposure to the SMT culture of teamwork. They had direct experience only of the proportion of the team's work which was public.

SMT leadership of the staff had to be carried out across the demarcation zone which was a consequence of adopting a team approach to school management. A key element in leading other staff was for SMT members to set parameters

Table 7.2 Permeability of the demarcation between the SMT and other staff

Direction of information flow

		Information flowing into SMT from other staff	Information disseminated by SMT to other staff
Source of information flow	Initiated by SMT	Consultation exercises, monitoring	Announcement, e.g. head's bulletin or minutes of SMT meeting, presentation by SMT of united front
	Initiated by other staff	Use of access to SMT, agenda item on middle management meeting (unofficial pressure group)	Use of access to SMT, agenda item on middle management meeting (unofficial lobbying of individual SMT members)

which fostered a two-way flow of information (including the opinions and concerns of other staff). Table 7.2 illustrates how SMT members were centrally implicated in the degree to which this demarcation zone was permeable to information passing in both directions. As we discussed in Chapter 6, SMT members used their authority to initiate two-way information flow: on the one hand gathering staff opinion and monitoring around the school while, on the other, disseminating information to other staff. We saw how much attention in the SMT was paid to the content of this information, and noted how SMT members were expected to present a united front in an attempt to control not only the range of information received by other staff but also the interpretation of it that they might make.

SMT arrangements for communication offered other staff more restricted opportunities to use their influence by initiating communication with the SMT. They could legitimately inform SMT members of their concerns and request a statement from them. Less legitimate means included informal lobbying of individual SMT members so as to tempt them to leak SMT confidences, and forming a pressure group (as we will discuss later in this chapter). Let us first consider how the demarcation between the SMT and other staff led to a continual concern within both teams over their credibility as the group providing leadership of the staff.

The possibility of a credibility gap arose because the central part of the SMT's work – largely conducted in the SMT meetings discussed in Chapter 6 – was invisible to other staff. Their information about this activity was restricted almost entirely to the limited announcements disseminated through the head's bulletin or published minutes about the issues being discussed by the SMT and accounts of SMT decisions and their rationale. Even when middle managers were invited into SMT meetings for consultation, they attended only while the relevant item was being addressed.

Credibility was of crucial importance to the SMT. While other staff accepted most or all aspects of the SMT's role in managing the school, their willingness to engage in the activities of staff membership necessary for SMT leadership was conditional on their perception that SMT members were doing their job as a team within the parameters that other staff found acceptable. A key concern, especially among middle managers, was that they should be consulted by the SMT over changes that would affect their responsibility and through this process have some influence over relevant SMT decisions. Other staff had to deduce, from the information they received from the SMT, how far views they had expressed during any consultation had been taken into account in making SMT decisions.

SEEKING CREDIBILITY AT MIDDLETON

An enduring myth outside the team at Middleton was that SMT members actually had their predetermined 'blueprint' for decisions even though they went through the motions of consulting other staff. None of the latter group whom we interviewed could offer evidence to support this notion. One middle manager indicated how he accepted the SMT's exclusive role in decision making, whatever the status of the blueprint myth:

> Whether or not the blueprints are there no one will ever know. The management team might not even be aware of a blueprint. Once it's there, the idea is difficult to get away from: they cannot disprove, nor can anyone prove it – a bit of a thorn in the side. Some people don't take on board the idea that there are people who are paid to take the decisions. They are going to make good ones; they are going to make bad ones. I am quite happy for them to do that.

He noted how the outcome of much consultation reflected his awareness of the view of most staff, consistent with the idea that SMT consultation was genuine in so far as staff views had apparently been taken into account. In many instances:

> One does not have to be very genned up to pick which might be the appropriate answer even before discussions have gone ahead. So therefore it is not decided upon but it is just the natural course and the right answer that eventually comes out . . . they are genuinely saying that we must consult everybody and get their views, and that is the way it should be done.

Peter was acutely aware that the SMT approach to policy making was open to cynical interpretation by those outside the team. Consultation over the pupil-support system had revealed a majority (but far from unanimous) view among other staff that the present system should not be radically altered. After the SMT decision had been taken, he commented:

> You go for consultation and you raise expectations. People can then turn round and say, 'Oh well. He used to be someone who consulted but had it all done in his bottom drawer, so there was no point in consulting. Now he consults and actually nothing happens.'

Much consultation activity was routine, the boundaries of SMT parameters being highlighted only on the rare occasions when other staff tried to step beyond them. The few instances we observed related to the unacceptability for some middle managers of the norm that the SMT had the exclusive right to make major decisions affecting them, after hearing their views. A middle manager commented on how the SMT procedure did not allow for an intermediate consultation stage about the decisions themselves:

> We have these big discussions about what we are going to do in the school on this, and we all talk to each other, and we all air our views. And that's it. Then a policy emerges from somebody else. Once the policy has emerged it is set in concrete very quickly. There's never: 'Here's the draft policy based on your consultation, would you like to make any amendments or comments?'

Immediately before the SMT was due to make a decision on the curriculum and staffing plan for the following academic year, heads of faculty requested an emergency meeting before the school day with Peter and Nick, where they expressed their concern that they would not be consulted over the curriculum and staffing-plan decision, arguing that it should take the form of a proposal which they could then discuss. Peter used his authority as head to reject the idea, which would have transgressed the boundary of the parameters set by the SMT for consultation. He restated the SMT norm that consultation was undertaken to inform the making of the SMT decision, over which the SMT would not consult. Adhering to this norm apparently helped to sustain a situation in which credibility of the SMT would remain an issue for other staff because they were excluded from the decision-making process.

A consequence of leadership of other staff being undertaken by a team was the possibility that individual SMT members might be viewed as symbolising the team as a whole in their dealings with other staff. Credibility of the team, and ultimately his credibility as SMT leader, was a central concern for Peter. He regarded the achievements or difficulties of individual SMT members in their work with other staff as having great significance for the credibility of the team. The staff we interviewed stated that, in principle, they would be willing to speak to the head about any concern over the performance of other SMT members (underlining their perception of a hierarchy within the team).

Peter noted how at the beginning of the autumn term of 1991 Colin and Jim were very popular with other staff, having made a great effort over the summer to have parts of the school redecorated and refurbished. Equally, Peter became concerned when a middle managers' meeting chaired by Nick had been unproductive. He also noted how Nick had gone on to re-establish high credibility with staff. He completed his round of consultative meetings with individual middle managers a week before the published deadline, allowing them more time than they had expected to be consulted as a group about the outcomes.

Other SMT members also perceived that their actions were taken by other staff as symbolic of the team. Julia participated in a working party set up to evaluate the thirty-five periods a week timetable. At one point a teacher asked her to visit a middle manager who was teaching in order to gather some information which the working party needed. It was suggested that Julia should undertake this task because she had high status as a member of the SMT. Julia declined because it would be setting a bad example for an SMT member to interrupt a colleague in the middle of a lesson. We interpret her action as withholding from operating with other staff in a way which was contrary to a public SMT principle.

Each SMT member represented the team in making public statements about SMT activity in the private arena. A high priority for the team was for all members to present a united front on team decisions. Other staff widely supported the principle that individual SMT members gave consistent messages, a middle manager indicating how it lay within the parameters of acceptability:

> It always strikes me that it is very much a collective responsibility principle that guides them and I am sure that there must be a line that they agree beforehand. I think that they behave tremendously professionally in that sense. It has not been my experience to find individual members of SMT gossiping.

A second middle manager commented favourably on the way consistency among SMT members stopped individuals among other staff from becoming 'favourites', suggesting to us that, for the SMT to have credibility with him, it must operate within the parameter of fairness in dealings with other staff.

We saw in the last chapter how, in the private arena, SMT members did practise their espoused team principles: for those in the know, consultation was indeed genuine. Members made great efforts not only to be fair, but also to *be seen to be fair* by other staff. Since other staff were unable to see for themselves much of SMT activity, team members perceived that their credibility with other staff rested on convincing them that SMT members were not being illegitimately manipulative behind their closed doors.

In Table 7.3 we have summarised our evidence of the components of SMT policy-making connected with the pupil-support system which were public within the school. (As with the relevant SMT meetings highlighted in Table 6.2, the process was actually more extensive. We were able only to sample activity during this period.) We described in Chapter 6 how the SMT took pains in their private discussions to ensure that the consultation process was not biased by the SMT, and attempted to forestall any misinterpretation of the account of the decision to be disseminated through the head's bulletin. The middle and right hand columns of the table show how SMT members took many initiatives to inform other staff about the process or content of the consultation, which included many opportunities for other staff to inform the SMT.

A concern for demonstrating the fairness of the SMT to other staff underpinned the consultation process itself. The SMT arranged for consultation to take place within the range of meetings designed to ensure that all interest groups in the school were represented, including two staff meetings. An in-service training day was devoted to the topic. In Peter's input at the beginning he stated how he wished to reassure staff that the consultation was genuine and there was no hidden blueprint possessed by the SMT. Both he and Harry refrained from participating in discussion groups on the grounds that they might be perceived by other staff to have a vested interest; they did not wish to risk any perception of SMT bias. The rest of the team participated as members

Table 7.3 Public components of SMT consultation about pupil support at Middleton School

Date (autumn 1991)	Component observed or surveyed	Source of information	Main direction of information flow
7.10.91	Head's bulletin – Julia announced programme for in-service training day and arrangements for collation of staff views	SMT	SMT→other staff
11.10.91	In-service training day organised by Julia – input by Peter and Harry	SMT Other staff	Other staff→SMT
28.10.91	Memo from Julia to group leaders from in-service training day inviting them to reconvene their group at full staff meeting and to join group collating staff responses	SMT	SMT→other staff
28.10.91	Meeting of INSET (in-service training) panel, Julia and other panel members planned procedure for full staff meeting	SMT Other staff	SMT↔other staff
28.10.91	Head's bulletin – Peter announced critical path for decision, including discussion at middle managers' meetings	SMT Other staff	SMT→other staff (other staff→SMT)
31.10.91	Full staff meeting – groups discussed their responses, SMT acceded to staff request for plenary session	Other staff	Other staff→SMT
2.11.91	Head's bulletin – Julia reminded other staff that individual views could be sent in to Peter	SMT	SMT→other staff
7.11.91	Governors' meeting – Peter reported on progress with review	SMT	SMT→governors
25.11.91	Head's bulletin – Peter announced procedure for moving towards decision including second full staff meeting on 28.11.91. Collated papers from in-service training day included as appendix	SMT Other staff	SMT→other staff Other staff→other staff
9.12.91	Head's bulletin – Peter announced that SMT decision made. Decision and rationale included as appendix	SMT	SMT→other staff

of groups led by other staff. When Colin was asked if would report back on the group's deliberations in a plenary session, he declined because he was a member of the SMT and did not wish to be perceived by other staff as influencing the consultation process. Several SMT members reiterated the plea that all staff views were welcomed.

At the first full staff meeting, several teachers argued that staff should be given an opportunity to discuss the issue in plenary instead of remaining in groups. SMT members immediately complied, holding a vote to determine majority opinion on whether to take this step, and then facilitating the discussion. The head's bulletin was used to keep staff informed about the various opportunities to offer their views, including writing direct to Peter, and to publish the collated group responses from the in-service training day.

SEEKING CREDIBILITY AT DRAKE

Here members of the SMT sought continuously to strengthen their credibility in at least four ways: through consultation; shaping the individual performance of other staff and management processes in the school; being present at meetings involving other staff; and becoming on occasions peers rather than line managers. Consulting, shaping and attending were often carried out by the team jointly through their presence at meetings held by other groups of staff, such as head of faculty and head of year meetings and senior staff meetings. Sometimes one or two individuals represented the SMT: at the teacher training day for pastoral heads, which Marian and Derek ran; or the 'guidance review team' where Philip was present as the person on the SMT responsible for coordinating records of achievement. Opportunities to become one of the staff again (and cross the demarcation zone completely) were less frequent but included all team members except Marian joining in the appraisal training day activities, leaving Marian mainly to respond to the management implications. Or, in the staffroom, Philip would usually sit with pastoral colleagues, whereas the deputies and head roamed, not wanting to identify too closely with any one group, to avoid accusations of favouritism.

SMT members were very conscious of the need to keep boundaries permeable while at the same time maintaining their integrity as a team. They were differentially approached by individual staff to express their concerns. Information was usually passed to Kate in her headteacher role: during what staff called the 'MOTs', the annual development interview she held with each member of staff; or during her termly interview with each head of faculty. Both these channels had been compromised, in the eyes of staff, by splitting the MOTs with Marian and the lesser frequency of Kate's meeting with individual heads of faculty. It was clearly important to other staff that, while respecting SMT members' desire to operate as a team, they should still have direct access to Kate as headtacher. Other members of the team were likely to be approached informally, in relating to their areas of responsibility or as a result of judgements about who was personally most accessible or could be influential in presenting a case at the SMT meeting. At the same time as team members strove to create a united front as leaders in managing the staff, individuals and groups of staff found it easier to atomise the team, in order to be more influential on thinking within it.

SMT members combined a strong concern, as leaders, to shape individual staff performance and that of the staff as a whole. By working with other staff in this way, they saw themselves contributing to improving children's learning experiences in the school. As a result of their discussions, they would agree on joint ways to work with individuals or groups to steer them towards a way of behaving that team members felt was more appropriate. They were particularly concerned to influence the ways in which heads of year worked together and operated with their tutor teams.

A whole day was given to this issue, led by Marian and Derek working with the pastoral heads. Ostensibly, the purpose of the day was to give the heads of year time and space to work out a policy and plan for their year and, together with colleagues, construct a framework for a coherent pastoral programme. The underlying agenda was to encourage the group to work more closely together as a team and share issues that some had thought about more than others. They had enjoyed less access to training opportunities than the faculty heads, and SMT members were keen to demonstrate support for their work through making available additional resources. The day's success lay in part in the delegated authority of Derek and Marian 'subject to SMT agreement' to commit resources to proposals for development arising from the pastoral heads' deliberations. The desire to shape was combined with the priority given by the team within the parameters set by Kate, to letting people get on with tasks for which they had been given responsibility, without too much interference. In some cases, staff would have welcomed more SMT involvement.

One head of faculty, who thought he could go a whole term without seeing the team, commented:

> I realise that they may be letting me get on with things because they think I'm managing well, but I don't know that and it could be that they're just not interested.

This policy of not intervening unless necessary meant that, when team members did become involved, they were perceived as trouble shooting, thereby establishing a negative basis for the intervention.

SMT members used their presence at meetings to reflect symbolically the value they attached to the activities of those involved. Although it was time consuming, Kate and the two deputies attended all year-review meetings, parents' councils, heads of faculty and heads of year formal meetings. Philip and Greg attended many of these meetings as part of their individual responsibilities rather than as SMT members. It was not technically necessary for all to be present; one would have sufficed, either to chair or represent the SMT. Being there was an important part of their strategy to strengthen their credibility and overcome the view of other staff that they were 'efficient and analytical' rather than 'human'. It showed they were keeping in touch and gave others a chance to keep them informed.

Their joint attendance at the heads of year and heads of faculty meetings allowed them to monitor but also to be challenged if they had not done something that their colleagues thought they should, such as clarifying criteria for the annual awards. At a faculty heads' meeting, they were reminded of staff concerns about the timing of the parents' evening. The item was introduced by a faculty head 'voicing my team's concerns'. Members of the SMT were keen to break down some of the barriers between staff with pastoral and those with academic responsibilities, by supporting the pastoral group's sense of belonging to a wider team. Their attendance at both meetings was an attempt to make the two groups feel more equal, even though the hierarchical structure (most of the pastoral heads were on C allowances) worked against this aspiration.

The senior staff meeting exemplified another forum for SMT members to demonstrate a desire to share leadership of the staff as well as consult. Kate regretted Marian's 'slip' when, at a senior staff meeting, she distinguished between 'senior management' and 'senior staff', thereby underlining a distinction which Kate preferred not to make. She wished to downplay the demarcation between the team and other staff through the language used to describe the SMT.

Although team members saw the SMT as the ultimate forum for decision making, they were concerned to secure staff involvement in as many ways as possible in contributing towards the final decision. One head of faculty described the autonomy he felt he was given, over the decision about assessment at the end of key stage 3 within the national curriculum. He knew Kate would prefer the school to have participated in the pilot tests but his decision that they were inappropriate was accepted. All the heads of faculty felt they strongly influenced decisions on staff appointments to their faculty. To have an impact on SMT decisions, it was clear that staff felt that they had to influence the team as a whole and not single individuals.

Marian's advent had contributed to other staff viewing the SMT as a team, particularly in how team members appeared at middle-management meetings. Then it was clear that they had often discussed issues beforehand and were coming 'not with a three line whip but with a plan of what they want'. Other staff approved of the strategy since it demonstrated the team working together. Indeed, they were disappointed when cracks emerged in the team façade and it was apparent that they did not always know what each member was doing. This confirmation of their legitimacy to lead as a team was accompanied, in some staff eyes, by the character of the staff as followers, who were generally not willing to challenge things about which they were unhappy. One head of faculty commented:

> I sometimes think we allow things to go through on the nod because they're almost presented as *faits accomplis*. They go through on the nod, though perhaps not everyone agrees with it but does not like to rock the boat.

Generally the SMT was perceived as a team, with both the advantages and disadvantages that identification as a discrete entity could bring. The timing of SMT meetings (before school three times a week), in the view of other staff, made it harder to pass things on to them. Team members were not always available when other staff were. One middle manager described them as 'a united front but in the positive way of not united against'. She perceived that breaking the front occasionally had a positive effect because it showed that the consensus decisions were really the outcome of discussion from different perspectives. The team boundaries appeared more permeable, the further up the hierarchy the staff were. One main-scale teacher was not sure exactly who was and was not on the team and had very little contact with SMT members: 'They are very helpful and supportive but at the same time I feel very remote from the decisions they are making.' She was not unhappy with that situation.

Middle-management responsibilities brought staff closer to team members and an understanding of how they worked, although one head of year confessed:

> I suppose when it comes to it, I don't know what really goes on behind the closed door of the management team. I don't know how often discussions are, or how hard fought some of the issues are, or whether there is such similarity of viewpoint that some issues don't get raised.

Much of the SMT's consultation took place in public arenas which, being more formal, could make it difficult for everyone to be open. The team's presence as an entity could be intimidating for the less secure. The decision that all but Kate should be present at the meeting where heads of faculty presented and justified their faculty plan was a sound one, in the eyes of SMT members, since it showed them acting as a team, sharing the task and the knowledge. For staff on the receiving end, there was a sense of being put on the spot, although they acknowledged this might have been because it was the first time it had happened.

Staff appreciated the opportunities provided by working-party membership to influence decisions, even though they might well arrive at decisions which, in one head of year's view, 'The SMT could probably have arrived at themselves'. Team members' concern that faculty and year heads should feel that curriculum and pastoral policy making was their responsibility was echoed by one year head's description of the process:

> In my view, major policy-making areas, including curriculum and pastoral, end up being dealt with by year or faculty heads, which is right and proper. For example, the national curriculum is not the responsibility of the SMT but of the faculty heads with perhaps the deputy in charge of curriculum having a say. I imagine the team discusses what the issues are and then says to Derek, 'This is your area. What do you think? Let us know what the heads of faculty have to say.'

The following example shows the extent to which his description was accurate. The staff had been challenged by an LEA adviser on whether religious education was adequately represented in the curriculum at key stage 4. The feedback had been to Kate as head, who then shared it with the SMT, with Derek taking particular responsibility for devising alternative proposals for finding time to meet this need. Inevitably someone's loss would be someone else's gain. The proposals were discussed at an SMT meeting but no decision taken. It was felt that the decision must come from the faculties. Representing the SMT, Derek distributed the proposals in advance to faculty heads and went over the issues with them in a meeting with other SMT members present. The faculty heads were unable to reach a consensus and Derek asked whether they wanted the SMT to make a decision. Kate urged the faculty heads not to take this route but to make the decision themselves. An emergency meeting of the SMT with faculty heads was devoted entirely to the issue, where Derek tabled a proposal he had already discussed with SMT colleagues. He had designed it as a consensus proposal and, with modifications from the faculty head destined to lose most by the changes, it went through.

The basis of his consensus proposal was his knowledge, through informal feedback, that the heads of faculty had opened up and explored individual and conflicting faculty concerns at a meeting held without the SMT being present. The catalyst for making the change was the faculty heads themselves. Their preferred solution was not that preferred by SMT members, but they were prepared to accept it. SMT members had alerted the pastoral heads to the problem and canvassed their views before it had been discussed by faculty heads. The situation provided SMT members with an opportunity to share the dilemma of finding a solution with which everyone could live, arising from their formal accountability to external demands. The pastoral heads were consulted to inform the SMT's consensus proposal but this decision was actually made by the faculty heads.

HEADS OF FACULTY AS A PRESSURE GROUP

The different relations between SMT and faculty heads in the two schools were reflected in part in the form taken by heads of faculty meetings that took place without SMT members present. In both schools the demarcation between the SMT and other staff, and its expression in the unity with which team members operated within their stated parameters, restricted the potential influence which individuals or groups could exert on the SMT. Team members legitimately crossed the demarcation zone within their management responsibility to monitor the arena of other staff. A key concern for groups of other staff was whether their legitimate sectional interests had sufficient impact on SMT decisions. Heads of faculty in both schools had formed a pressure group exclusively to represent their shared interests. At Middleton they perceived that the combination of the additional interests of cross-curriculum coordinators and the SMT presence at the regular curriculum middle managers' meetings diluted their ability as a group to influence school management. A head of faculty argued that

> We needed a time when we were not overlooked by SMT. I think there need to be moments of freedom. As all members of SMT are in faculties [as teachers] there is still that 'over your shoulder'. You cannot be as free. However nice they are, we know they are members of SMT.

This pressure group was directed towards influencing the SMT.

At Drake, the heads of faculty saw themselves more as making opportunities to talk openly and to support each other with problems arising from their faculty responsibilities. Like the Middleton heads of faculty, they appeared to be seeking a similar level of privacy to that experienced by SMT members in their team meetings. We interpret heads of faculty in both schools to have empowered themselves as a group by forming a coalition within the dialectic of control between the SMT and other staff. Their corporate power rested upon the development of a collaborative culture which entailed forsaking an interest in maximising advantage for one faculty for the shared interest of the group (mirroring the SMT culture of teamwork). At Middleton, one head of faculty commented:

> It's amazingly collaborative. There are times when you are going to be at a stalemate, inevitably. Because what you want is probably counter to what the rest of the heads of faculty want. But people are extremely accommodating. With the recent discussion about the curriculum . . . everybody was trying to make life easier for each other. We know that we are all under massive pressure and it is trying to lessen that pressure across the school.

Synergy within the group was often aligned with SMT school-wide interests, as in this instance, so contributing to their mutual empowerment. At other times, the Middleton group was united in putting forward a view for the SMT to consider. Minutes of the meetings were forwarded to Peter and Nick, with items asterisked to which they wished the SMT to respond. Even when attempting to counter the SMT, their influence as a group was limited because of the authority of SMT members to protect their exclusive power to make major decisions. Heads of faculty put forward a proposal for a two-week timetable after the SMT had made a decision to retain the present thirty-five period week. The proposal was immediately rejected because, Peter argued, its timing lay outside the parameters for consultation within the evaluation exercise.

The synergy of the heads of faculty group at Drake was less evident. One member commented: 'At the end of the day faculty heads feel they need to fight their own corner.' Their informal lunches held a week before the faculty heads' meetings with the SMT provided the opportunity to build a united front on issues to be addressed at the meeting, but this opportunity was rarely taken up. One head of faculty reported:

> We would not normally get together beforehand either to agree a strategy in the meeting or to influence people outside the meeting. We did discuss things in advance last year when it was a question of who would lose time on the timetable to make way for more integrated home studies. It wasn't a case of a united front, however, since whoever was going to lose the time wasn't going to feel united about it. As a group we don't challenge the SMT very much, not because it's unchallengeable but because we are a fairly placid group.

We observed one lunchtime meeting when the group built up towards challenging the SMT on distribution of the budget but, when it came to the heads of faculty meeting, the issue was not on the agenda. The person who had taken responsibility for taking it forward had not done so. Usually the head of faculty who convened the group met with Derek afterwards to pass on how the group was feeling about issues and to suggest any items for the heads of faculty meeting agenda. It was an informal arrangement, with the head of faculty concerned only reluctantly acknowledging that he was both 'convenor' and 'go between'. Attendance at the meetings was voluntary; not everyone attended. In contrast to Middleton, the existence of the group at Drake owed much to SMT members' conviction of the desirability of such an event for team building amongst the heads of faculty. The value they placed on a forum for expressing sectional concerns without their presence was reflected in the constant encouragement they gave to the heads of year to do something similar.

At Middleton, SMT members had respected the concern of heads of faculty to have their exclusive forum and, although it remained unofficial (not appearing in the diagram of the staffing structure reproduced in Figure 3.1), the group had become legitimated, the times of meetings appearing in the staff diary. When SMT members published the critical path for major decisions, without prior consultation outside the team, it included agenda items for forthcoming heads of faculty pressure group meetings. One head of faculty perceived that the group's own agenda had been 'hijacked' by the SMT – an ironic consequence of legitimacy!

When SMT members at Drake asked the heads of faculty to decide among themselves how the money allocated for in-service training should be divided between faculties, no one objected to this item being the focal point of one of their meetings. Empowering the group in this way also encouraged the growth of a unity in the face of what heads of faculty perceived as the failure of SMT members to commit adequate funds to faculties. The challenge (as we saw above) failed to materialise, in part because generally all heads of faculty confirmed their sense of being highly involved in any decisions concerning them.

CHECKS AND BALANCES – THE GOVERNING BODY

The link with governors was more complex than the relationship with other staff but also less directly related to the SMT than to the head as its formal leader. The composition of the governing body (mainly by legislative design) both cut across the school management hierarchy and reached into the local community. We have seen how the SMT was formally accountable to the governing body via the head, yet there was some ambiguity over the balance of authority for school management held by the head and governing body. Our observations of meetings involving governors in the second phase of the project confirmed that they largely supported the professional staff, rather than taking their own initiatives, but required proposals for school policies to be justified before being approved.

The relationship between the SMT, other staff and governors is depicted in Figure 7.1. The permeability of the demarcation between the SMT and other

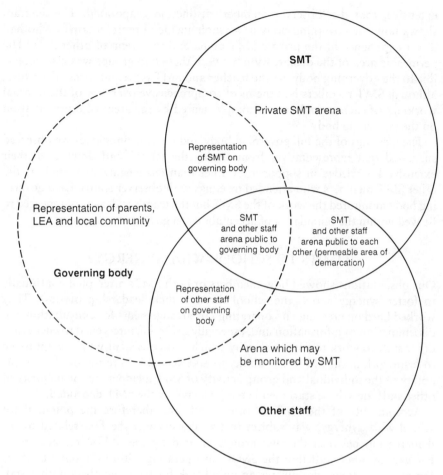

Figure 7.1 Relationship between the SMT, other staff and governors

staff is represented by the overlap between the SMT and other staff arenas. A considerable private SMT arena remained in both study schools, while the equivalent arena for other staff was variably monitored by the teams. The governing body of each school had representatives from both SMT and other staff, alongside groups not employed in the school including parents, the LEA and local business people.

In contrast to their hierarchical status within the school, SMT and other staff representatives had equal status within the governing body. Both heads represented the SMT but, at Middleton, Julia also served as teacher governor. Her position spanned both SMT and other staff. Teaching staff at this school were also represented by a head of faculty, and one co-opted governor was a member of the office staff. At Drake, as well as the two staff governors and the head, the two deputies attended governing body meetings as observers. In a staff governor's view, the deputies' contribution to governors' meetings was so extensive, that the 'observer–member' distinction evaporated. The diagram shows how the governing body as a whole included representatives who had direct experience of the private SMT arena and the arena of other staff. The permeable area of the demarcation between these two groups was also access-ible to the governing body via the teacher and SMT representatives. Therefore, although SMT members had the most comprehensive overview of the internal workings of each school, it was complemented by the areas of representation on the governing body.

The meetings of the full governing body and the subcommittees we observed suggested that representatives from among the school staff drew upon their extensive knowledge in supporting (rather than challenging) the head, as did other SMT members who attended meetings with observer status. Each govern-ing body monitored the work of the SMT but the team's endeavours appeared to lie well within the boundaries of acceptability to governors as a group.

LIMITS TO SCHOOL-WIDE SYNERGY?

Our observations showed how members of both SMTs attempted continually to foster synergy across the school through their leadership of staff. They worked hard on creating and operating fair arrangements for consultation and dissemination of information and, especially at Drake, intervened to encourage other staff to work together in a way which was consistent with the approach to teamwork in the SMT. The ability to take such a lead rested on the accept-ability of the individual and group activity of SMT members to the majority of other staff, on whose staff membership behaviour the SMT depended.

Acceptability of the SMT to other staff, and therefore the potential for school-wide synergy, was subject to two constraints: the first related to the demarcation between the two groups created by the SMTs' private arena. Persuading other staff that the SMT was operating within the bounds of ac-ceptability to them was always an uphill task for team members. Other staff had to make a leap of faith to cross the credibility gap posed by their uncer-tainty whether the invisible component of the SMTs' practice matched the account given by their members. The impossibility of removing the conditions whereby individuals might interpret the SMT to be guilty of illegitimate ma-nipulation was indicated by the way the blueprint myth lingered on at Mid-dleton despite the efforts of SMT members to dispel it.

The extent of the private arena and the degree of permeability of the demar-cation zone appeared to be broadly similar in the two schools. The account summarised in Chapter 1 of how Taylor (1992) opened up the SMT to other staff suggests that it may be possible to reduce the extent of the SMT private arena by letting in more other staff on more SMT deliberations, so increasing the permeability of the demarcation zone. Where such a strategy is seen as desirable, there still appear to remain limits. Taylor regarded certain staffing issues as too sensitive to discuss openly. Respondents among SMT members and middle managers in all six of our study schools pointed to the imprac-ticability of large groups for consultation and decision making.

The second constraint concerns substantive sectional interests: within their staff membership role, followership among other staff depended not only on acceptance of the SMT consultation and dissemination procedures but also on the belief that their sectional interests were being adequately served compared with those of colleagues. SMTs were charged with finding an acceptable balance between sometimes incompatible interests, not all of which could be fully met within the existing level of resources. Heads of faculty in both schools grouped together to maximise their ability to protect such sectional interests as they shared.

At Middleton the group had taken on some characteristics of a team, seeking compromises on individual members' interests and, with a largely united front, promoting to the SMT what heads of faculty perceived was in their best combined interest. One area of contention was the proposal to purchase IT hardware, which met the interest of the IT coordinator, but not the top priority interests of heads of faculty. They united in questioning whether the money should be spent on this innovation rather than being shared among the faculties. Heads of faculty at Drake had moved some way in this direction, but first allegiance to fighting individual faculty corners remained more prevalent.

Members of both SMTs had accepted this grouping of interests and the creation of another private arena, legitimating a way of operating amongst other staff that mirrored their wish to work within a private arena of their own. While SMT members had authority to prevent any sectional interest among other staff from dominating, they had limited ability to create conditions where other staff might embrace the SMT value of giving lower priority to any sectional interest than to the balance of interests across the school. Other staff did not have full access to the whole-school perspective which informed adherence to this value by SMT members.

Since SMTs achieve their joint tasks mainly with and through other staff, a seemingly inevitable strain accompanying a team approach is rooted in the out-group that is the flipside of creating a cohesive management team. In such large organisations there appears to be limited possibility of extending the comprehensiveness of the SMT overview and the face-to-face decision-making process much beyond the team, without diluting its ability to perform as a team and the ability of other staff to concentrate on their more localised primary tasks. Even the governing body, which is structured in such a way as to offer a safeguard against the SMT overstepping the boundaries of acceptability to representatives of a wider range of interest groups connected with the school, can have very limited knowledge of how the SMT actually works.

8

Team Development at Drake School – a Question of Balance

During the year that we observed the Drake SMT at work, we focused in part on its members' attempts to develop as a team. Here we describe what team development involved, and explore what members' experiences tell us about teamwork and the cultural and political factors affecting its progress.

In Chapter 5 we characterised this SMT as a 'developing' team. We showed how each person's role in the team and her or his commitment to teamwork changed during the year so that at the end no one's team contribution was the same as at the beginning. Derek opened out, Marian became more cautious, Philip was more comfortable with his 'manager' role and Greg more confident with his new responsibilities; Barbara felt more integrated with the team and Kate, as leader, reviewed and refined her approach to leadership of the team. These changes stemmed from the events that constituted each team member's daily experience of managing and teaching at Drake (as well as those in their private lives). Structured attempts at individual and team development were just one element of that experience but perceived by some as having the potential to bring more radical change. This chapter focuses on these attempts and discusses the reasons why team members considered development necessary and desirable, the form taken by development activities and their impact on individual and team performance.

Development took a number of forms, including induction, coaching and the annual residential meeting. Our research project coincided with the team decision to focus for one year on individual and team self-development through joint use of a distance-learning package produced for managers in industry, and provided by LEA staff. The focus on development differentiated the SMT at Drake from others in our study. The content and the process of team members' discussions of how they operated (stimulated by the package) illustrated many of the gains and strains of teamwork.

Individuals varied in their interpretation of their responsibility in bringing about development. They each used authority or influence to support their own and others' development and to resist being developed in ways with which they were uncomfortable or which they considered unnecessary.

ACHIEVING BALANCE AMONG PERSONAL STYLES

Kate's decision to adopt a team approach required changing her managerial style as a head in addition to supporting others' development, in order to facilitate their equal contribution to the team. Since becoming head at Drake, she had replaced departing team members with 'suitable' people:

> People I could use as sounding boards to bounce ideas off, and to whom I could delegate effectively in areas of the school's work that I could not undertake myself; and making the most of opportunities as they arose to grow on some talent. I had also read Belbin, and I looked at team roles and where we were deficient in terms of personalities and what people could contribute to the team.

She chose individuals who would bring varied qualities of knowledge, skill and personality to the SMT.

One question for Kate was: what mix of personalities would make a balanced team? We suggested in Chapter 2 that contrasting personalities may be interpreted as being expressed in interaction through varied individual preferences in the use of power according to equally varied beliefs and values. Individuals in SMTs express their personality through their preferred use of power, reflecting their relevant beliefs and values, within their personal managerial style. We interpret Kate to have selected members according to a belief that personal styles among team members must cover both task completion (addressed by Belbin) and seeing to the needs of people, both inside the team and outsiders to whom the team must relate. It did not matter if members' personal styles leaned more towards tasks or people's needs, as long as individuals complemented or balanced each other in covering both between them. She appeared to have extended the idea in Belbin's work of complementarity among preferred team roles in achieving a shared task to complementarity among personalities in so far as they affected personal managerial styles.

Striving for 'balance' was a characteristic of team members' development efforts, informing Kate's early attempt to create an SMT. Kate soon realised that team members were perceived by other staff as distant and formal, despite her endeavour to counterbalance what both she and Derek recognised as their almost austere and aloof personal managerial styles (perceived as 'very efficient but perhaps a little inhuman') with the greater integration of Greg and Philip with staff outside the SMT. Marian's appointment represented an attempt to restore a desirable balance among members' personalities. Existing team members saw her as bringing the warmth, people skills and outgoing personality which the rest of the staff saw as missing.

Combined with the authority associated with her status as deputy (which, in the eyes of staff, Greg and Philip did not have) her appointment created the potential for transforming the culture of teamwork, and the image of the team held by other staff. Kate's mission had been to create the team; Marian's was to change it. Although changing was something other team members, including Kate, recognised as desirable, the experience proved both painful and positive.

The search for balance, as the dominant cultural characteristic of team members, went beyond their range of personalities. For Kate, valuing balance was linked with the norm she embraced that harmony and equilibrium were to be preferred to discord and upheaval. At one development session she was surprised that some teams engage in 'slanging matches' since none she had been in had ever done so. At another, she warned Marian against 'throwing ideas in the air for the sake of it'.

Kate's preferences for harmony and balance were also an outcome of her judgement about the needs of the school after a long period of continuous innovation. Her approach to creating the team was as a cook to her ingredients; having identified and weighed them, they needed careful mixing and blending to produce the desired outcome: efficient teamwork that accomplished the school's objectives. The challenge was to blend in a way that created the synergy of which she believed teams to be capable, without losing the unique contribution of each ingredient.

A consequence of the operation of Kate's selection criteria was a team whose members displayed six contrasting temperaments, which had the potential to disrupt teamwork at times. Although in Belbin's terms it was a balanced team in representing the range of preferred team roles he described, team members also possessed other qualities. His work offered little guidance for the challenge now faced by SMT members at Drake: how were they going to work together, having been selected for different qualities? Although Marian's appointment was intended to complete the balance among members, it actually raised a question over how far harmony and balance contributed to creative teamwork.

The impact of a new member was to polarise the 'separate togetherness' of the team (Chapter 5), highlighting the contrast between the personal styles in expressing leadership of the team and team membership preferred by Kate, Derek and Barbara, and those preferred by Greg and Marian. Structured development activities had represented for all members an attempt to strengthen the team's capacity for joint work, but an unanticipated outcome was to highlight the effect of this polarisation on the teamwork process. Differences between members were constrained by the introspection demanded by the development materials, which supported the belief of the majority of team members in the appropriateness of separate togetherness. The development effort highlighted the effects of enduring personal characteristics on attempts to create a shared culture of teamwork. Moreover, the shifting balance of power in the team led one or other set of characteristics to dominate at any one time.

The acquiescence of Greg and Philip to hierarchy shifted the balance of power back to most team members' preferred way of working and on many occasions left Marian out on a limb. The potential for structured development activities to tip the culture of teamwork in a new direction was enhanced when Kate delegated leadership of the activity to Marian; but the latter's reluctance to lead within the team on this issue by making a substantive contribution, in addition to facilitating the deliberation process, and other team members' resistance to change in the directions suggested by the materials, meant that such a shift was not realised.

One stimulus for team development was the need to get the balance right in terms of individual contributions to the process of teamwork. New additions to the team could unsettle the balance which their presence was designed to achieve. Greg and Philip, who had taught in the school for over twelve years, had gone through the challenge posed by membership of the team to their historical identification with staff other than senior management. Greg reported:

> I was aware of discomfort when I first moved from one camp to the other so that when I first went back to the staffroom sometimes people would stop talking. People would come up to me and say, 'I want to speak to you now as a member of the senior management team.' And I would say, 'Just speak to me now as you did three months ago.'

His induction and development as a manager was achieved mainly, in his view, by participation in SMT meetings. Philip confirmed as one positive feature of the team's approach: 'If your name is on the agenda you jolly well prepare yourself, it's part of the indoctrination.' Kate believed in encouraging the retention of differences rather than inducting newcomers into what she considered as a dangerous conformity. When Marian joined the team, Kate felt it would be an affront to her obvious capability to induct her formally. Similarly Kate recognised the discomfort of Philip and Greg at their new team status, but was adamant they must accept their greater allegiance to the SMT. The question of induction did not arise when Derek joined the team as he had worked with Kate since she took over the headship, she knew his track record, and their individual managerial styles were similar. Barbara, too, had never been inducted, having worked in the school for twenty years and being a member of the SMT before Kate's arrival. We saw in Chapter 5 how her partnership with Kate, combined with ambiguity about how far she was a team member, put her on the margin of the team.

Kate knew that Marian's presence would initially create discomfort in the SMT. Retrospectively she concluded: 'It's eighteen months since Marian joined the team and it's clear it takes at least a year for a new member to shake down.' She also revealed to Marian:

> When you were appointed there were very clear criteria. I knew we needed someone who would fill the role which you do fill. I also knew that it would not necessarily be comfortable for me personally to work with your style all the time because it's not my style; but that made it even more important that you brought a different approach.

Colleagues supported her decision to select an outsider, though all recognised the risk in appointing someone who was radically different in personal style. The development sessions revealed the tensions created by bringing in someone with a different personality, style and institutional history. When she joined the team, it was developing within parameters set by the team leader. Inevitably, some difficulties arose at first in coping with the different style of a newcomer. This difference was particularly marked between the two deputies. According to Derek, 'Marian likes to fling herself into everything immediately while I prefer to sit tight for a while and see how the land lies.'

Marian was also the first woman to be brought on to a team whose leader was a woman. We saw little in the team's work methods to contradict the hypothesis we proposed in Chapter 2 that a team's commitment to equal contribution also contributes to neutralising the effects of gender factors on group work. The similarities of Derek's and Kate's styles and marked contrast between Kate's and Marian's precluded any easy association between style and gender. Derek, Philip and Greg had all worked with woman heads before and were used to women in leadership positions. The lack of casual comments and gender jokes that so often characterises mixed group interaction might be attributed to the same professional, almost 'polite', interaction that was so highly valued within the culture of teamwork. Just as it constrained openness about deeply held values, it also set norms about appropriate behaviour between members, whether men or women. We are not arguing that some of the same issues about men and women working together were not present, but that they rarely surfaced or were allowed to surface.

A RANGE OF DEVELOPMENT ACTIVITIES

It was clear that team members had work to do on the tensions created by different personalities and perceptions of the extent of equal contributions within the SMT, and by changes in the dynamic of an established team. Marian's advent also led to reallocation of job responsibilities. The development agenda was heavy, particularly when set alongside individuals' career and professional development concerns. In making a team decision to engage with a development programme, a balance had to be struck between individual and team needs.

They were not always congruent, as revealed by difficulties arising in reviewing and allocating team roles. Greg and Philip were concerned how the chosen distance-learning package could support their own development as managers. Although this aspiration was on Kate's and Marian's agenda for the allowance holders, the head and deputy wanted to use the programme to raise issues about how the team was operating, an aim with which Derek agreed. Marian perceived that: 'Everyone here in our team could move on except Kate. We are all at different stages of our careers and each individual is highly motivated.'

She was the most motivated to further her development, ambitious to achieve a headship in the near future and therefore keen to strengthen and extend her range of management skills. She was also committed to teamwork as the best way to manage a school: 'I tend to adopt a team approach to anything that I do. That's the way I get people to work best with me and that's the way I like to work.' Marian had a vested interest in the successful use of the distance-learning programme, both as the staff-development coordinator and, as a result of Kate's delegation, leader within the team of the development programme. Her vision for teamwork, which both complemented and contrasted with her colleagues' approach, meant that she was keen to shape the culture of teamwork 'to that of which I want to be a member' while conscious of being shaped and developed by it.

Kate's decision to let her take the lead on the development programme empowered her to focus team members' attention on areas where she thought change was desirable. Although she and Kate discussed some issues arising from its use, Kate's main commitment was to having them aired. There was no prior agreement on how they should be taken forward.

Activities other than the distance-learning package aimed at individual development were often covert, controlled in the main by Kate's perception of her central role in providing development opportunities for her colleagues. Job allocation was her primary means of ensuring a balance between the imperative to manage the school and individuals' career development needs. We suggest that her part in allocating responsibilities was, from her perspective, legitimate manipulation. Although aspects were discussed in the team, they were likely to have been preceded by discussions between Kate and individual team members. For her, leadership of the team included the continual search to fit the right people to the right responsibilities, while simultaneously preserving enough flexibility for team members to change them when appropriate.

The main forum for reviewing SMT members' responsibilities was the annual residential meeting, although Marian's arrival provided an extra stimulus, since she brought new skills that had to be incorporated. Kate used her authority to delimit the responsibilities any colleague might be allocated. Her preferred strategy was to make small adjustments to individual responsibilities among team members each year, to avoid the danger courted by job rotation of square pegs in round holes. It was primarily her decision which pegs fitted into which holes. Her judgement about people's ability to perform well in a particular task area was paramount. For her it was a necessary extension of her commitment to full delegation, once a responsibility had been allocated, and her priority that any decision should be in the interest of the school, even if it clashed with individual team members' expressed interests.

Philip had been disadvantaged when Marian joined the team because of the decision to incorporate his 'plum job' as professional tutor into Marian's personnel role. He accepted without dissent that the reallocation was in the interests of the team and school, though he privately acknowledged that it was at the expense of some of his job satisfaction. A year later his new responsibilities still failed to meet this personal interest. He told the others at the team's annual job review:

I found relinquishing my head-of-year role harder than I thought. No one comes to me any more, but goes to others. The problem with being in charge of evaluation is that it is at the bottom of everyone else's list of priorities. Records of achievement are the same. I have to keep prodding people. It's the same with health and safety; I'm trying to look at it positively and not as a chore. I miss doing personnel and working with new teachers.

The impact of this apparent cry from the heart was deflected by Philip's belief in hierarchy that led him not to push his personal interests in the face of team interests.

Barbara's expression of concern about her role had a similar fate. As the three men had already left to teach, only Kate and Marian listened to her comment: 'I am not sure how I fit into this whole set up. I don't feel I make the contribution I should.' Both women reassured her that what she was doing was of immense value: to Kate in managing the budget and resources, and to Marian in managing personnel. Unlike Philip's plea, Barbara's was for more development and support in a role that was becoming increasingly complex and demanding. Philip expressed his concern in terms of job satisfaction but his position reflected judgements not only about where he was most appropriately placed but, implicitly, also over who might be even better placed.

Job review and allocation were not only about managing the school and meeting individual development needs; they were also about individuals staking a claim for responsibilities that best served their personal interests in career development and job satisfaction. Until Marian arrived, all members subscribed within the culture of teamwork to the norm that Kate had the right to make unilateral decisions on job allocation and the norm that they should take collective responsibility for sharing out mundane tasks. Marian challenged these norms in a way that threatened to upset the balance of the team; this time the scales were tipped almost entirely against her.

At one of the team's development sessions, Kate expressed concern at team members' tendency to see themselves as specialists, differentiated rather than integrated. Team interest expressed through greater flexibility was in conflict with individuals' interests in their individual development for their careers and for job satisfaction. Both Marian and Derek agreed that a review of job descriptions was desirable but each had a different vested interest in the outcomes. One person's gain was potentially another's loss. Factors affecting recognition of the force of their claims was influenced by seniority accorded to Derek, length of time on the team and the extent to which each claim fitted with Kate's perceptions of what was possible and desirable.

Marian expressed the wish to give up responsibility for arranging staff cover. Other members combined resources, according to beliefs and values which were incompatible with hers, to reject this proposal. The articulated justification was that only Marian had the necessary skills to do the job and it was highly valued. However, though not made explicit at the time, there was dissatisfaction on the part of three team members with Marian's expressed reluctance to continue with a responsibility for which, in their view, she had been appointed. As the only member of the team currently applying for promotion elsewhere her actions were interpreted as demonstrating personal interest at the expense of team unity. One claimed: 'It wasn't unpleasant, just a quiet closing of ranks.' For them, Marian's claim ran counter to the team norm that each member should accept a share of mundane responsibilities. Kate described the boundary of acceptability to her that Marian had transgressed, 'rather than one person having all the grotty jobs, we need to share them out.'

THE RESIDENTIAL MEETING: FOR TASK ACHIEVEMENT OR TEAM COHESION?

Team members' search for balance continued in their annual residential meeting and their work on the distance-learning package. While they collaborated in building an agenda for the residential, responsibility for facilitating use of the development package was delegated to Marian. The main purpose of this meeting was perceived as an opportunity to reach consensual decisions about policies and issues that had evolved during the year and needed resolution. In this respect, the annual review meeting was not unlike other SMT meetings held during the year; it was the equivalent of eight meetings held consecutively with short refreshment breaks between.

Where it might have been expected to be different was in being residential. This arrangement offered opportunities for decision making away from the immediate pressures of the school, and had potential for a different kind of team interaction as a result of social as well as professional discourse (potential which, as we saw in Chapter 4, was realised in other schools in Eastshire). Constraints on 'opening up' imposed by the usual school setting would disappear in a country house location where SMT members breakfasted and dined together as well as meeting professionally. Philip alone chose not to stay. He welcomed the time to fulfil team tasks, but experience had taught him that being residential did not alter how SMT members behaved together. He perceived that he would miss nothing by not staying overnight. Other team members were happy to stay, but most were more committed to the decision-making tasks of the two days than to the potential of a residential event to help members develop as a team.

The heavy emphasis on task achievement was dictated partly by the huge agenda built up beforehand, and also by individuals' continuing preference for separating professional and social life. The residential was defined exclusively as professional by all members except Marian. Kate justified the heavy agenda: 'It provides an atmosphere where the team can be together and some frank talking can develop without it being terminated by clock watching.'

The previous year's residential provided an opportunity for working through tensions created between the two deputies by Marian's arrival. The attention to team process necessitated by these tensions focused on difficulties between two individuals. In Kate's view both Marian and Derek learned from the experience and followed up with the necessary adjustments to their personal styles as well as accepting the clarification of job boundaries that threatened their working relations and harmony. The 'bloodletting' was an individual rather than team experience with the two allowance holders as embarrassed onlookers and Kate as referee. Philip perceived that the tension was a matter for the deputies to sort out between themselves and then with the head, not something that should be dealt with by all team members. Kate too was uncomfortable with the open expression of conflict:

> When the clash emerged, I then intervened to open it up, to let blood and let what needed to be said be said. But I don't usually intervene in that way unless I really have to.

A key norm within the culture of teamwork appeared to be that confrontation should generally be excluded from the SMT arena.

Since the residential offered opportunities for debating issues at length, a type of team process could emerge to which Kate, as team leader aspired, but which was not always possible in the confines of the school day. For her, the residential in January was 'about visioning, setting the tone, thinking ahead, planning, dreaming a bit – all for implementation next October!'. An outline agenda was already evolving the previous September, to include faculty action plans, areas for audit, strategic planning, and resources for the school-development plan. This opportunity for the team to develop through residential experience did not extend to Barbara who, as usual, attended only those items that impinged directly on her areas of responsibility.

Our observation confirmed Philip's claim that interaction during these two days differed little from SMT meetings in school. The culture of teamwork appeared to include the norm that joint work was confined to meetings; discussions of work issues rarely extended into refreshment breaks. The sessions were typically businesslike and efficient, issues being discussed thoroughly and often heatedly and decisions being reached through consensus.

There were attempts outside the development session during the residential to engage in the open-ended creativity that study of the management package had shown to be missing in the team's approach. Kate introduced the first item, 'a future structure for the school', as a brainstorming session. She handed over leadership of the item to Marian on the grounds that 'my mind after all these years is probably set in the system we have'. Marian played devil's advocate for radical changes to the pastoral system, behaviour not fully approved of by Philip who revealed at the end of the day his irritation at '*agent provocateur* tactics that can waste time'. From his perspective, Marian had transgressed the norm within the culture of teamwork that individuals should challenge but not deliberately take up a position they did not hold (whereas playing devil's advocate was valued at Middleton as a means of stimulating creative thought). Equally, he did not make his perception explicit to her at the time, which would also have gone against the norm ruling out confrontation. Marian's defence of her method, supported by Kate, was team members' need on behalf of the school to capitalise on their creative potential and not allow complacency to set in.

In contrast, Kate led on the item dealing with the school's current structure by tabling a paper outlining the parameters for the discussion and options for action. Her outline gave no indication of her preferences and the debate ranged freely, mainly between Marian and Derek, with interjections from Kate, and Greg and Philip as attentive listeners.

During breaks, the chat circled around the surface details of private lives with, characteristically, Derek and Kate being the least self-revealing and Philip and Marian the most. None tried to compete with Marian's energetic exposition of her recent parachute jump! At the development session set aside for a 'team health audit', the ambience resembled that of similar sessions back in school.

Such sessions were timetabled twice a term as the last item in the usually long agendas of the regular SMT meetings after the school day ended. Inevitably, team members were tired at the end of a long day and constrained by the concern of the three men in particular to get home to their families. Greg and Derek had young children and Philip often argued that work should not impinge unreasonably on non-work time. Neither of the women were heard to express similar concerns or reservations.

EXPERIENCE WITH THE DISTANCE-LEARNING PACKAGE

We analysed use of the development package over three terms in which it was a regular item on the SMT agenda. It was Marian's idea to use this package which she had employed in her previous school. The package was designed for use by individuals, supported by group meetings in which the outcomes of private study were shared and, if appropriate, decisions on future action agreed. This combination of individual and group study complemented the majority of team members' preference for separate togetherness, allowing most of the development work to be done in private with only occasional public disclosures of experiences and self-discovery.

Individual members were further protected from disclosure within the SMT by Kate's delegation to Marian of leadership of the exercise. For Marian, facilitating compromised her substantive contribution within her team membership role, making her less vocal than she might have been if Kate had assumed leadership. Consequently, each time team members arrived at a point of joint enlightenment, no one took responsibility for identifying implications and securing commitment to action. Marian held back because she did not want to compromise Kate's position as leader of the team. Kate held back because 'it was Marian's baby and I agreed she should take us through it. I felt it might have been a put down for her if I had taken over'.

Although Philip, Derek and Greg agreed to participate, they were sceptical about the programme's potential for team development. They looked to Marian for guidance on what they individually 'should' do next and for approval when they had done it. Rarely was the question 'What should the team do next?' posed, other than by Marian, despite Kate's commitment to the programme as a way of shaping the culture of teamwork so that 'it could become something beyond its component parts'.

All were aware that disclosures encouraged by the programme could make them individually vulnerable, especially Kate as leader of the team. She was prepared to accept disclosure for the sake of team development but was not entirely comfortable when it happened. While committed to equal contribution as a team member, the development activities revealed her concern that as the leader of the team there had to be constraints on sharing and the degree of collaboration.

The development-programme materials highlighted throughout the separate role of the team leader, drawing attention to Kate's different role in the SMT, even though her practice did not reflect this separateness. The boundaries that she drew around self-disclosure set the tone of those sessions that required it, despite Marian's attempts to encourage self-disclosure through her example in being ready to reveal thoughts and feelings. Disclosure of feelings about self and team colleagues appeared to transgress the norms within the culture of teamwork promoted by Kate, and largely accepted by others except Marian, that interaction should be cordial and polite and feelings – especially negative ones – should not be expressed within the SMT arena. Unless the latter norm could be replaced, we suggest that the existing culture of teamwork constituted a barrier against the the form of team development encouraged by the materials. Yet it must be borne in mind that this culture also underpinned the ability demonstrated by team members to fulfil the role of the SMT in managing the school.

The pattern for using the development programme varied little. Other SMT members agreed with Marian on the materials to be covered before a given date, when team development would appear as the final item on the SMT agenda. Barbara left and the group spent up to an hour discussing points arising from their reading and completion of written exercises. Marian led the discussion, sometimes with a flip chart to record points. There was no other formal record of the discussions or ideas for action. Discussion was slow at first, despite Marian's exhortations for SMT members to be 'brutally honest'. Participation required each individual to come to terms with personal doubts about the possible impact of the activities. Philip and Greg considered themselves relative novices as managers and did not at first wish to appear naïve. Derek's personal style did not generally encourage self-disclosure although, in the exceptional circumstances of the previous year's residential, he had been prepared to open up a conflict of interests between himself and Marian. Kate felt vulnerable as team leader. Marian alone was confident about revealing personal weaknesses and commenting on what she perceived as weaknesses in the team as a whole. She attempted to combine the tasks of facilitator (by keeping team members to time and task) and catalyst (using the materials to raise issues about the team). Kate sometimes picked up on and supported a team weakness identified by Marian, such as the fact that team members were 'self-limiting' in their ambitions for the school.

This revelation led to a sharing of concerns about the constraints felt to be on the school in determining its own direction. In Derek's view, due to the constraints on school managers imposed by central government policies, 'you feel more and more like His Master's Voice and less and less like someone who believes in something'. The opportunity provided by such statements to explore more deeply held values was not taken. It would have meant transgressing the boundaries of individuals' right to keep their personal beliefs and values to themselves, a norm which the culture of teamwork defined as inviolable. Team members recognised a fundamental divergency of values but accepted they had not been selected for their values but their skills. Kate said:

> We have talked a lot about values regarding the school's mission statement and what the school stands for, but we haven't linked them to personal value positions. I would be worried that we might find some person's position so different it would cause a polarisation. It's important to leave people room for their personal opinions.

The norm that agreed team values should be given primacy over individual values (accepted by SMT members), combined with the norm of consensual decision making, meant that any team member would agree to support a team decision supported by the majority (say, to become a grant-maintained school), even if he or she disliked it in principle.

The residential development session revealed members' different perceptions of the team, since it involved an audit in which they identified the team's state of health. It was measured in terms of degrees of satisfaction with different aspects of team process such as clarity of mission, helpfulness of intergroup relations, and appropriateness of leadership style. (Unusually, Barbara stayed for this session and was able to contribute her views.) Marian began by warning the group that the audit's purpose was to increase the openness of the group. Critical observations might come to the surface. The team leader, as the most vulnerable member, should state openly how the process should go and whether they needed to fear disclosing their true viewpoints. A moment's silence followed, then much jocularity about whether they should leave now or wait to be sacked. Kate responded by saying, 'I can't sack you'. Marian was reassuring: 'If we are not open and honest, there's not much point doing this – and Kate won't sack us!'

SMT members perceived the team as relatively healthy in all the identified areas. Their joint score indicated they thought they were weakest on 'closed and open thinking': the ability to stand back and review critically what they did. Derek disagreed, arguing that they spent too much time being self-critical and not enough on saying well done to themselves. Others supported his view, quickly reaching a consensus that they should celebrate success more, a theme which resurfaced throughout the session.

The item on levels of team satisfaction and dissatisfaction picked up on a theme raised earlier in the year about the extent to which team members provided each other with emotional support. Greg was sceptical about whether, given their very different personalities and jobs, they could offer each other emotional support. He and Kate felt that there were times when they were not supported emotionally and Kate wondered 'if in some teams who were more similar in sex and age the social interaction might be different.' This was the sole reference made to gender as a potential factor influencing interaction. Differences in personal style, with equally strong contrasts between the men and between the women, dominated team members' self-analysis. They debated whether interaction would be different or better if they met more socially but their resistance to this strategy continued to be strong, apart from Marian.

Three months later, at the residential, they continued to skirt around the same issue. Derek confirmed that he felt much happier this year as a result of more collaboration on the school development plan which he had previously done alone. Kate disagreed with Marian that the team continued to work 'in their own pockets', constraining Marian in pushing for more work on collaboration between team members. There was little response to a question about how good they were at developing people in the team. Discussion focused on the validity and reliability of the scoring mechanism, apparently deflecting team members away from an uncomfortable issue.

At this point the session was being used to confirm the positive elements of the culture of teamwork, rather than explore the implications of conflicting views or agreed weaknesses. Marian, Philip and Greg agreed 'the team has a good blend of personalities' and 'enough team members to get the job done'. Consensus emerged on the efficiency of SMT members in achieving their joint tasks, leaving the affective side of teamwork unexplored. Members were in agreement at this stage about 'a balanced team', the item on which they scored highest.

By the end of the session, the balance was less clearly discernible. They disagreed on the team's clarity of mission. Collectively they appeared to think it was clear, individually they did not. Kate was concerned: 'I know what I'm aiming to achieve, but I worry a lot that we may not all be focused in the same way.' Derek pointed out the difference between *knowing* what the team is aiming at and *agreeing* with it. Team members confirmed the acceptability of agreeing after debate a direction or decision that individually they may not strongly support. This willingness to compromise they felt accounted for their tendency not to be 'fired' with a sense of joint purpose but, in Derek's words, 'We are professional, we come in and do a job and go home and spend the money.'

It was easier to arrive at agreement and action points on the effectiveness of their meetings. Their main concern was that meetings were getting longer. They decided to meet additionally on Fridays for one period and shorten the after-school meeting on Monday. The item on team role clarity showed they were all aware of their own objectives but were not sure of each other's. Marian pushed for more openness. Greg confessed that he was sometimes very aware of disagreeing with others' objectives and not saying anything. Again, the culture of teamwork seemed to discourage the further disclosure of differences and they moved on to safer ground: their need to congratulate themselves more on a job well done.

PERSONAL STYLES QUESTIONED

The most difficult item, reflected in long silences, addressed the appropriateness of leadership style. Kate acknowledged it was a difficult issue for them to examine honestly. From the beginning, the item was discussed by identifying leadership solely with Kate. No one used their practice of sharing leadership within the team on particular issues to challenge the package's association of leadership with an individual. Kate too accepted that leadership was about how she operated as head within the team. After a silence, Marian concluded: 'So we're saying that's fine, the statements are often true.' Even within the parameters for openness invited by the development package, other SMT members were not prepared to discuss aspects of Kate's leadership style with which they were not comfortable, either as a group or individually. At the end of the session, Kate commented:

> Clearly this had to be a threatening situation for me. Most of you indicated in the question on leadership style that it's true for the most part that I adopt an appropriate one. In return for my having submitted myself to that quite threatening situation, given the mix of personalities in the team, what do you think is the best style of leadership?

At this point Derek took the initiative by disclosing that other members experienced discomfort on the few occasions when Kate deviated from her style: 'So when you move from chairman [sic] of the group style to directive style it is always difficult to cope with.' The debate switched to discussion of different team members' impact on others. Later Kate revealed to us that the comments had touched on her own concern about achieving a balance between delegating and directing and her desire to be consistent within one style.

Having reviewed the separate items, Marian tried to move team members towards agreement on action to be taken on weaker areas. Since no one else volunteered points for follow up, Marian identified areas from the flip chart to which others responded, such as whether they were open enough or hiding things. Kate said that as a team they were fairly frank and honest with each other and certainly not hiding things. However, her comment that 'we're probably not a very extrovert group of personalities and you can't change your personality, nor should you try' set in motion a heated debate about how team members perceived each other (excluding Kate). The harmony and balance that had been confirmed throughout the session, in part by avoiding issues which threatened it, was destabilised through the polarisation created by openness about the impact of different personalities on others' behaviour in the team.

Greg and Marian perceived that, within the group, the more extrovert personalities were suppressed. Philip attributed constraints on his own behaviour to his desire in the team to be professional: being attentive at meetings led to him being 'less effusive about things, just keeping your mind on the job'. Kate repeated her assertion that 'If we were all extrovert or all introvert it wouldn't be a well-balanced team'. The discussion increasingly associated negative qualities with extrovert teams: extroverts swamp people; they have slanging matches. Marian's attempts to defend alternative styles and her reservations about some aspects of the existing mix threatened to set her apart. For the others, the audit had confirmed the appropriateness of the present culture of teamwork. Philip wondered whether Marian's discomfort stemmed from joining a team that differed greatly from her previous one with which she often made comparisons.

Marian appealed to Greg for support over feeling some suppression by the team of their more extrovert personalities. Greg agreed but considered it not a bad thing. He apparently chose to subjugate his preference for being extrovert in favour of harmonising with the dominant personal styles within the team. Marian defended her interest, thereby compromising her facilitator role in order to assert her right to make an equal contribution. Her challenge led other team members to affirm their preference for a 'calm, businesslike, safe' approach over styles they had jointly experienced which 'involved throwing a lot of things up in the air and not being sure if and where they would all come down'.

At this point, Marian was excluded from part of other SMT members' shared history and made aware that her style at times unwittingly reminded team members of past experiences that they preferred to forget. The contribution of personal styles to the process of teamwork had been shaped by Kate, with others' support, as a contrast to what had gone before. Any attempts to move it back in that direction were unwelcome. Kate, nevertheless, expressed concern about what the discussion had revealed:

> It's a little alarming to hear you and Greg saying that you feel inhibited, because if you do, the balance isn't quite right. It would suggest that the rest of us are balancing to one end of what you might call a range of personality traits.

Her colleagues refrained from exploring the issue further. Greg confirmed the right of other team members to shape his performance and Marian returned to her facilitator role. Following their custom, team members brought the issue to a close by reaching a consensual decision to distinguish some meetings as more appropriate for creative thinking and critical review and others for business. The issue of different personalities and their impact on team process was not addressed again, either within the meeting or in the pub later that evening.

We suggest that, as before, key norms within the existing culture of teamwork had inhibited individuals from the transgression which pursuing the debate would have represented, resulting in a reinforcement of the existing culture of teamwork. It appears that Marian (and to a lesser extent Greg) frequently withheld from expressing some of her teamwork values, including most of the time when leading the development activity, so as to accommodate her preferred personal style to those expressed by other team members. In other words, where balance within the team was achieved, complementarity of personal styles entailed Marian displaying inaction by not expressing parts of hers. She did not fully share colleagues' culture but, within the dialectic of control in the team, had either refrained from using influence to change team norms, or had little impact when doing so in the face of the authority and influence used by others to sustain their culture of teamwork. From their perspective, any imbalance related more to Marian's personal style as a new member than to norms within their culture which limited their willingness to accommodate certain of her beliefs and values concerning teamwork. However, over the period of our observation there was evidence of mutual accommodation.

While Kate shared some of Marian's concerns, she chose not lead on follow-up action. A later session focused on their communications with the school rather than in the team. This time commitment to action followed. All agreed to be about the school more (rather than leave it to the two 'people' people) and to review their communication systems. The issue about individual responsibilities was simmering at the time, having been postponed from the residential. As we described earlier, it involved much discussion between individuals outside the SMT arena, possibly militating against team members being willing to make their feelings and perceptions about each other explicit within the development sessions.

DEVELOPMENT OR REAFFIRMATION OF CURRENT PRACTICE?

The next development session was fitted into the new meeting time of a middle period on a Friday afternoon, creating tight time parameters as Greg had to teach the last period. Development was the only agenda item. The background reading for this session proved particularly apposite to a problem members were encountering. A decision they took at the residential to create a new post (to be advertised internally) had gone wrong. The materials helped them analyse faults in their decision-making process. They thought they had considered the decision with their usual thoroughness, but realised they had suffered from tunnel vision and a failure to share what was in each other's minds. This realisation echoed what had been revealed in the team audit: that they tended to assume shared aims whereas in fact their aims were different.

Marian invited colleagues to highlight learning points from the experience, and Greg commented that they had all been writing their own notes rather than sharing their thinking on a flipchart. The development activity indicated how members adopted different approaches to something they aimed to do collectively. Marian made a substantive contribution, suggesting that their staff selection decisions also needed revising, to include clarification that they were all looking for the same thing. Kate agreed to a list of selection criteria 'as long as it's clear it's just a tool'; she was not prepared to relinquish her flexibility to take account of gut reaction. Marian summarised that they had agreed to try the new system out and, since no one agreed or disagreed, moved on to the next item. In this case, she had led the team to an agreement to revise selection practices but not to action on the decision-making process.

The section in the package on problem solving stimulated a review of monitoring and evaluation. Kate was confident from her appraisal feedback that other staff felt secure with the present systems. Marian challenged whether systems also prevented creativity and taking an overview. The debate followed the pattern we have described: Marian pushing for more radical change, Kate and Derek urging caution and incrementalism. Marian reminded colleagues of suggestions in the development package for increasing creativity, such as bringing new people into the team on a short-term basis. Derek supported her and the seed was planted for the change, though it was still under discussion nine months later. Kate commented:

> I am quite attracted to the idea of having a fresh mind, and from the point of view of development of a member of staff it has much to commend it. But it would change this team. There would be a long process of rebuilding with another person which would be unsettling if they were only with us for a year and there are many issues I wouldn't be prepared to discuss with another member of staff.

She demonstrated her intent to define the boundaries of teamwork by controlling membership. Although the session had highlighted individual differences, there were none of the tensions that had characterised the sessions requiring more personal disclosures. Team members felt the team was finally gelling and were confident enough to consider expanding, raising for us the question: when is a developing team developed, and in whose eyes? Kate was concerned about team members becoming stale or complacent, and about not destabilising what she had carefully nurtured over six years. The three men who had worked with her during this time shared her concerns whereas Marian, as newcomer, did not have the same ownership of the processes characterising the team's work. Other team members had asked her to join them but she appeared to be regarded as someone to be nurtured by the longer serving members until she had developed by integrating into their existing ways. The team's experiences with the development package continued to reveal a tension between achieving balance between personal styles, leading to harmonious interaction, and the necessity of accepting temporary instability as a way of opening up the possibility of new ways of operating.

The final two books of the development package addressed time management and personal action plans. Marian's leadership stopped at the point where they were completed and she suggested the action plans form part of their personal staff interviews with Kate. This idea separated Kate from the development activity in which she had engaged equally as a team member, since no one was given responsibility for discussing Kate's action plans with her.

By this time, there had been a number of changes impinging on the team's work. Good exam results and a full intake had taken immediate pressure off competition with the neighbouring school. Swingeing cuts in LEA funding and discussions about whether to seek grant-maintained status meant that demands on the team's skills were, in their view, being tested to the maximum. Derek was not at the final meeting to discuss the development materials on time management. Philip welcomed the opportunity the session gave to switch back to the more personal aspects of management, like stress and personal organisation, and members shared freely their experiences of stress and strategies for coping. The more experienced and older trio (Kate, Philip and Marian) spent some time advising Greg who confessed to being stressed 'up to the eyeballs' as a result of combining an extremely conscientious approach to teaching with management responsibilities and the demands of a new baby.

Kate was reluctant to accede to Marian's suggestion that all members of the SMT should have a day when they did not teach. Her own best thinking time was early mornings and away from school, a pattern which, by implication, others might adopt. The recognition of equal contribution implicit in Marian's suggestion, particularly where the two allowance holders were concerned, took second place to hierarchy.

Marian found herself in a minority when she used the materials on meetings to propose staff meetings which were more than an information exchange. In Kate's view the value of these meetings was as 'a celebration of staff coming together'. Kate's role in them was symbolic, a chance for staff to come together with the head (not the SMT). As previously, Marian moved from acting as catalyst to facilitator, summarising: 'So we think our meetings are fine then?'

SMT members' discussion of delegation revealed Philip's concerns in view of the demands on teachers relating to the policy adopted by Kate of spreading management responsibilities widely. He asked Kate whether she did not worry that there were lots of people doing things on her behalf. She replied, 'I'm quietly confident'. This time the schism in the group was between the allowance holders (with feet still planted firmly in the camp of other staff) and the deputies and head, firmly committed to delegation. The opportunities for development offered by the doubts of the allowance holder about their approach to delegation were not explored further, yet delegation was a central plank of the team approach.

OUTCOMES OF THE TEAM DEVELOPMENT EFFORT

We summarise team members' reactions to their shared development experiences in terms of impact on individual and group behaviour, hierarchy in the team and the culture of teamwork. The impact of development experiences will depend on commitment to change and support for change. Individually, all members of the team were keen to extend their management knowledge and skills. None, however, contemplated the change of personality towards which so many of their discussions directed them! There was readiness to consider changing some team practices but several attempts to do so petered out through lack of commitment among team members. Reaching consensus by compromising individual preferences did not necessarily result in dedication to follow-up action.

Team members did not continue with formal development efforts once the programme had finished. In Kate's view it had strengthened the cohesion of the team:

> We'd had enough navel gazing, we were all equally committed but now the feeling is 'let's move on'. At its best the team now functions with a dynamic of its own, so when all six are together and discussion takes off the team is operating fully. The component bits couldn't operate in that way. It's like a

seabird taking flight. The programme had helped by creating a degree of trust in team members who were now more prepared to discuss short-comings and challenge each other. Each person had made themselves vulnerable and then helped each other to bob back up. At the same time they continue to remain very much individuals.

She perceived that some pointers to action had emerged. Having noted Greg's concerns about being the least experienced in the team, she had reviewed his job description within her leadership of the team and started making changes, mindful of the longer term and the need to make use of 'his undoubted talents in marketing and public relations'. The programme had helped strengthen the two allowance holders' confidence and they were 'now much more complete members of the team than before'. As leader, she had also come to the conclusion that the team was ready for expansion, even though 'it would put the team back'. She had ideas about whom she wanted to bring onto the team but was not sure all members would support her in the choice. She had seen each member about his or her personal action plans but none had chosen to discuss them within the framework proposed by the development package. Apart from Marian, who was actively seeking promotion elsewhere, team members' main concerns were how to avoid getting stale and how to continue to grow and develop.

Kate's response suggested that the programme's impact had been less to herald change, more to reaffirm the appropriateness of the way most SMT members had been operating. Our observation suggested that at a number of points during the development sessions team members could have chosen, as a result of shared concerns, to take one path or another. In the end, as a group, they kept mainly to the same path that we described in Chapters 5 and 6 and which we have characterised as one of harmony and balance. The culture of teamwork that was the backcloth for the development programme was too powerful and in most members' eyes too successful to risk change. Whatever fissures were revealed by the 'navel-gazing', they did not justify the risk of creating a chasm. Had Kate felt otherwise, things might have gone differently.

Instead, her participation in the programme was accompanied by personal introspection and feedback from her own appraisal as head. Together these experiences had led her to be more confident about the appropriateness of her leadership style but also to move towards more emphasis on her role in providing leadership of the team rather than team membership; indeed it was something to which all the others in different ways subscribed. It was different too from the kind of leadership 'lapse' the others had mentioned, when she deviated from her normal style. This feedback had taken her by surprise and she had been henceforth vigilant in ensuring that it did not happen again.

Derek concurred that the team was working better than it had ever done, though he was less willing to ascribe change to the impact of the programme. In his view the activities comprised just one of a number of factors influencing team members' behaviour, not least of which was the length of time they had been working together. It was still a team of five and occasionally three plus two, with the allowance holders waiting to see which way to jump. Barbara continued to be on the margins but Marian was fully integrated. Derek commented: 'There's no sense now of her being a new person. She has her own interests but is no longer really challenging the boundaries.' Although the programme had little effect on his own behaviour, the team's joint introspection had increased the amount of interaction and provided a basis for constructive dialogue.

Both Philip and Greg agreed about the impact on the team as a whole, which they described as more open and more appreciative of what made each person tick. Philip was dubious about whether hierarchy in the team had changed, but due mainly to his own reluctance to change: 'I know my place . . . I put myself there . . . it suits me to be like this.' He had enjoyed the development experience but recognised that to have an impact on his own behaviour, he would have to make more effort to follow learning points through. In contrast, Greg was more confident that the hierarchical division in the team affecting equal contribution of members was breaking down, as he matured as a manager and debate within the team became more open. The experience had been a 'culture shock' for him and, he thought, other members: 'We are now much more aware of each other . . . in the past there were tensions, and suggestions could be brutally put down because not everyone was aware of all the background.'

In Marian's view, the hierarchical schism in the team had sharpened, not as a result of development, nor of Kate's revision of her leadership of staff, but because of changes in the job and people's personal circumstances. The allowance holders were partly protected from the increasing demands on senior management by their different conditions of service. The programme had strengthened her own skills of facilitating and leading a team. Although she regretted the constraints on pursuing development ideas further, she commented: 'It wasn't my place.'

We suggest that Marian may have perceived it as inappropriate to have pushed colleagues towards taking action in the light of awareness raised through the team development materials. While leadership within the team on the issue of team development had been delegated to her, this issue was unlike most others addressed within the SMT since it concerned the very nature of the team. To have pushed for action would have edged into the role of leadership of the team since it implied reconsideration of some present parameters for teamwork. Leadership in setting such parameters had hitherto been primarily Kate's prerogative.

The programme had set in motion some of the changes in the culture of teamwork for which Marian had hoped: people were more prepared to criticise and less defensive. The enjoyment they had all derived from discussing individual and team issues as part of the programme had continued, partly because they saw its value, and partly because

> We're more open and confident with each other in discussing each other's area of responsibility. We've moved out of our boxes and become more of a team, less five individuals. We're more ready to take advice on our own areas and more familiar both with the head and each other.

Team members' attempts to develop had helped them address 'people' issues that had stood in the way of accomplishing team tasks. The experience had often been uncomfortable, even painful, but the gain had made it worthwhile. Development activity had reaffirmed rather than shifted the existing culture of teamwork. Members felt able to continue, as a team, meeting the increasing number of demands more effectively, not as a result of radically changed practices, but through the more subtle development of stronger bonding. Balance and harmony had been restored, in part through Marian adapting her personal style, but also by everyone else shifting position in some degree.

9

Restructuring the SMT at Middleton School

The early chapters of this book have demonstrated how commitment of all SMT members to a team approach and a shared culture of teamwork featuring complementarity between team leadership and membership assist an SMT in achieving synergy as a team. One of the severest tests of the potential for synergy, even for an SMT with a strong culture of teamwork, must be the task of working together towards a consensual decision where the stakes are very high for all team members, yet some of their interests and assumptions are incompatible. Debating the future membership of the SMT at Middleton, and individual responsibilities within it, proved to be just such a threat. No decision could reflect all members' views on what was best for the school or the SMT, or serve all their personal job satisfaction and career interests. Yet the urgency of these views, since individuals' professional future was inseparable from that of the SMT, made it very difficult for individuals to compromise their interests for the sake of consensus.

The acceptance by LEA staff of Harry's application for early retirement at the beginning of 1992 meant that a decision had to be made about the structure of the SMT and members' responsibilities once he left at the end of the summer term. Possibilities for the SMT included whether to appoint another deputy, which might give the two E allowance holders the chance to apply for promotion if they so wished (but not the opportunity for both to be successful), or to adopt a new structure with the two remaining deputies. As noted earlier, Peter had resisted pressure from some governors by insisting that all SMT members should be fully involved in making the decision, which would take the form of a proposal for the approval of the governing body. He led the SMT in working towards this decision, following the approach that team members perceived had served them well until now.

The ensuing deliberations exposed the fragility of the culture of teamwork where a mutually acceptable outcome could not be achieved. Something had to give: the deadline for the SMT-restructuring decision, the decision itself, or the cohesion of the team. The experience illustrates the strain that may still occur within a well-established team approach where all members are working with full commitment to teamwork, giving rise to the possibility of mutual disempowerment and collapse of the culture on which teamwork depends. Addressing the issue together over four weeks took almost twenty hours of often heated debate, just a couple of these hours being within the school day. This marathon effort was made alongside the normal heavy SMT agenda and the presentation of a united front to the outside world.

We will follow the course of the debate, using concepts introduced in earlier chapters. The aim is to show how delicately balanced are the conditions which can make or break teamwork, even in an SMT with a strong history of cohesion and task completion.

OPENING THE DEBATE

Peter had carried out a round of staff development discussions with each SMT member the previous term and had collated summaries of what each person had said. With colleagues' permission he circulated the collation document within the team, but the planned SMT discussion had been overtaken by the new priority of restructuring. Most of the information in the document was common knowledge to members but they varied over which interests should be considered within the debate. Jim wished to continue with his responsibility for LMS, whereas Nick was interested in job rotation – specifically to become more involved with finance. Colin sought a less fragmented set of responsibilities, to include pupil assessment, and was keen to become a deputy head. Julia wished to develop further her staff development work and had not ruled out the possibility of applying for a deputy headship in the future. It was unlikely that all these interests could be accommodated within a restructuring decision.

Within his habitual interpretation of the chairing role, Peter first checked that all colleague members agreed with participation by the entire team in making the decision. Harry stated that he wished to act in an advisory capacity only; for the first time, the other five SMT members would have to make a major decision without his full participation. Peter set a deadline to give time for approval by governors and advertising for any post they might decide to create. In a preliminary paper for discussion he proposed groundrules, including:

- all members of SMT *must* be involved in the debate;
- there must continue to be equal recognition of our views, despite the fact that our 'status' is different;
- the debate will open up areas/issues which could cause 'conflicts' of loyalty/ interest especially for Colin and Julia;
- the harmony, good humour, efficiency and effectiveness of SMT are all valued by us and we must give the debate time to ensure we end up with what we want for ourselves and for the school;
- we must submit proposals [to the governing body] upon which we agree.

Through this means, Peter used his authority within the management hierarchy to underline the SMT norm that all team members had the right to make an equal contribution to this major decision (even though they had differential status within the management hierarchy), and the duty to reach consensus. He also made public to colleagues the possibility of a tension between the career interest of the E allowance holders and their judgement about what was best for the team and the school. The paper set out options for the decision as a starting point for discussion. Contextual information included the fact that all heads of year now held a D allowance as an outcome of the consultation exercise over pupil support the previous term (see Chapters 6 and 7), and a reminder of the financial constraints which would limit any proposals for expansion of staffing.

In opening the debate during an SMT meeting, Peter drew colleagues' attention to these groundrules, inviting Colin and Julia to be as open as they felt they could be. Team members began to explore the range of options. More were added, including Colin's idea that, instead of replacing Harry, they could upgrade the two E allowance holders to deputies, so meeting the career interests of Julia and himself in creating a team consisting of head and four deputies. Peter checked the national regulations on salaries and reported that such a structure was only possible where a school was split between three or more sites. Julia commented, 'Nice try!' One SMT member's career interest had been articulated.

The following week a meeting was held after school. Peter, typically, recapped on the debate so far and asked colleagues how they should proceed. No strong ideas about process emerged, but Jim pointed to the need to improve the gender balance in the team, which Peter acknowledged as a significant issue. SMT members discussed what present SMT responsibilities could be removed. Harry outlined the tasks connected with his responsibility for pupil support which included making a rapid response to issues arising for individual pupils and parents. A second individual interest was made explicit: Peter stated how he wished to continue having the high quality support in this area for which Harry was renowned throughout the school. He suggested that more of this work could be done by heads of year, within their newly enhanced responsibilities, and commented on the difficulty of selecting someone to replace Harry. Julia suggested that the responsibility could be shared.

As the end of the meeting drew close, Peter asked all colleagues except Harry to write a list of responsibilities that should be covered within the SMT, which he would collate ready for the next meeting in a week's time. At this meeting, the collated list was circulated and the team continued to focus on which areas of management the SMT should cover.

Peter highlighted a third individual interest on behalf of Colin and Julia: whether to bring about parity of teaching load between the allowance holders and deputies, in line with their equal contribution as team members. He suggested that existing teaching commitments should be reduced by varying amounts so that deputies and allowance holders were all doing the equivalent of two days' teaching a week, whereas he would continue to do one day. There was unanimity on this principle, reflecting the strength of belief that all members other than the head made an equal contribution to the work of the team.

He also put forward two new ideas: creating a post with responsibility for the community and pupil assessment; and improving academic monitoring of individual pupils by giving each SMT member overall responsibility for pupil support within a year group. He had picked up on Julia's comment about sharing pupil-support work. Nick had argued the previous term that curriculum and pupil support should not be separated, but the issue had not been resolved within the consultation exercise on the pupil-support system. There was little reaction from other SMT members, though Nick questioned how heads of year would fit into such an arrangement. The meeting concluded with Peter asking the others what they should do next, Nick suggesting that they go through all the options again at the evening off-site meeting to be held after the half-term break. No movement towards a decision had yet been made.

Peter elaborated on his individual interest with us after the meeting. He assumed it would be hard to replace Harry with someone as competent. He wished to avoid becoming embroiled in responding to pupil-support issues. If he was to protect his ability as head to act strategically it was essential to delegate pupil-support responsibility within the SMT, as much rapid response work could not be done by heads of year. This interest was stated in a memo that Peter wrote to SMT colleagues just before half term:

> There is a permanent and daily need for quick response from SMT. At the moment the role is taken by Harry and me, to a great extent. When Harry goes, the need for quick response does not disappear with him . . . we have to be reactive in areas which simply *cannot* be delegated.

He developed the idea of sharing pupil support, with each member supervising one year group and having a reduced teaching timetable. Peter's memo was his first move to narrow the range of ideas but there was no time to discuss his proposal before the evening meeting immediately after half term.

PROPOSAL FOR A DECISION

Peter took a further step over the holiday, firming up his ideas into a much fuller proposal which he circulated to SMT colleagues on the day before the evening meeting. He commented later, 'It had just been cooking in my head over the whole of half term . . . I just copied it straight out from my head . . . it was all coming together.' He had felt responsibility as chair for the decision-making process. Few ideas had been contributed by colleagues and he now felt obliged to begin moving towards a decision on the new SMT structure.

We saw in Chapter 6 how, in working towards a major decision, Peter often wrote a proposal after consultation and the decision would be built around colleagues' reactions. He had deviated from his normal approach to chairing only in having circulating two papers, one building on the other, without consulting colleagues on the first. Whereas his colleagues had been expecting to look at all options again, they had now received both an outline proposal and a detailed version with implications for each of their jobs, which implied a narrower focus for debate.

Peter's stated rationale for the content of the proposal was that 'I believe it combines the need to be developmental with the need to be realistic and pragmatic'. It was a mixture of new thinking and development of ideas that had already been mooted, and included:

- a structure consisting of the head, two deputies and three 'assistant heads' on E incentive allowances. One assistant head would therefore be a new appointment;
- a link for each SMT member to a different faculty (other than the one where members currently taught);
- a link for each member with a different year group. Rapid-response pupil support would therefore be shared between all six SMT members (and some of the existing separation between curriculum and pupil support within SMT roles would be removed as each team member would also have familiarity with two faculties);
- a major responsibility (tallying with existing members' responsibility, with the addition of 'community' for the new appointment);
- several minor areas (related to existing responsibilities and taking into account some of SMT members' interests articulated in the earlier staff development interviews);
- parity of teaching loads as suggested in his memo.

Amongst a list of Peter's 'unanswered questions' were:

- How do we ensure continuity across year groups?
- Should we make . . . any position positively in favour of women?
- Have we considered all the options?

Finally, Peter acknowledged that parity of teaching responsibility and school-wide importance of responsibilities did not give parity of status within the management hierarchy (the proposed structure consisting of three levels, as in the present SMT) and asked colleagues to consider this sensitive issue.

While the proposal did not name any SMT member, it appeared that a new embryonic job description was being put forward for each person. The deputy headship responsibilities did not preclude the possibility of rotation between Jim and Nick but, as the proposed structure did not include a third deputy headship post, there was no opportunity for Julia or Colin to apply for promotion. As team leader Peter, typically, had been more equal than other members in putting forward the first substantial proposal designed to funnel the debate towards a decision. He and Harry met before the evening meeting to explore how adequately the structure could cover pupil support.

The SMT came together for the evening off-site meeting the day after Peter circulated his proposal. As chair he began by recapping, inviting colleagues to be frank in their response to his proposal, and stating how important it was for them to place 'all cards on the table'. This phrase symbolised the high value he placed upon openness among all team members, which would include individuals making explicit both personal interests and concerns for the future of the team. He asked colleagues how they wanted to proceed, commenting afterwards that he took great care to gain consensus on process because the stakes were so high.

MIXED RESPONSE

Other SMT members gave their view on Peter's proposal in turn. Jim reacted positively, approving of parity in teaching load but expressing the wish that his status as deputy be preserved. His response illustrates a concern both for equity (in teaching load) and an individual interest in retaining some hierarchical differentiation from assistant heads.

Julia circulated a critical paper written the previous night. Her arguments included a view that the debate was being conducted in the wrong way. The SMT should be less restricted to pragmatic response (a reference to Peter's rationale for his proposal) and more concerned with articulating a philosophy to underpin policy making:

> Whereas much philosophy, in the form perhaps of shared values, is implicit in the present team, there is a serious lack of discussion on important policy matters. These include aims of the school . . .

She also predicted that sharing pupil support would lead to fragmentation in the work of each member, and proposed that the community responsibility of one assistant head be replaced by responsibility for pupil support. She made explicit her personal interest in protecting time to focus on her staff-development responsibility; implicitly, taking on rapid-response pupil support work might distract her from a major responsibility for which she already had too little time to fulfil to her satisfaction.

Julia questioned the idea of having just two deputies and raised the issue of gender balance in the team, while acknowledging her difficulty because she might be perceived to serve her personal interest:

> What about the case for a woman deputy? I'm sure there are many women on the staff on whose behalf this point should be forcefully made, though perhaps I'm not in the best position to make it.

While Jim had earlier highlighted the need to redress the present gender imbalance in the SMT in general terms, none of the men had referred to the level within the management hierarchy for which a suitable candidate might be sought. Expressing a preference for appointing a third deputy who was a woman would have clashed with Colin's articulated career interest, given the restriction on the number of deputies it was possible to appoint.

Nick's response was also critical. He questioned why there should be fewer deputies when pupil numbers were rising; pointed to the opportunity to redress the present gender imbalance within the SMT; predicted that shared responsibility for pupil support would be impossible to coordinate effectively; and argued that the new community responsibility was unclear. In contrast, Colin was content to take a share in pupil-support work, having had a similar responsibility in the past, and approved of the idea of two deputies and three assistant heads. The proposal would offer him a less disparate set of responsibilities than he had at present, another of his personal interests. Since Harry had excluded himself from decision making, two of Peter's colleagues were for and two were against his proposal.

He debated the sharing of pupil support at great length with Nick and Julia. His predictions about how the arrangement would operate were diametrically opposed to those of his two colleagues. He perceived that SMT members would act strategically, much of the detailed work being done by heads of year within their enhanced responsibility. They argued that SMT members would be forced into being largely reactive, and so would be distracted from addressing their other responsibilities. Resolution was rendered difficult because each party had to rely on assertion, no evidence being available to substantiate or refute any prediction.

At one point Peter referred to his difficulty in leading the process, because there had been no reaction to any ideas he had put forward until after he had worked up a detailed proposal as the deadline approached. Other SMT members seem to have expressed followership in expecting Peter to lead through his normal procedure of consulting and putting forward proposals to which they would then respond. Our subsequent interviews with each SMT member indicated that, from the perspective of most members other than Peter, there had been an unintended gap in this procedure. They had not been consulted over Peter's memo (because half term had intervened) before receiving the detailed proposal with profound implications for their future work only a day before the evening meeting, giving them very little time for reflection. Nor had they been sounded out individually by Peter before the meeting about their proposed responsibilities.

A high priority for Peter, as team leader, was to meet the deadline for the decision, prompting him to make a detailed proposal which took into account many interests of which he had so far been made aware:

> I felt the responsibility for organising everything was up to me and therefore I was going to move it on. Suddenly when I moved it on [my colleagues] felt pushed because I was setting the speed.

Nick commented:

> After half term, from the Monday onwards, I felt continually under pressure to make a decision for which there wasn't time . . . I don't want to suggest for a moment that it was deliberate; I'm sure it wasn't. Had there been more time in the general timetable [for the decision], I'm sure we would have been given more time.

We interpret Nick's assumption that Peter had not been manipulative to reflect the high level of trust built up within the team through previous experience. The time pressure felt by Peter was exacerbated by the requirement that in the meeting he should both display team leadership through the chair and contribute equally as a member when the issue on which he was leading had proved to be controversial: 'I think it is very difficult chairing, watching and ensuring that everybody feels involved as well as putting your own personal views. To be honest I think it's actually impossible.'

Deadlock over the proposal remained unbroken after several hours of debate and no process which was acceptable within the culture of teamwork could be found for breaking it. At one point Jim asked Peter whether a comment he had just made about not replacing Harry with a deputy was a categorical statement as head, meaning that he would not allow further debate on this issue. Nick interjected that Peter had never made categorical statements of this kind before, and should not start now. Peter replied that he did not wish to exclude debate. We note that for Peter to have used his authority within the management hierarchy to decide unilaterally not to have a third deputy would have contradicted the norm that members should be entitled to make an equal contribution to the team decision. Nick's interjection suggests that he, as a team member, would not readily accept such a move. Peter avoided the risk of conflict, implicitly confirming his commitment to the norm of equal contribution through his response. The limit of Nick's willingness to express followership might have been reached had Peter's leadership of the team transgressed such a deeply held norm within the culture of teamwork. It was essential for team cohesion that he practised what he preached, even if it was at the expense of a quick decision.

Towards the end of the meeting, Peter reasserted the necessity of meeting the deadline and Nick responded by arguing that more time must be given to get the decision right. Unless all SMT members were agreed, the outcome would have a detrimental effect on the team. We suggest that Nick was referring to the importance of adhering to the norm of consensual decision making if the culture of teamwork was to survive. As we portrayed above, Peter included this norm among the groundrules in his original paper.

Julia's response to this pressure was to begin seeking to compromise, querying whether a temporary arrangement could be put in place with a review after a year, and suggesting that a seventh member could be appointed to the SMT, with pupil-support work shared between two people. In winding up the meeting Peter reiterated his fear that the SMT might not be able to handle all Harry's work after he left (so laying down his key 'card' once more).

COPING WITH DEADLOCK

The SMT met again the following morning, beginning before the school day. Peter circulated a short paper summarising the debate the night before, and commented that nearly – but not quite – all cards were now on the table. Jim responded by reaffirming his personal interests relating to job satisfaction, including the wish that he retain responsibility for LMS (which would preclude Nick from involvement in this area). Nick tabled an alternative proposal that he had written overnight. He had developed Julia's suggestion that the pupil-support responsibility (including academic monitoring of pupils) be shared between two SMT members. His proposed structure included a third deputy but excluded a community responsibility.

Julia reiterated her criticisms of Peter's proposal and stated that she was no longer willing to compromise. She referred to putting her cards on the table: it would be too difficult to carry out her staff-development responsibility if she took on pupil-support work, and a majority SMT decision would 'damage the teamwork model'. Colin said that he did not want the responsibility outlined for him in Nick's proposal, and that he preferred shared responsibilities.

Peter noted that deadlock remained. He perceived that to use his 'casting vote' would threaten the good working relationships within the SMT and he would not take the risk of losing colleagues' goodwill. As the end of this meeting drew near without progress towards a shared decision, Nick asked him what the 'rule book' would say about breaking a deadlock. We note that Nick expected Peter, as team leader, to set new parameters for teamwork in a situation which the SMT had not previously encountered. Peter stated that he did not wish to push through a majority decision and suggested that they look at the possibility of a temporary arrangement. The deadline for a decision on the new permanent SMT structure would have to be abandoned.

He declined Colin's suggestion that he be more directive, saying that he did not wish to get tough with the people on whom he depended, otherwise 'the SMT would become a colander!' Peter used his authority as head to resist the influence of a colleague who was attempting to persuade him to express this authority in a way he did not think appropriate. Within the dialectic of control inside the SMT, he appeared to acknowledge his dependency as the formal leader (despite his exclusive level of authority) on the synergistic – as opposed to antagonistic – use of influence by other members.

At the next meeting the following day, Peter put forward another paper, setting out options for staff to take on temporary 'acting responsibilities' after Harry's departure. In contrast with the last two meetings, there was consensus among all SMT members in reaching a temporary arrangement which avoided having to make acting appointments. They opted unanimously to shoulder for a term the pupil-support responsibility for a different year group, Julia and Nick accepting on a temporary basis an arrangement to which they had been steadfastly opposed as part of a permanent SMT structure. In addition, team members shared out Harry's remaining responsibilities equitably between them, so potentially adding to their existing workload. The culture of teamwork seemed to have been reasserted in working synergistically, as usual, towards a solution which was acceptable to all members and entailed considerable compromise for two people.

After the meeting, Peter informed us that all other members had come to speak with him individually in the last few days, reaffirming their loyalty to the SMT and to him. This action implies to us that members perceived the recent experience to pose a serious threat to the team approach. They all valued it highly enough to use their influence in reassuring the team leader of their allegiance to the culture of teamwork.

Until this point, inability to reach consensus on a major decision had resulted in top priority being given by the head to sustaining teamwork in the SMT, so avoiding the threat of mutual disempowerment. The immediate outcome seemed to be the re-emergence of mutual empowerment in making a temporary decision which would not commit any SMT member indefinitely to a pupil-support responsibility. The new arrangements were approved by the governing body and their rationale and details were published in the head's bulletin for staff. It was agreed that Harry would take charge in school for a day to enable other SMT members to have an off-site meeting to come to a decision on a new permanent structure for the SMT.

The interviews we conducted with each member prior to this next meeting enabled us to explore further some of the issues we had observed. Members were unanimous that for this decision, where their professional lives were so deeply affected, it was vital that consensus was reached if the team approach was to be sustained. Julia underlined the likely consequences if Peter had pulled rank by using his authority within the management hierarchy to impose a majority decision. The equal contribution of team members in the minority would have been denied:

> Peter cannot suddenly change the rules without there being a changed dynamic within the team . . . it would have demotivated me . . . I would have felt that my voice within SMT had been discounted. I suppose I would have resented the new relationship that would have been created between me and Peter, because he would have said, 'I'm the head and I'm instructing you to do this.'

She indicated further how in the past: 'Even when he's been directive it has been with the consent of the team. We have allowed him to be directive; none of us really minded.' This acknowledgement illustrates our interpretation that, within the dialectic of control inside the SMT, the head as team leader is dependent on the willingness of other members to display followership as well as membership. Despite heads' exclusive authority within the management hierarchy, leadership of the team actually works by mutual consent.

Other members acknowledged Peter's authority within the management hierarchy to direct their work, yet both Julia and Nick would have found it difficult to commit themselves fully to implementing a decision which, on their prediction, could not be made to work effectively. Nick commented how he would have lost faith in the teamwork process and added: 'Although I would accept cabinet responsibility for the decision I think I would have a lot of inner turmoil – as I had during the process [of the meetings] – about working with it.' Mutual empowerment requires mutual commitment.

For his part, Peter's belief in the principle that this decision should be made by consensus was reflected in his actions:

> It is inviolable. And I can remember writing in the first briefing paper that whatever else we do we must present a unanimous view to governors . . . I would not have used a casting vote.

He regarded the way his colleagues had worked so hard on the decision as symbolising their commitment to the SMT, which would have been 'detonated' had he used a casting vote approach: 'There's a tremendous commitment and loyalty, and you tamper with that at your peril.'

Another concern for Peter, once the division of views between other team members became evident, was to avoid the possibility of deteriorating relationships among them. He was the most recent arrival in the school and, as we have seen, when he first took up post he had insisted on existing SMT members making a fresh start. He had learned enough of the institutional history for him to decide to ban reference to any differences existing before his arrival, and to work on creating conditions through his leadership of the team which supported colleagues in operating collaboratively within it. Peter was unwilling to risk any legacy of past conflicts resurfacing in the present debate.

His priority now was to secure a decision by the new deadline date. He was prepared to raise the issue of what to do if team members could not reach agreement and to announce that he would remove the decision from the SMT arena if necessary and make it himself. This stance suggests that, as a last resort, the head was ready to revert to directing colleagues (as his position at the top of the management hierarchy allowed) even if it jeopardised the potential for synergy within the SMT. Should this contingency arise, it seems likely that the contradictory norms relating to differential status within the management hierarchy and equal contribution as team members would be brought together in the same interaction, resulting in the kind of conflict that the head had so far avoided. The stakes seemed to have become higher for Peter than for any other team member. Unless agreement on a permanent SMT structure could be reached, he was faced with some degree of disempowerment as head. If he took back the decision he risked loss of the empowerment he enjoyed through the team approach he had nurtured for three years. If he allowed the debate to go unresolved he risked losing the credibility of the SMT, and therefore himself as team leader, in the eyes of governors and other staff.

It is often said that a team is as strong as its weakest member. We indicated earlier how any incompetent or uncommitted team member could inhibit a team approach to school management. In terms of individual empowerment or disempowerment, however, heads appear to be potentially the most vulnerable member of their SMT since they have most to lose if they make a strong commitment to teamwork which then fails. Arguably, Peter was ultimately more dependent upon the rest of the team to empower himself in carrying out his responsibility as head, than any other members were dependent on their team membership in order to fulfil their individual management responsibility.

TEAMWORK IN JEOPARDY

How close was the culture of teamwork to falling apart? Each member reported that they still valued the team approach, Julia regarding the way priority was given to reaching consensus over keeping to the decision deadline as an indication of how well it had worked under duress. Nick, however, had lost some confidence in the SMT and the policy-making process. Different values of SMT members about whether to adopt a philosophical or purely pragmatic approach, which were not normally expressed within the team, had surfaced: 'For the first time I felt some of the differences of opinion, different philosophies that have existed historically within the institution, had come to the fore.' It appeared that potential conflict between the 'philosphers' and the 'pragmatists' had been avoided hitherto because all members had colluded in keeping this issue out of the SMT arena. Harry noted that it was debatable how far agreement on fundamental educational and managerial values was actually necessary to carry out the SMT role. The culture of teamwork may have included shared values about what was to be left unsaid for the sake of harmony.

While Jim's belief in the team approach had not been dented, like Peter he was concerned about the credibility of the team with other staff if SMT members proved unable to reach a unanimous decision. (Since details of the temporary arrangement had been published in the heads' bulletin, other staff expected the SMT – rather than the head alone – to come up with a decision on a permanent structure.)

As researchers, we were in a privileged position to determine how different interpretations of Peter's request to put all cards on the table had led to some disjunction between perceptions of SMT members. Peter was uniquely aware of all colleagues' personal interests as a result of the earlier staff-development interviews. Although the collation of individuals' interests and concerns, including his own, had been circulated, it was not brought into the debate. He perceived that no interest should be ineligible for consideration, but he had not expected everyone to 'put their entire pack out'. As chair, he had referred obliquely to others' unstated interests where relevant within the discussion, to give them an opportunity to assert them if they wished. He had repeatedly mentioned his priority interest in protecting himself from becoming too caught up in pupil-support work.

All members had articulated interests relating to the team and the school, but they differed over how far they felt it appropriate to mention personal job satisfaction and career interests. Jim had made clear his interest in retaining responsibility for LMS early on, leaving it to Nick whether to push for his incompatible interest in job rotation (to include finance). Nick was aware that both his and Jim's personal interests were already known to other members; he decided to forego pursuing his own, so did not respond to Jim's statement.

There was divergence over whether to mention career interests. The issue was highly salient for Julia and Colin. If the decision was to replace Harry with another deputy for pupil support, Colin's previous experience in this area might favour his chance should he apply for the post. If the decision was to have a third deputy, and a woman was to be preferred (if a suitable candidate came forward) to redress the gender imbalance, Julia would be advantaged should she apply. Arguments for different SMT structures, based on the interests of the team and the school, would inevitably have different implications for the possibility of promotion for both allowance holders.

Colin had made his career interest explicit at the outset, but felt he need not reiterate it, as colleagues were aware of his aspiration to become a deputy. He believed that his duty as a team member was to put forward his view solely on the grounds of what was best for the team and the school: 'I tried very hard not to promote ideas that I thought would lead to jobs for me and I tried to be very school-based and objective.' We interpret him as attempting to avoid manipulation through any assertion that might be overtly in the team and school interests while covertly promoting his personal interests. He had accepted Peter's proposed SMT structure even though it excluded a third deputy post. An issue for Colin and Julia was whether colleagues would accept at face value their judgement, based on what was good for the team and the school, or interpret it as a covert and illegitimate attempt to advance their promotion prospects.

Julia took a similar stance to Colin but, as there turned out to be little debate about a third deputy, she had not put her career interest forward. She wondered whether Peter had kept a card back in proposing a model with no third deputy. The card might have been to avoid possible contention by ruling out the possibility of promotion for either allowance holder. She perceived that it would have been appropriate for her to argue for a third and preferably female deputy if she perceived it to be in the interests of the team and the school. However, she felt inhibited by the possibility that she might be interpreted as promoting a career interest under the guise of her contribution as a team member. Julia and Colin did not make the groundrule they had adopted explicit in the debate, leaving their motives open to misinterpretation.

Individuals appeared to subscribe to different norms governing which interests they were willing to express within the team. The combination of interests that any member could feasibly hold, coupled with the possibility of varying perceptions about each other's unarticulated interests, left room for considerable disparity over how far members might perceive their colleagues to be overt about what they wanted. It seems likely that such a situation could precipitate a loss of trust in each others' integrity and so withdrawal from full commitment to teamwork in the SMT.

A related issue for SMT members was whether individuals might have formed a coalition to promulgate a shared view or protect a shared interest, rather than operating as individuals whose views happened to coincide. All members stated that they had acted individually and that others should do so, indicating that this norm was shared within the culture of teamwork. None perceived that a coalition had definitely existed among other members who appeared to be in alliance, although two members pointed out that they could not be certain. A greater concern for all members was whether they might be perceived by others to have formed a coalition, an action which lay firmly outside the parameters of acceptable behaviour in the team. Colin commented:

One thing that nobody knows is that Jim and I never spoke to one another. [After the evening meeting] we talked about this at the dinner table and Jim said, 'You realise that if we said it, nobody would actually believe us!'

As with the request to put cards on the table, room for suspicion over the integrity of others' behaviour arose through the possibility of illegitimate manipulation, since each member could not prove whether others had formed a coalition. We suggest that the high level of trust previously established in the SMT may have enabled team members to give each other the benefit of the doubt in re-establishing synergy to reach a temporary decision.

SEEKING A RESOLUTION

In order to come to a consensual decision on the permanent SMT structure within the new deadline, something had to happen: a greater willingness to compromise, a change in priorities among individual interests, or a shift in the parameters for the decision so that more interests could be met. All members apart from Harry met for a day meeting off-site, starting the decision-making process again from scratch. This time personal job satisfaction and career interests were given greater prominence alongside consideration of a structure which would be good for the team and the school, and the frame for debate posed by Peter's proposal was removed.

Colin alone expressed dissatisfaction with his current situation, restating that he wanted a more coherent set of responsibilities. Then SMT members debated again which SMT responsibilities could be delegated outside the team, paying particular attention to those currently falling to Colin. Nick suggested that whoever undertook pupil support could also be given assessment to give the person an opportunity to develop a new area. Peter noted that the new structure could consist of five members: head, two deputies and two allowance holders – Colin possibly taking the pupil support and assessment responsibilities. Although it was not stated, Peter's stance indicates that he was now prepared to compromise on his earlier proposal that the pupil-support role should be shared among all members.

Colin argued that if the SMT was reduced to five members they would all have a heavy workload. He suggested, 'putting my cards on the table', that the status structure should be head and four deputies. He pointed out that not only were SMT members other than the head increasingly working as equals, but also that the national regulations restricting the number of deputies in a school had been lifted. The principle of parity between SMT members other than the head had resurfaced. We note how Colin's proposal would meet Jim's interest in retaining the status of deputy head. Colin stated that he would be willing to take on a heavier responsibility in return for equal status with the deputies, and that this option was cheaper than appointing a sixth SMT member on an E allowance. Peter asked Julia for her view, referring to her possible career interest, but her response did not refer to it: she said that she was glad the issue had come up, but was still concerned about having a heavy workload.

The debate had come full circle, SMT members reconsidering an option which Colin had originally put forward during the initial meeting. In supporting the proposal, Nick articulated his individual interest in sharing out dinner duties among more people, since only the head and deputies undertook this task. He asked how far the proposal would redress the gender imbalance, and Julia replied that the gender balance would be improved – though only marginally – with one woman and four men.

A key question was whether the legal parameters which had ruled out consideration of Colin's proposal in the first place had now shifted. Peter made several telephone calls to check, and reported that the idea was now possible, but that all deputy headships must be nationally advertised (so ruling out the simple and more rapid process of internal promotion). Colin's response was to suggest that he and Julia were appointed as acting deputy heads, with no specified time limit. Peter made another phone call and confirmed that this arrangement could be made. Team members then worked out how to cover Harry's teaching load through appointing a science teacher. The responsibility for examinations, which Colin was to drop, would be advertised internally and awarded a D allowance. Jim reported that the proposal would not pose an extra burden on the LMS budget.

Peter checked that each member approved of the proposal. The decision was made, ready to be put to governors and, subject to their approval, the temporary SMT structure could now be cancelled. He wound up the meeting by acknowledging that the last few weeks had been the toughest within his headship; the situation had been very tense, but everyone had worked extremely hard to reach the decision.

THE PRIMACY OF THE PARITY PRINCIPLE

The final outcome of the debate shows that the culture of teamwork had survived the test. Since not all individual interests could be accommodated, SMT members had to be willing to compromise in order to find a 'best fit' between them, those connected with careers being included in the debate. The change in parameters represented by the new national regulations freed up the constraints which had earlier precluded the principle of parity being fully applied to both Julia and Colin. According to the individual interests which were made explicit each member had gained, but some also lost:

- Peter had abandoned sharing out pupil support and given up on the original deadline for a decision, but had regained a united SMT, committed to implementing the decision;
- Nick had voluntarily foresaken the opportunity to push for job rotation, but there was some consolation in the prospect of extra support with dinner duties;
- Jim had retained his responsibility for LMS;
- Julia and Colin had gained a deputy headship and a smaller teaching load, in line with their equal contribution with the existing deputies, enabling Julia to direct more energy to staff development and Colin to enjoy a more coherent set of responsibilities.

The five SMT members who were to form the restructured SMT had survived the experience of making their first major decision together. Our final interviews the following term indicated that they were generally satisfied with the outcome. Julia expressed some concern about her 'quasi-promotion', being wary of the possibility that other staff might perceive two SMT members to have been manipulative in serving their career interests by promoting themselves. For her, the issue remained one of retaining credibility with other staff through being seen to set a good example. Other members reported that several teachers had expressed relief that the temporary arrangements announced in the head's bulletin had been revoked. They shared the concern of Julia and Nick that fragmentation within pupil support might have occurred if these arrangements had been implemented.

Jim referred to the importance of increasing parity within the team:

> The principle of restructuring was to create parity because it was quite obvious to everybody that we operated as a team. But we had different people on different allowances with different time allocations and yet we were expecting them to contribute, in discussion at least, to everything that was going on in the school. So to all intents and purposes they were deputies anyway. So what we've done is faced that one squarely and said, 'If we are a team, and we acknowledge that we are – we work like that – then it's a team of deputies and a headteacher, or just a team of which one person is more equal than others'.

The balance between the contradictory norms of differential status within the management hierarchy and equal contribution as a team member (see Figure 2.1) had shifted in the direction of a more egalitarian team, in so far as the SMT structure had been changed. Members of the new team could now look forward to the challenge of developing their practice together in order to fulfil the promise of the new structure.

10

Making SMTs Work

In the first part of this book we looked at a range of team approaches within six SMTs whose members expressed a commitment to working together within a team; in the second part we immersed ourselves in the detail of teamwork in two of them, revealing diverse ways of operating. We have experimented with a combined cultural and political perspective to help us grasp some of the complexities of interaction within SMTs, and between them and other staff. For it is through interaction that the entity of a team is created, developed, and sustained or destroyed. It is beyond the scope of a qualitative study of this scale to generalise about SMTs or determine what team structures and processes are effective under particular circumstances. We are able, however, to extract ideas from our findings which may inform practice. The first stage in considering what makes SMTs work is to review what we have learned so far. What is the picture?

OVERVIEW OF THE FINDINGS

What we saw of the teams we studied was, of course, part of a wider canvas. SMTs represent a response up and down the country to the greater managerial complexity of secondary schools following from their large size as organisations; to a staff culture which values people having some say in making the decisions that they will be expected to implement; to the way the benefits of teamwork within industrial management have been held up as a shining example for school managers to emulate; and to massive changes, mostly imposed by central government reforms. Coordination is required to implement a multiplicity of innovations (many of which are designed to interrelate) and to arrange for the necessary staff development, within limited resources (Wallace, 1991b; Wallace, Hall and McMahon, 1993). Several major innovations, once implemented, demand continuing coordination since they have increased the range of decisions to be made at school level. Unpredictable reversals in central government policy require coordination to undo or modify what has just been implemented. It is also necessary because action required to cope with the reforms does not always fit neatly within individual management responsibilities of senior staff. A team approach to management offers one way of achieving a coherent strategy for implementing multiple innovations.

The creation of SMTs implies superimposing new working practices for senior staff upon a hierarchy of formal status which is structurally reflected in salaries and conditions of service. This hierarchy, because of its long lineage, is deeply embedded within the staff culture. To the extent that participation by SMT members in decision making entitles them to contribute equally, it cuts across the management hierarchy to which they also belong.

We found many ways in which the structure and practice of our SMTs reflected a variable balance between contradictory norms connected with the management hierarchy and equal contribution of members. Hierarchy was strongly evident in the differential status of team members and their level of individual management responsibility. The clearest hierarchical distinction lay between heads and other members. Without the commitment of heads, teamwork could not exist; they alone had the authority to create the conditions for other senior staff to participate in fulfilling a shared role in managing the school. We chose to go where the going was good; all full team members displayed competence in their individual contribution as well as commitment to a team approach. While the evidence of other studies (e.g. Weindling and Earley, 1987) suggests that heads may work around uncommitted or incompetent SMT members and may even succeed in persuading them to adopt more positive values in respect of teamwork, the other members have considerably fewer resources to make a teamworker out of a head who is not enamoured with a team approach.

Equally, heads alone could be held externally accountable for the team's work, a factor which stimulated them to find safeguards against the possibility of their team colleagues contributing as equals to outcomes which the heads might find unacceptable. Equal contribution was most evident in the process of teamwork: all members regarded as fully within the team were encouraged to contribute to the agenda, offer their knowledge and opinions, and work towards consensus on major decisions. However, heads were more equal than colleagues in having delegated the authority to other members that entitled them to make such a contribution; if heads perceived that the process was failing, they could take back this authority, leaving other members with recourse solely to the use of influence.

There was room for manoeuvre (within the limits of national legislation and institutional history) to express differing degrees of hierarchy or equality in team structures and working practices, and to change them, depending upon the beliefs and values of heads and other members. At one school we studied opportunities were sought to create a less hierarchical structure and more equitable working conditions for members; at the other they were not, partly because allowance holders wanted what they perceived as the benefits of being at the bottom of the SMT hierarchy. Although the balance between hierarchy and equal contribution varied between SMTs and shifted over time, diversity was limited: both norms were expressed in all six teams.

Under-representation of women in senior managerial positions in co-educational secondary schools is as old as mixed secondary schooling, with patchy attempts to redress the gender imbalance, a situation reflected in the composition of SMTs. Our sample was highly unrepresentative of the national picture, in containing an equal number of heads of either gender. Even in the teams led by women, men still outnumbered women among full SMT members, and women were notably under-represented at middle-management level. There was variable awareness of gender issues connected with management among women and men in the SMTs, but no evidence of women having 'caring' responsibilities because of any restrictive expectations about 'women's work'. We found little evidence of direct discrimination inside the two teams we observed: while the experience of women and men may have differed, interaction within the teams did not conform to stereotypical differentiation in behaviour between men and women. Throughout our fieldwork, we found a common allegiance to collaborative norms associated with teamwork in all the schools (reinforced in some cases by adherence to the norm of promoting equity in the workplace) which appeared to be the key factor explaining the degree of androgyny that interaction in the teams displayed.

Since our SMTs were the brainchild of the headteachers, it is hardly surprising that they played such a critical part in creating them and promoting a shared culture of teamwork. Their methods were subtle and manifold: both overt, as in laying down groundrules for the team-meeting process; and covert, as in their attempt to manipulate the setting for joint work and the degree to which they symbolised, through the example of their behaviour, what they wished other members to embrace. The norms relating to teamwork which emerged, though heavily influenced by heads, were the outcome of negotiation between all SMT members. No member could simply determine the actions of colleagues; they all had some power to accept or reject others' norms or to try and introduce their own. Consequently the cultures of teamwork varied, the 'separate togetherness' of one team we observed contrasting with the more group-oriented culture of the other.

The SMTs were in no sense a fixed entity; they evolved as their team history unfolded through shared experience, previous institutional history having a major impact on current interaction. Most striking was the mutual adaptation which occurred with change of team membership. Heads took institutional history (including any past team history) into account when setting out to develop their own version of a team; other members inherited by one head were expected to bury 'historical memory' to help build a new culture; and externally appointed newcomers, whether heads or other members, had to let go of their past experience elsewhere and come to terms with the history of the current team. At the same time, members' interaction made team history;

experiences which were interpreted as good or bad informed their current perception of each other and their related feelings.

The culture of teamwork was conservative, developing gradually, primarily through SMT members' job experience rather than through any structured development activity. Attempts to stimulate a rapid cultural shift, whether made by a new member bringing in foreign norms drawn from the culture of teamwork of another SMT, or an individual trying to stall or force a decision when there was disagreement by advocating a different procedure, were met with a closing of ranks among the majority of members to protect the existing culture.

Yet our observation suggests that heads were potentially the most vulnerable members if teamwork failed. Teamwork is about interdependence, whatever any member's position in a management hierarchy. The heads needed other SMT members to commit themselves to the team approach as much as the latter needed the head's sponsorship for the opportunity to be in the team. Failure of teamwork stands to make a bigger dent in the credibility of heads with other staff and governors than in the credibility of their SMT colleagues, since heads are accountable as SMT leader. Therefore adopting a team approach in more than name is a high-risk strategy for them. Although they have the resources to fall back on a more hierarchical mode of working, collapse of teamwork may cost heads some of the empowerment they may otherwise enjoy through the synergy of an SMT where all members are committed to working in the same direction.

To a considerable (though varied) degree, the two SMTs we observed had developed the necessary foundation of a shared culture of teamwork. Norms within it covered both what was encouraged or tolerated and what was not. We guessed at what was disallowed either from its absence (party political values underpinning individual stances on education issues were never mentioned in one SMT) or from disputation (the lack of input of wider educational philosophies to debate was highlighted by two members in another SMT).

This foundation was never more solid than the last few days' experience of working as a team. The threat of transgression of key norms was enough for one or more members either to question their commitment to the team, or to use their resources to bring the transgressor back into line. It was unusual for such a threat to arise, being most likely to appear when working towards a decision where the stakes were exceptionally high for all team members, so that they were unwilling to compromise, and their preferences were likely to differ. Such situations included selection for a post which included SMT membership; a structured development exercise requiring a degree of self-disclosure beyond the limit within the existing culture of teamwork; and reallocation of SMT members' individual responsibilities. SMT restructuring entailed a heady mix of all three!

A key to the smooth operation of SMTs was complementarity between the expression of individual team leadership and team membership roles, which varied between the two teams we observed. Leadership of the team with an emphasis on intervention, including monitoring of SMT members' work, required willing followership behaviour within the team membership role alongside equal contribution and leading within the team on particular issues. Light-touch leadership of the team, based on a conception of delegation which excluded close monitoring, featured non-intervention (a form of deliberate inaction) more strongly once parameters had been set. This style relied on team membership behaviour which included competence to lead within the team without close supervision, while remaining within those parameters. The different combinations of complementary team roles were expressed in SMT meetings, the arena where most of the SMTs' joint work took place. We observed how the varied approaches to chairing adopted by each head set a different tone for others' contributions.

A third role – team support – was fulfilled in different ways in these two schools by non-teaching staff with major responsibility for administration, whether from a position within the SMT or outside it. While this role did not appear to be a necessary condition for team functioning, there was evidence that team support could greatly facilitate the work of the SMT, especially where the role was unambiguous and the person providing team support operated in a way which was congruent with the internal culture of teamwork.

The shared role of the SMT to which individual team roles were directed was quite similar in the six schools, differing only in the degree to which particular types of agenda item were addressed. The teams constituted the locus of school-wide policy making within an overview to which all members contributed. At the heart of their joint work lay consensual decision making on school-wide policy issues, creating a framework for more detailed policies covering sectional interests within the school to be made at middle-management level. Such decisions were generally subject to the formal approval of governors, but governing bodies in all cases were largely supportive of heads and, through them, the SMTs. Representation on governing bodies encompassed constituents from various interested parties including other staff. Teacher–governors had equal status with the head, in contrast with their position in the management hierarchy, giving them the authority in principle, with other constituents, to provide a check on the SMT if members overstepped the boundary of acceptability to the majority of governors. We never witnessed such an event.

A major consequence of creating a team and preserving a private arena for much of its work was, at the same time, to create a demarcation characterised by limited permeability between the SMT and other staff. The possibility of a credibility gap arose because outsiders' direct experience of the joint work of the SMT, which often had a major impact on their professional lives, was limited to the arena that SMT members chose to make public in the school. The hierarchical organisation of the schools meant that SMT members were empowered to monitor the work of other staff, but not the other way round. The potential therefore arose for a sense of distance between the SMT and other staff.

Yet we did not find the degree of distancing noted by Bowe and Ball (1992), which they attributed in part to the increasing preoccupation of senior staff

with management issues following from central government reforms. Stren-
uous efforts were made by SMT members in our study schools to ensure that
the demarcation remained at least semi-permeable. At the same time they
presented a largely united front to outsiders, whatever internal disagreements
there may have been, reflecting the norm of collective responsibility within the
SMT culture of teamwork. The retention of a private arena meant that SMT
members could not prove to other staff that consultation was genuine and their
views really were taken into account in making major decisions. Consequently
SMT members had continually to work at both being fair and being seen to be
fair in their dealings with other staff, in order to retain the credibility on which
the SMT depended. Other staff supported the SMT only if (as far as they could
tell) team members operated within the boundaries of acceptability to them.

The possibility of SMT members extending teamwork to the whole staff,
and so directly orchestrating the development of synergy throughout the
school, appeared to be limited for several reasons. SMT privacy constrained
the opportunity to model the collaborative culture that members wished other
staff to adopt. The latter did not have access to the overview enjoyed by SMT
members, and they also had sectional interests which it was their responsibility
to promote. Consequently they were less likely than SMT members to perceive
what was in the interest of the school as a whole. Nevertheless, there was some
evidence that the 'balkanised' staff culture of isolated departments
(Hargreaves, 1992) had shifted to the extent that heads of faculty, in both the
schools we studied in depth, had formed a pressure group to represent their
combined interests. Their voluntary collaboration entailed compromising on
the sectional interests of each faculty to get the best deal for the group.

THE CULTURAL AND POLITICAL PERSPECTIVE

The concepts forming the building blocks of our interpretation inevitably
framed our picture of SMTs at work. The experiment with making two
perspectives go into one was designed to support us in asking a wider range of
questions than either a cultural or political perspective alone would allow.
How successful was it? Combining the two enabled us to explore who had the
power to define, build or change a culture; how allegiance to particular
cultural norms affected the use of power; and the interplay between culture
and power in the relationship between interacting individuals and groups. The
same action could be interpreted as expressing both the use of power and
cultural norms, as in the deliberately symbolic behaviour of heads in attempting to persuade team colleagues to accept the norms implicit in their exemplary
action or non-intervention.

The dual metaphor avoided the narrowing of focus, that we judged to follow
either from the assumption that cultural consensus underpinned surface political conflict or from the assumption that superficial accord overlaid a silent
struggle. Which way the interpretation would go became a matter for investigation, and we suggest that, in many instances, there was a mixture of conflict and consensus. For an SMT member to compromise a minority personal

view, for the sake of a working consensus in the team, might imply a conflict of views on the substantive topic and allegiance to the cultural norm that compromise should be sought where necessary for consensus. For an SMT member to refuse to compromise might imply not only a conflict of views on the substantive topic but also the expression of conflict within the culture of teamwork. For example, cultural conflict might follow from rejection of the team norm concerning compromise, in favour of allegiance to the contradictory norm that members should make an equal contribution by expressing their sincerely held beliefs. It may be less productive to go for either consensus or conflict as necessarily the bottom line explanation for social interaction, than to embrace the possibility that both may be present.

This assertion was reinforced by our understanding of the relationship between parties to interaction which we gained by adopting a stipulative definition of concepts taken from a political perspective. First, viewing power as transformative capacity rather than a zero sum formulation enabled us to address the possibility of mutual empowerment, as we observed to happen much of the time in the two SMTs we examined in depth. In such circumstances of synergy, we suggest that the power shared by team members to maintain the status quo or make changes was greater than the sum of their power as individuals to work towards the same ends. Conversely, where SMT members were in conflict, their shared power as a team was less than the sum of their power as individuals to realise different interests.

Second, the idea that the control of interaction follows a dialectic directed our attention to the way all parties made use of resources to realise their interests. Control by any individual was far from absolute. It meant attempting to delimit the boundaries of a range of possibilities for others' actions, rather than simply determining them. Ball and Bowe (1991) argue that headteachers are faced with the task of 'achieving control over subordinates while also maintaining their cooperation' (p. 44). Much depends on what is meant by control. We found heads typically to seek a *measure* of control over other SMT members through *delimitation of a range of possible behaviours* rather than by direction. Equally their SMT colleagues (and other staff) sought a measure of control by delimiting the actions of the head and each other. Power was distributed throughout the SMT and beyond. Struggles for control were evident only where there was a threat of one party overstepping another's boundary of acceptable possibilities. Much of the time, heads, other members and other staff expressed satisfaction that others were acting within the bounds with which they were comfortable.

Third, the notion of authority was treated as a matter of degree, rather than an all-or-nothing affair. Delegated authority of SMT members other than heads was clear cut in relation to their line responsibility for other staff, but the boundary had to be negotiated between their individual authority to make decisions within this responsibility and the authority of the team as a whole to have an input into such decisions. Authority shaded into influence, where they used the authority delegated by the head to make an equal contribution to debate in advocating a proposal which ran counter to what the head favoured.

Their action was legitimated by the parameters of their team membership set by the head, but their delegated authority was not accompanied by formal sanctions. They could, however, use influence to pose the threat of informal sanctions, such as withdrawing their commitment to teamwork.

Fourth, we eschewed the term 'micropolitics' (as often used to denote a covert and illegitimate world of underhand manoeuvres and dirty tricks) to allow for a grey area between the wholly 'up front' and the wholly 'behind the back'. We distinguished two dimensions underlying the notion of manipulation: the degree to which an action had a covert intention, and whether either party to interaction perceived an action as legitimate or not. We were able to identify a variety of actions which amounted to legitimate manipulation, such as the heads' attention to the setting for team meetings, but very little which counted as illegitimate, the stuff of much that is commonly included within accounts of micropolitics. A sizable proportion of interaction may be manipulative, in not being fully overt, without being perceived as illegitimate.

CAN SMTS MAKE A DIFFERENCE?

As we showed in Chapter 4, our six SMTs were regarded as quite, or very, effective by informants inside and outside the teams. (In Table 4.1 we summarised the criteria they used for judging SMT effectiveness.) Our study over a year of two of these SMTs suggested that, although they operated very differently, the teamwork process usually went smoothly; members kept to task and fulfilled their shared role. An overview was maintained, consultation with other staff was genuine, consensual decisions got made, there was evidence of efforts to implement them, and credibility with the other staff we interviewed remained solid. The externally imposed reforms demanded the coordinated response which they received. In one team, members unanimously reported how much they enjoyed the experience of working together. Equally, we were aware of some difficult moments when consensus could not be reached, soaking up time; or when grappling with new ideas which, for most members, posed a threat to the existing culture of teamwork.

The two SMTs mostly demonstrated various characteristics of effective teams outside the education sphere that, in Chapter 1, we suggested could provide some pointers as long as they were not taken as gospel. There were examples of principled leadership, shared through opportunities to lead within the team on particular issues; unified commitment to teamwork; competence among individual members; and a collaborative climate. On the other hand, in the past there had been some competition between two members in one team (which they had largely resolved); openness was constrained in both teams when the stakes were high for individuals; and we witnessed how, in each case, the degree of unity on goals for the team and for members within it was questioned.

Beyond these observations we can go no further in judging the effectiveness of the six teams. Their different practices and the lack of evidence which would imply that they were ineffective suggests that there is likely to be a variety of ways of working that are effective within particular secondary school contexts. We have explored at some length the possibility of complementarity among individual team roles being an important factor in promoting effectiveness, rather than any team role taking a particular form.

Defining SMT effectiveness, never mind identifying it, is not a simple matter. We mentioned at the outset that we did not follow the causal chain of SMT effectiveness all the way from the contribution of team members, through their impact on other staff, to the learning of pupils. Another qualifier relates to the fact that the SMTs were working within externally imposed constraints. Our fieldwork indicated how central government reforms and the level of resourcing limited the ability of SMT members to operate as they would have preferred. How far could staff be consulted and kept informed when decisions, for reasons beyond school level control, had to come so thick and fast?

It is also worth reminding ourselves that, to some extent, effectiveness lies in the eye of the beholder. Teamwork in SMTs is not simply technical: it reflects values connected with process and direct or indirect outcomes; no one has a monopoly on which values to hold. To a Conservative central government minister, an SMT which achieves synergy in working towards the outcome of protecting comprehensive educational and public service values may be seen as more subversive than effective!

Values connected with process may be contradictory, depending on how much one value is expressed at the expense of the other. Consensual decision making may be valued because it tends to promote commitment of all team members to implementing decisions. Critical thinking may be valued because the more factors a complex decision takes into account, the less likely implementation is to be foiled by failure to think things through. Too high a value placed on consensus, rather than being prepared to argue the toss between perspectives, is widely held to lead to ineffective outcomes through 'groupthink'. Janis (1972) defines this term as

> a mode of thinking that people engage in when they are deeply involved in a cohesive in-group, when the members' strivings for unanimity override their motivation to realistically appraise alternative courses of action.

(p. 9)

A concern expressed in several of our study SMTs was whether individuals were overly ready to compromise. The opposite extreme – impasse between contested views – may result either in a majority decision, with the possibility that those in the minority will not be fully committed to its implementation, or in no decision at all. Effectiveness may lie in allegiance to both values, but how much to accord to each is not easily determined.

SMTs are not simply a means to an end. Many team members reported on the intrinsic benefit gained from the intellectual challenge of debate or emotional support from colleagues. Teamwork, despite the strains, can be an enjoyable and personally fulfilling experience in a senior manager's professional life. There is a strong ethical argument for enabling staff to participate in

Table 10.1 Linked hypotheses about effective SMTs

<hr>

Input: Team members

Individual

1. Members are committed to teamwork.
2. Members are competent in fulfilling their individual management responsibility.
3. All areas of each member's individual management responsibility are school wide.
4. Members are concerned both with management tasks and with the needs of those inside and outside the SMT with whom they work.
5. Heads set explicit parameters for teamwork and ensure that their boundaries are monitored.
6. Heads attend to building a shared culture of teamwork.
7. New members receive planned induction into the SMT.

Group

8. Members display a range of strengths in terms of the knowledge, skills and attitudes they bring to the team.
9. The team is small enough to facilitate face-to-face discussion and large enough to include all individuals necessary for making major decisions.
10. There is a single-tier structure of SMT meetings.
11. All members contribute to the selection of new team members within explicit groundrules.
12. Membership reflects attention paid to promoting equal opportunities for women and men and the main ethnic groups represented among pupils and staff.
13. Attention is paid to the development of individual members as teamworkers and to the development of the team as a whole.

Process of teamwork

Internal

14. Heads provide conditions which encourage all members to contribute fully to the work of the team while negotiating the boundaries of acceptability to them.
15. Other members facilitate the teamwork process.
16. There is complementarity between the individual team roles of 'leadership of the team' and 'team membership'.
17. Arrangements for chairing do not inhibit any member from making an equal contribution to debate.
18. All members make an equal contribution to making major decisions and to sustaining an overview.
19. All members take the lead on particular issues, especially those connected with their individual management responsibility.
20. The work of the team and its members are monitored as a team concern, without constraining individual initiative.
21. Major decisions are made by consensus reached after the open expression of individual views.
22. Contingency procedures are established in case consensus is not achievable.
23. All members keep to task in SMT meetings, while allowing sufficient relief to sustain concentration.
24. There is a high degree of trust, mutual respect and cordiality among SMT members and disagreements focus on issues rather than personalities.
25. Members gain intrinsic benefit from working in the SMT.

Table 10.1 *Continued*

26. Individual educational and managerial beliefs and values are made explicit and consensus is reached on broad team goals.
27. Steps are taken to avoid the creation of enduring coalitions within the SMT or the expression of favouritism.
28. SMT members address a manageable agenda and keep the time spent on joint work within bounds as far as is possible.

External

29. A communication structure is established which enables other staff to have a real impact on school-wide policy making.
30. Ground rules for consultation and decision making are negotiated between the SMT, other staff and governors, which are respected by SMT members.
31. All members attend to sustaining a permeable demarcation between the SMT and others by making themselves accessible, promoting positive relationships and seeking outsiders' views.
32. The private SMT arena is kept to a minimum, while overloading other staff with managerial concerns is avoided.
33. Activity within the private SMT arena is consistent with the public account members give about what they do behind closed doors.
34. Other staff are encouraged to consider their sectional interests within as much of a school-wide perspective as they can plausibly achieve.
35. SMT members follow through with other staff on issues connected with the implementation of major decisions.
36. Members present a united front to other staff on decisions that have been taken within the SMT, while acknowledging the range of views taken into account.

Direct outcomes

37. The SMT has high credibility with other staff and governors based on evidence of members' joint work that is available to them.
38. The governing body supports the work of the SMT.
39. The agenda of the SMT encompasses all areas of school-wide policy.
40. Major decisions are reached and backed by all SMT members.
41. Major decisions are communicated to those outside the team to whom they are relevant.
42. Attention is paid to the implementation of major decisions.

school management on the grounds that, as human beings, they should be entitled to humane work experiences of intrinsic worth. Bottery (1992, p. 175) refers to all teaching staff in suggesting that, on these grounds, ' "good management" becomes a concern for the morale, self-esteem, commitment, enjoyment, and personal, social and political fulfilment of those engaged in the process'. Teamwork that succeeds can be effective for the people in the team.

Both technical and ethical arguments relate to the question of who gets to be in the team and what they do in it. If we accept that women and men are equally capable of contributing as senior managers in secondary schools, we shall see that an effective SMT should not exclude members of either gender. To the extent that senior managers provide a role model for pupils and staff, both men and women are needed in the SMT to encourage others of either gender to aspire towards such positions. Ethically, if women and men have the same right as citizens to equal access to any job in schools, the composition of SMTs should reflect this right as far as possible within local circumstances. Values connected with the effectiveness of SMTs therefore connect with a range of wider social and political values.

Rather than make wild claims, we have drawn up a (far from exhaustive) list of hypotheses about effective SMTs. Table 10.1 is based on findings reported throughout the book (and builds on the earlier list of judgements discussed in Chapter 4). A number of features should be noted:

- they form a linked set of criteria, and should be taken together. Isolated statements don't take us very far: clearly, there is more to effectiveness than, say, SMT members having a great time together (No. 25);
- they cover inputs to the SMT (both individual characteristics and those of the entire group), the process of teamwork among SMT members and in relation to outsiders, and the immediate outcomes of their work;
- some, like unified commitment (No. 1), may be necessary. Others, such as new members receiving planned induction (No. 7), may not;
- some, say, all members contributing to the selection of new members (No. 11) imply action. Others, including the avoidance of coalitions or favourites (No. 27) imply withholding from it;
- several, perhaps a single-tier structure of SMT meetings (No. 10), will be contentious, depending in part on the values determining what counts as effectiveness;
- a few, like keeping the private SMT arena to a minimum while avoiding overload for other staff (No. 32) imply a balancing act between contradictory values.

We speculate that SMTs can make a very positive difference: to the working conditions of SMT members; to the range of factors taken into account in making school-wide policies; and to the degree of coordination in managing the school. A team where synergy is achieved and credibility with outsiders is sustained can lead school staff in keeping ahead of the game by making a coherent and sophisticated (rather than reactive and piecemeal) response to national reforms and other changes. Teamwork among senior staff may well not be a necessary condition for school effectiveness, but we are willing to hazard the guess that heads without the support of teamwork among senior staff are likely to have even greater difficulty in promoting synergy across the school in the current climate than those who are successful in going for a team approach.

IMPLICATIONS FOR RESEARCH AND DEVELOPMENT

Given the prevalence of SMTs in secondary schools for at least the last decade, and the strong evidence of greater managerial workload for senior staff in all state educational institutions as a result of central government reforms, it is striking how little research has been done on team approaches to management at senior- or middle-management levels. We need to know far more about teamwork in a wider range of settings, whether secondary schools, educational institutions in other sectors, or other public sector and commercial organisations. There was no shortage of evidence in our small sample that teamwork is problematic even in favourable situations. It seems likely that there are other difficulties, and ways of resolving them elsewhere, that research could identify for the benefit of practitioners. A $64,000 practical question, for example, is how to foster greater collaboration among individuals who are not committed to it. Ultimately, there has to be an element of voluntariness for collaboration to work, since any individual has access to resources to assist or resist collaborative overtures. How is the necessary culture of teamwork to be nurtured where the going is not good?

We have questioned the adequacy of research into teams outside the education sphere which does not get close to the real action but relies either on simulation or on team members' accounts of the secrets of their success. There is an urgent need for observational studies of teams which can track what happens when they are at work in their everyday organisational setting. On the other hand, many studies of teams elsewhere (unlike our own research) have included measures of team output. There is scope for work on management teams in educational institutions which attempts to compare teams according to direct outcomes. More research is needed also on the impact of women and men working together in teams, that takes into account similarities and differences in their approaches to management.

The cultural and political perspective seems worthy of further development and application to other fields of enquiry. Our conceptualisation was exploratory, but the powerful analytic lens it provided suggests that this dual metaphor has promise as a way of interpreting interaction in a range of group settings.

IMPLICATIONS FOR POLICY MAKERS

Many LEAs in this country have provided some form of training and development support for secondary school SMTs in recent years, including both those in the present study. It was also apparent in our research that structured development activities, while offering the potential for facilitating teamwork, played a relatively minor part compared with ongoing and unstructured team development in our study SMTs. Structured development activities may not be necessary for teamwork but they can certainly promote it where they provide a sound framework for an enduring attempt to improve team effectiveness.

We noted at the beginning of the book that SMTs do not feature in central government policy. This policy vacuum is unfortunate, given the plentiful evidence that national reforms have added very significantly to the managerial load in every school. We highlighted earlier how close coordination among senior managers and strong links with other staff are imperative, not just for dealing with multiple innovations and coping with frequent reversals of reform policy, but for mere existence within the new context. Coordination is certainly facilitated through teamwork in SMTs, so those that work well in this way may be one key both to getting reforms implemented and to promoting high-quality education in the brave new world of devolved decision making and quasi-markets. The problem is that effective teamwork is not easy to achieve. Can central government ministers afford to ignore a situation where, according to evidence reported in Chapter 1, perhaps a third of SMTs are not effective teams? The support that LEA staff can provide is increasingly constrained by central government policies, resulting in the increasing devolution of in-service training budgets to schools. Direction of funds by central government towards the implementation of specific reforms means that little money is available at school level for generic management-development activities. SMT members are unlikely to be willing to take a large slice of the in-service training budget for their own development as a team when there are demonstrably so many other needs to be met among other staff. Therefore the initiative for increased support must lie with government ministers.

There is a strong case for targeting management-development support on SMTs rather than solely upon individual managers, and it is equally important to ensure that this support is effective. Abundant evidence from research and training experience (Wallace, 1991a), supported by some of the findings from Chapter 8, implies that structured development activities should ideally include:

- a focus on intact teams, rather than a few individuals within it;
- a central concern with the reality of SMT members' working lives, as opposed to the abstraction that simulations represent;
- the services of facilitors who are unconnected with the team in question, rather than relying on team members who have a substantive interest in the team issues being addressed;
- opportunities for extensive interaction, rather than always fitting activities into the working day;
- feedback on actual performance of the team, rather than merely on what SMT members perceive about their practice;
- a sustained programme, rather than a one-off event.

A tall order? Quite possibly, for a government whose ambitions for reform so demonstrably outstrip the resources made available to realise them. Any additional strain on the education budget would though, in our view, be more than outweighed by the gain that greater synergy within SMTs could achieve.

IMPLICATIONS FOR SENIOR STAFF AND GOVERNORS

SMTs can be a mixture of good news and bad news for those at the managerial chalk face. In Table 10.2 we have summarised some of the possible consequences for SMT members of going for a team approach, drawing on the overview above. If the prize seems worth the risk, the difficult trick to bring off is to minimise or safeguard against experiencing the strains while maximising the chance of enjoying the gains.

Table 10.2 Teamwork – a balance sheet for SMTs

Potential strains	Potential gains
• Disempowers head to act unilaterally	• Empowers head through support of other SMT members
• Disempowers SMT if unresolvable internal conflict	• Empowers all SMT members if operate synergistically
• Head risks greatest loss of credibility if teamwork fails	• Enhances all SMT members' job satisfaction
• Drains resources since time consuming	• Mutual support constitutes a resource for all SMT members
• SMT divorced from other staff	• SMT enhances possibility of creating school-wide synergy
• Management hierarchy inhibits contribution of SMT members	• Equal contribution maximised for all SMT members
• Makes SMT members more accountable to each other	• SMT members' development enhanced by learning from each other

The hypotheses about effective SMTs may be useful as a starting point for heads who are considering whether to adopt a team approach or for SMT members who are reviewing their work. Key questions for heads at the team design stage, who are taking up a new post or otherwise wishing to move towards a team approach, include:

• What is my rationale for adopting a team approach?
• What is the role of the team as a whole in managing the school?
• What educational and managerial values should underpin its work?
• How far will the SMT's operation reflect different status levels within the management hierarchy?
• What are the boundaries of acceptability to me in terms of the teamwork process and outcomes for the school?
• How far should the institutional history be taken into account in the composition and working practices of the SMT?
• What should be the range of individual management responsibilities within the SMT?
• What SMT structures and processes will be required?
• What communication links need to be established between the SMT, other staff, governors, and other parties with a stake in the school?
• What range of criteria should be adopted for selection of team members?
• What groundrules for working together must be spelled out from the beginning?
• How may a shared culture of teamwork be promoted?
• How may the credibility of the SMT with other staff and governors be developed and sustained?
• How will the teamwork process and outcomes of the SMT's work be monitored and decisions taken to modify practice?

The research poses a practical question for governors: how should the governing body relate directly to the SMT (as opposed to the head or other individual members)? In so far as the management of the school is carried out through a team approach, SMT members are accountable for their joint work, through the head, to the governing body. Equally, the support of governors is needed to back the efforts of SMT members. Yet the workings of the SMT were something of a mystery for most chairs of governors interviewed in our study. Not surprisingly, they were most familiar with those SMT members who attended governors' meetings or subcommittees. Apart from one chair of governors who had observed the SMT at work, they had never been inside the private SMT arena. The heads formed the main link between governing body and SMT. Is this link enough?

Perhaps the most important implication of this study for members of SMTs is that it underlines the Achilles' heel of teamwork alongside its potential. Individuals, whatever their status in the management hierarchy, have greater ability to inhibit synergy, through withdrawing their commitment, than the remainder of the team has collective resources to persuade them to contribute to making synergy happen. Together, team members make the team; individually, they can break it. The culture of teamwork is no stronger than individuals' commitment. So having accepted team membership, the onus is on every member to accept equal responsibility for making the SMT work.

References

Bacharach, S. and Lawler, E. (1980) *Power and Politics in Organizations*, Jossey-Bass, San Francisco.

Bagley, C. (1992) *Back to the Future*, National Foundation for Educational Research, Slough.

Ball, S. (1987) *The Micropolitics of the School*, Methuen, London.

Ball, S. and Bowe, R. (1991) Micropolitics of radical change: budgets, management, and control in British schools, in J. Blase, (ed.) *The Politics of Life in Schools*, Sage, London.

Barnett, B. (1984) Subordinate teacher power in school organizations, *Sociology of Education*, Vol. 57, no. 1, pp. 43–55.

Baron, G. (1975) Some aspects of the 'headmaster tradition', in V. Houghton, R. McHugh and C. Morgan (eds.) *Management in Education 1: the Management of Organizations and Individuals*, Ward Lock, London.

Belbin, M. (1981) *Management Teams: Why They Succeed or Fail*, Heinemann, London.

Bell, L. (1992) *Managing Teams in Secondary Schools*, Routledge, London.

Blase, J. (ed.) (1991) *The Politics of Life in Schools*, Sage, London.

Bolam, R., McMahon, A., Pocklington, K. and Weindling, D. (1993) *Effective Management in Schools*, HMSO, London.

Bolman, L. and Deal, T. (1991) *Reframing Organizations: Artistry, Choice and Leadership*, Jossey-Bass, San Francisco.

Bottery, M. (1992) *The Ethics of Educational Management*, Cassell, London.

Bowe, R. and Ball, S. with Gold, A. (1992) *Reforming Education and Changing Schools*, Routledge, London.

Briault, E. and Smith, F. (1980) *Falling Rolls in Secondary Schools: Part One*, NFER, Windsor.

Burnham, P. (1968) The deputy head, in B. Allen (ed.) *Headship in the 1970s*, Basil Blackwell, Oxford.

Bush, T. (1986) *Theories of Educational Management*, Paul Chapman, London.

Chaudrey-Lawton, R., Lawton, R., Murphy, K. and Terry, A. (1992) *Quality: Change through Teamwork*, Century Business, London.

Cohen, M. and March, J. G. (1974) *Leadership and Ambiguity*, McGraw-Hill, New York.

Coleman, G. (1991) *Investigating Organizations: A Feminist Approach*, University of Bristol School of Advanced Urban Studies, Bristol.

Corson, D. (1992) Language, gender and education: a critical review linking social justice and power, *Gender and Education*, Vol. 4, no. 3, pp. 229–254.

Critchley, B. and Casey, D. (1984) Second thoughts on team building, *Management Education and Development*, Vol. 15, no. 2, pp. 163–175.

Cuthbert, R. (1984) *The Management Process, Block 3, Part 2, E324 Management in Post-Compulsory Education*, Open University Press, Milton Keynes.

Dahl, R. (1957) The concept of power, *Behavioural Science*, Vol. 2, pp. 201–215.

Davies, B., Ellison, L., Osborne, A. and West-Burnham, J. (1990) *Education Management for the 1990s*, Longman, London.

Deal, T. (1985) The symbolism of effective schools, *Elementary School Journal*, Vol. 85, pp. 601–620.

Deal, T. and Kennedy, A. (1982) *Corporate Cultures: the Rites and Rituals of Corporate Life*, Addison-Wesley, Reading, MA.

Department of Education and Science (1977) *Ten Good Schools: a Secondary School Enquiry*, HMSO, London.

Department of Education and Science (1987) *School Teachers' Pay and Conditions Document 1987*, HMSO, London.

Department of Education and Science (1988) *Secondary Schools: an Appraisal by HMI*, HMSO, London.

Department of Education and Science (1992) *Statistics of Education: Teachers in Service England and Wales 1989 and 1990*, DES, London.

Earley, P. and Baker, L. (1989) The recruitment, retention, motivation and morale of senior staff in schools. Report for the National Association of Headteachers. NFER, London.

Earley, P., Baker, L. and Weindling, D. (1990) *Keeping the Raft Afloat: Secondary Headship Five Years On*, NFER, Windsor.

Earley, P. and Fletcher-Campbell, F. (1989) *Time to Manage?* NFER-Nelson, Windsor.

Evetts, J. (1992) The organization of staff in secondary schools: headteachers' management structures, *School Organization*, Vol. 12, no. 1, pp. 83–98.

Fullan, M. with Stiegelbauer, S. (1991) *The New Meaning of Educational Change*, Cassell, London.

Giddens, A. (1976) *New Rules of Sociological Method*, Hutchinson, London.

Giddens, A. (1984) *The Constitution of Society*, Polity Press, Cambridge.

Gillborn, D. (1989) Talking heads: reflections on secondary headship at a time of rapid educational change, *School Organization* Vol. 9, no. 1, pp. 65–83.

Greenfield, W. (1991) The micropolitics of leadership in an urban elementary school, in J. Blase (ed.) op.cit.

Gronn, P. (1986) Politics, power and the management of schools, in E. Hoyle and A. McMahon (eds.) *The Management of Schools*, Kogan Page, London.

Hall, V. (1993) Women in education management: a review of research, in J. Ousten (ed.) *Women in Education Management*, Longman, Harlow.

Hall, V., Mackay, H. and Morgan, C. (1986) *Headteachers at Work*, Open University Press, Milton Keynes.

Hall, V. and Wallace, M. (1993) Collaboration as a subversive activity: a professional response to externally imposed competition between schools?, *School Organization*, Vol. 13, no. 2, pp. 101–117.

Halpin, A. (1966) *Theory and Research in Administration*, Macmillan, New York.

Hargreaves, A. (1991) Contrived collegiality: the micropolitics of teacher collaboration, in J. Blase (ed.) op.cit.

Hargreaves, A. (1992) Cultures of teaching, in A. Hargreaves and M. Fullan (eds.) *Understanding Teacher Development*, Teachers College Press, New York.

Hearn, J., Sheppard, D., Tancred-Sheriff, P. and Burrell, G. (eds.) (1989) *The Sexuality of Organization*, Sage, London.

Hough, J. (1986) Gender bias in educational management and administration, *Educational Management and Administration*, Vol. 16, no. 1, pp. 69–74.

Hoyle, E. (1986) *The Politics of School Management*, Hodder and Stoughton, London.

Inner London Education Authority (1984) *Improving Secondary Schools*, ILEA, London.

Janis, I. (1972) *Victims of Groupthink*, Houghton Mifflin, Boston, MA.

Kanter, R. (1983) *The Change Masters*, Unwin Hyman, London.

Kanter, R. (1990) *When Giants Learn to Dance*, Unwin Hyman, London.

Larson, C. and LaFasto, F. (1989) *Teamwork: What Must Go Right, What Can Go Wrong*, Sage, London.

Lawley, P. (1988) *Deputy Headship*, Longman, London.

Leithwood, K. and Jantzi, D. (1990) Transformational leadership: how principals can help reform school culture. Paper presented at American Educational Research Association annual meeting, Boston.

Litawski, R. (1993) The 'nappy and noses' brigade, *Times Educational Supplement*, April 2nd, p. 6.

Louis, K. S. and Miles, M. (1990) *Improving the Urban High School: What Works and Why*, Teachers College Press, New York.

Mangham, I. (1979) *The Politics of Organizational Change*, Associated Business Press, London.

Maw, J. (1977) Defining roles in senior and middle management in secondary schools, in A. Jennings (ed.) *Management and Headship in the Secondary School*, Ward Lock, London.

McBurney, E. and Hough, J. (1989) Role perceptions of female deputy heads, *Educational Management and Administration*, Vol. 17, no. 3, pp. 115–118.

Merriam, S. (1988) *Case Study Research in Education*, Jossey-Bass, London.

Miles, M. and Huberman, M. (1984) *Qualitative Data Analysis*, Sage, London.

Morgan, C., Hall, V. and Mackay, H. (1983) *The Selection of Secondary School Headteachers*, Open University Press, Milton Keynes.

Morgan, G. (1986) *Images of Organization*, Sage, Newbury Park, CA.

Murgatroyd, S. (1986) Management teams and the promotion of staff well-being, *School Organization*, Vol. 6, no. 1, pp. 115–121.

Nias, J., Southworth, G. and Campbell, P. (1992) *Whole School Curriculum Development*, Falmer, London.

Nias, J., Southworth, G. and Yeomans, R. (1989) *Staff Relationships in the Primary School*, Cassell, London.

Nicholson, R. (1989) *School Management: the Role of the Secondary Headteacher*, Kogan Page, London.

Oldroyd, D. and Hall, V. (1991) *Managing Staff Development: a Handbook for Secondary Schools*, Paul Chapman, London.

Perrow, C. (1986) *Complex Organizations: a Critical Essay* (3rd edn), Random House, New York.

Peters, T. (1988) *Thriving on Chaos*, Macmillan, London.

Peters, T. and Waterman, R. (1982) *In Search of Excellence*, Harper & Row, London.

Radnor, H. (1990) Complexities and compromises: the new ERA at Parkview School. Paper presented at American Educational Research Association annual meeting, Boston.

Reitzug, U. and Reeves, J. (1992) 'Miss Lincoln doesn't teach here': a descriptive narrative and conceptual analysis of a principal's symbolic leadership behaviour, *Education Administration Quarterly*, Vol. 28, no. 2, pp. 185–219.

Richardson, E. (1973) *The Teacher, the School, and the Task of Management*, Heinemann, London.

Scottish Education Department (1988) *Effective Secondary Schools*, HMSO, London.

Secondary Heads Association (1992) *If it Moves Again: a Further Study of the Role of the Deputy Head*, SHA, Leicester.

Sergiovanni, T. and Corbally, J. (eds.) (1984) *Leadership and Organizational Culture*, University of Illinois Press, Chicago.

Smith, W. F. and Andrews, R. L. (1989) *Instructional Leadership: how Principals Make a Difference*, Association for Supervision and Curriculum Development, Alexandria, VA.

Spencer, J. and Pruss, A. (1992) *Managing your Team: How to Organize People for Maximum Results*, Piatkus, London.

Straker, N. (1984) The role of the senior teacher in secondary schools, *School Organization*, Vol. 4, no. 1, pp. 55–64.

Taylor, P. (1992) Striking a better balance, *Times Educational Supplement*, January 3rd, p. 7.

Times Educational Supplement (1992) Deleting the deputy, May 22nd, p. 23.

Torrington, D. and Weightman, J. (1989) *The Reality of School Management*, Blackwell, Oxford.

Trethowan, D. (1985) *Teamwork*, Industrial Society Press, London.

Wallace, M. (1986) The rise of scale posts as a management hierarchy in schools, *Educational Management and Administration*, Vol. 14, no. 4, pp. 203–212.

Wallace, M. (1987) Principals' centres: a transferable innovation?, *School Organization*, Vol. 7, no. 3, pp. 287–295.

Wallace, M. (1991a) *School Centred Management Training*, Paul Chapman, London.

Wallace, M. (1991b) Contradictory interests in policy implementation: the case of LEA development plans for schools, *Journal of Education Policy*, Vol. 6, no. 4, pp. 385–399.

Wallace, M. (1992) *The Management of Multiple Innovations, Module 1, Unit 3, Part 2, Open University course E326 Managing Schools: Challenge and Response*, Open University, Milton Keynes.

Wallace, M. and Hall, V. (1989) Management development and training for schools in England and Wales: an overview, *Educational Management and Administration*, Vol. 17, no. 4, pp. 163–175.

Wallace, M., Hall, V. and McMahon, A. (1993) School development planning in a turbulent environment: reconciling coherence with flexibility, in H. Busher and M. Smith (eds.) *Managing Educational Institutions: Reviewing Development and Learning*, Sheffield Papers in Education Management Series No. 95. Sheffield Hallam University Centre for Education Management and Administration on behalf of the British Educational Management and Administration Society, Sheffield.

Wallace, M. and McMahon, A. (1993) *Planning for Change in Turbulent Times: the Case of Multiracial Primary Schools*, Cassell, London.

Weber, M. (1947) *The Theory of Social and Economic Organizations*, Collier-Macmillan, London.

Weindling, D. and Earley, P. (1987) *Secondary Headship: the First Years*, NFER-Nelson, Windsor.

Wilson, B. and Corcoran, T. (1988) *Successful Secondary Schools*, Falmer Press, London.

Woodcock, M. (1979) *Team Development Manual*, Gower, Aldershot.

Woodcock, M. and Francis, D. (1989) *Clarifying Organizational Values*, Gower, Aldershot.

Yaseen, M. (1993) Tears and fears for Section 11, *Education*, July 9th, p. 30.

INDEX

MANAGING BETTER SCHOOLS SERIES

The need for good school management and for development and training has never been greater. In the last few years schools have had to deal with change on an unprecedented scale: school closures and reorganisations, TVEI, computer studies, profiling, GCSE, TRIST and GRIST. Now, Government policy has produced a whole new agenda for change – appraisal, new conditions of service, the National Curriculum, regular testing, local financial management, new roles for governors, and grant- maintained schools – all of which have major implications for the management of change in schools and LEAs and therefore, for management development training.

Produced by the NDC/EMP in Bristol, **Managing Better Schools** *is a series of practical handbooks for management development in schools. Based on successful practice and relevant research, each book is designed to enhance the quality of management development and training, areas of current concern for school managers and management trainers.*

Titles available in this series:–

INSIDE THE SMT
Teamwork in Secondary School Management
Mike Wallace and Valerie Hall

1 85396 208 2 Paperback 216pp 1994 £16.95

SCHOOL-CENTRED MANAGEMENT TRAINING
Mike Wallace

1 85396 099 3 Paperback 192pp 1991 £14.95

LOCAL MANAGEMENT OF SCHOOLS
David Hill, Brian Oakley Smith and Jim Spinks

1 85396 073 X Paperback 80pp 1990 £10.95

A HANDBOOK FOR PRIMARY SCHOOLS
Agnes McMahon and Ray Bolam

1 85396 081 0 96pp Paperback 1990 £11.95

A HANDBOOK FOR SECONDARY SCHOOLS
Agnes McMahon and Ray Bolam

1 85396 080 2 96pp Paperback 1990 £11.50

A HANDBOOK FOR LEAS
Agnes McMahon and Ray Bolam

185396 082 9 Paperback 1990 £11.95

MANAGING STAFF DEVELOPMENT
A Handbook for Secondary Schools
David Oldroyd and Valerie Hall

1 85396 112 4 Paperback 224pp 1991 £14.95

MANAGING HEADTEACHER APPRAISAL
Victor Gane and Alun Morgan

1 85396 191 4 Paperback 224pp 1992 £13.95

Other titles of interest in Staff Development and Educational Management

MANAGING CHANGE IN EDUCATION
Individual and Organizational Perspectives
edited by Nigel Bennett, Megan Crawford and Colin Riches

1 85396 211 2 Paperback 320pp 1992 £10.95

TEACHERS' CASE STUDIES IN EDUCATIONAL MANAGEMENT
edited by Margaret Preedy

1 85396 069 1 Paperback 320pp 1989 £13.50

MANAGING THE EFFECTIVE SCHOOL
edited by Margaret Preedy

1 85396 210 4 Paper 256pp 1993 £9.95

EFFECTIVE DISCIPLINE IN PRIMARY SCHOOLS AND CLASSROOMS
EFFECTIVE DISCIPLINE IN SECONDARY SCHOOLS AND CLASSROOMS
Pamela Munn, Margaret Johnstone and Valerie Chalmers

1 85396 174 4 Paperback 160pp 1992 £12.95 (PRIMARY)
1 85396 175 2 Paperback 176pp 1992 £12.95 (SECONDARY)

THEORIES OF EDUCATIONAL MANAGEMENT
Tony Bush

1 85396 041 1 158pp Paperback 1986 £9.50

EFFECTIVE SCHOOL MANAGEMENT 2/e
Bertie Everard and Geoffrey Morris

1 85396 086 1 288pp 1990 Paperback £12.50

MANAGING PRIMARY SCHOOLS IN THE 1990s
A Professional Development Approach 2/e
Chris Day, Patrick Whitaker and David Johnston

1 85396 110 8 240pp Paperback 1990 £11.95

THE SEARCH FOR QUALITY
Planning for Improvement and Managing Change
Del Goddard and Marilyn Leask

1 85396 190 6 Paperback 224pp 1992 £14.95

LEARNING, ADAPTABILITY AND CHANGE:
The Challenge for Education and Industry
John Heywood

1 85396 067 5 Paperback 224pp 1989 £11.50

HEALTH AND SAFETY IN SCHOOLS
David Brierley

1 85396 130 2 Paperback 240pp 1991 £11.95

THE PRIMARY HEAD: Roles, Responsibilities and
Reflections
THE SECONDARY HEAD: Roles, Responsibilities and Reflections
Peter Mortimore and Jo Mortimore

1 85396 140 X Paperback 144pp 1991 £11.95 (Primary)
1 85396 141 8 Paperback 192pp 1991 £11.95 (Secondary)

MANAGING WITH APPRAISAL
Achieving Quality Schools through Performance Management
David M Trethowan

1 85396 135 3 264pp Paperback 1991 £13.50

APPRAISAL AND TARGET SETTING
David M Trethowan

1 85396 043 8 Paperback 224pp 1987 £12.95

MANAGING AUTONOMOUS SCHOOLS
The Grant-Maintained Experience
Tony Bush, Marianne Coleman and Derek Glover

1 85396 202 3 Paperback 256pp 1993 £14.95

LEADERSHIP AND CURRICULUM IN THE PRIMARY SCHOOL
The roles of senior and middle management
Christopher Day, Carol Hall, Philip Gammage and Martin Coles

1 85396 214 7 Paperback 176pp 1993 £12.95

SCHOOL MATTERS
The Junior Years
Peter Mortimore, Pamela Sammons, Louise Stoll, David Lewis
and Russell Ecob

0 7291 0194 0 314pp Paperback 1988 £9.95

MANAGING ASSOCIATE STAFF
Innovation in Primary and Secondary Schools
Peter Mortimore, Jo Mortimore with Hywel Thomas

1 85396 231 7 Paperback 240pp 1994 £14.95

SHATTERING THE GLASS CEILING
The Woman Manager
Marilyn J. Davidson and Cary L. Cooper

1 85396 132 9 192pp Paperback 1992 £12.95

BREAKTHROUGH
The career woman's guide to shattering the glass ceiling
Margaret L Flanders

1 85396 233 3 160pp 1994 Paperback £10.95

ORDER FORM

Order through your local bookseller or complete the following order form and return to:

PAUL CHAPMAN PUBLISHING LTD.,
144 LIVERPOOL ROAD,
LONDON, NI ILA.

TEL: 071 609 5315/6   FAX: 071 700 1057

* I enclose my cheque for £   , made payable to
Paul Chapman Publishing Ltd.

* Please charge my Access/American Express/Barclaycard/Visa.

ACCOUNT NO: ....

EXPIRY DATE: ....

TITLE .... INITIALS .... SURNAME ....

INSTITUTION: ....

DEPARTMENT: ....

ADDRESS: ....

* ....

* ....

* .... POSTCODE ....

SIGNATURE .... DATE ....

PLEASE SEND ME A COPY OF COMPLETE EDUCATIONAL
MANAGEMENT CATALOGUE

——	1853962112	BENNETT et al: Managing Change in Education	£10.95
——	1853961302	BRIERLEY: Health & Safety in Schools	£11.95
——	1853960411	BUSH: Theories of Educational Management	£9.50
——	1853962023	BUSH: Managing Autonomous Schools	£14.95
——	1853961329	DAVIDSON/COOPER: Shattering the Glass Ceiling	£12.95
——	1853961108	DAY et al: Managing Primary Schools in 1990s 2/e	£11.95
——	1853962147	DAY: Leadership and Curriculum in Primary School	£12.95
——	1853960861	EVERARD/MORRIS: Effective School Management 2/e	£12.50
——	1853962333	FLANDERS: Breakthrough	£10.95
——	1853961914	GANE/MORGAN: Managing Headteacher Appraisal	£13.95
——	1853961906	GODDARD/LEASK: The Search for Quality	£14.95
——	1853960675	HEYWOOD: Learning Adaptability and Change	£11.50
——	185396073X	HILL et al: Local Management of Schools	£10.95
——	1853960810	MCMAHON: A Handbook for Primary Schools	£11.95
——	1853960802	MCMAHON: A Handbook Secondary Schools	£11.95
——	1853960829	MCMAHON: A Handbook for LEAs 2e	£11.95
——	185396140X	MORTIMORE: The Primary Head	£11.95
——	1853961418	MORTIMORE: The Secondary Head	£11.95
——	1853962317	MORTIMORE: Managing Associate Staff	£14.95
——	0729101940	MORTIMORE el al: School Matters	£9.95
——	1853961752	MUNN et al : Effective Discipline Secondary Schs	£12.95
——	1853961744	MUNN et al : Effective Discipline Primary Schs	£12.95
——	1853961124	OLDROYD: Managing Staff Development: Hndbk Sec Sch	£14.95
——	1853960691	PREEDY: Teachers' Case Studies in Educational Mngt	£13.50
——	1853962104	PREEDY: Managing the Effective School	£9.95
——	1853960438	TRETHOWAN: Appraisal and Target Setting	£12.95
——	1853961353	TRETHOWAN: Managing With Appraisal	£13.50
——	1853960993	WALLACE: School-Centred Management Training	£14.95
——	1853962082	WALLACE/HALL: Inside the SMT	£16.95

The publisher reserves the right to alter prices without prior notice.